More Fun and Games

Anthony Dowson,
BSc, MSc, PGCE

Human Kinetics

Library of Congress Cataloging-in-Publication Data

Dowson, Anthony, 1975-
    More fun and games / Anthony Dowson.
          p. cm.
    Includes bibliographical references.
    ISBN-13: 978-0-7360-7730-9 (soft cover)
    ISBN-10: 0-7360-7730-8 (soft cover)
    1. Sports for children.   2. Games.   3. Physical fitness
for children.   I. Title.
    GV709.2.D694 2009
    796.083--dc22

    2009015390

ISBN-10: 0-7360-7730-8 (print)   ISBN-10: 0-7360-8763-X (Adobe PDF)
ISBN-13: 978-0-7360-7730-9 (print)   ISBN-13: 978-0-7360-8763-6 (Adobe PDF)

Copyright © 2009 by Anthony Dowson

The Web addresses cited in this text were current as of April 1, 2009, unless otherwise noted.

Acquisitions Editor: John Dickinson, PhD; **Developmental Editor:** Amy Stahl; **Assistant Editor:** Lauren B. Morenz; **Copyeditor:** Patsy Fortney; **Proofreader:** Jim Burns; **Graphic Designer:** Nancy Rasmus; **Graphic Artist:** Kathleen Boudreau-Fuoss; **Cover Designer:** Keith Blomberg; **Photographer (cover):** Tom Roberts; **Photographer (interior):** © Human Kinetics; photo on p. 77 © Ingo Jezierski/age fotostock; **Photo Asset Manager:** Laura Fitch; **Photo Production Manager:** Jason Allen; **Art Manager:** Kelly Hendren; **Associate Art Manager:** Alan L. Wilborn; **Illustrator:** Alan L. Wilborn; **Printer:** Versa Press

Printed in the United States of America   10   9   8   7   6   5   4   3   2   1

The paper in this book is certified under a sustainable forestry program.

Human Kinetics
Web site: www.HumanKinetics.com

Europe: Human Kinetics
107 Bradford Road, Stanningley,
Leeds LS28 6AT, United Kingdom
+44 (0) 113 255 5665
e-mail: hk@hkeurope.com

United States: Human Kinetics
P.O. Box 5076, Champaign, IL 61825-5076
800-747-4457
e-mail: humank@hkusa.com

Canada: Human Kinetics
475 Devonshire Road Unit 100,
Windsor, ON N8Y 2L5
800-465-7301 (in Canada only)
e-mail: info@hkcanada.com

Australia: Human Kinetics
57A Price Avenue, Lower Mitcham,
South Australia 5062
08 8372 0999
e-mail: info@hkaustralia.com

New Zealand: Human Kinetics
Division of Sports Distributors NZ Ltd.
P.O. Box 300 226 Albany, North Shore City, Auckland
0064 9 448 1207
e-mail: info@humankinetics.co.nz

Contents

Preface

Fun and Games, which I co-wrote with Keith E.J. Morris (2005), is an excellent resource that, as expected, has been well received by teachers and coaches alike. It has been very rewarding to speak to others working in sport, physical education and coaching who have found this out for themselves and are using the ideas regularly in their own work. *More Fun and Games* will prove to be another invaluable resource, containing more of the same . . . yet much more!

Every day in my teaching and coaching I use the games and ideas from *Fun and Games,* yet I continue to learn and develop more games. This is so that I can continually keep my coaching sessions and physical education lessons fun and enjoyable and ensure that those that I teach or coach experience a variety of entertaining activities. All those who lead children's sport, whether they are trained experts or enthusiastic amateurs, must have a resource to refer to and include in their work. With another book of *Fun and Games,* they can now have two! Following from the first book, *More Fun and Games* includes more fantastic ideas for those leading children's games, ideas that will help them enthuse and activate children. Children will enjoy playing these games and will ask to play again and again!

The activities and games in this book are easy to set up and require only common sports equipment; this means that even novice teachers, coaches and activity leaders can put them into practice. With many years of coaching and teaching experience, I have realised the need for children's sporting encounters to be *fun*. Children love to play games, and entertaining activities help in the following ways:

- They keep children focused and on task.
- They help children to form positive attitudes towards physical activity.
- They keep children active.

This book contains a range of warm-up and cool-down ideas, games, skill practices and sport-specific activities to enthuse and motivate youngsters. All the games and activities are fully inclusive, involving each participant throughout. I find that with greater involvement, participants enjoy themselves more and are more receptive to learning.

It is important that children develop technical skills in sport and physical education (e.g., passing and dribbling in hockey) so they make progress in relation to their peers. This should lead to greater levels of self-confidence and self-esteem, which are associated with improving in sport. The ideas in this book will help you develop children's motor abilities and techniques as they participate in fun and enjoyable activities. I guarantee that children will leave the session having had fun and wanting to come back for more.

Many activities and games in this book require minimal equipment and are easy to set up. They can be used as part of a one-off session when you may have a group on only one occasion, or included in longer-term planning.

With a reported increase in childhood obesity worldwide, many children need to have healthier lifestyles, which involves being physically active more often. I hope that using these games and activities regularly with your groups will help in the development of positive attitudes towards physical education and sport, which could lead to children who participate in more lifelong physical activities.

Reference

Dowson, A., and Morris, K.E.J. 2005. *Fun and Games*. Champaign, IL: Human Kinetics.

Acknowledgements

To Marie-Anne: Again, I owe you so much for your love and support throughout the writing of this manuscript. You are still amazing!

This book is also dedicated to the many teachers, coaches and leaders in sport and physical education whom I have met and learned from. Whenever I need inspiration, I need look no further than my friends and colleagues. I have been privileged to work with many people who share my passion for sport and physical education: Dave Bullock, Steve Hall, Dr. Steve Harvey, Ralph Grant, Bruce Vause, Guy Wnuk, Bob Holmes, Carol Gordon and Dan Wortley.

Once again, gratitude is offered to those at Human Kinetics, most notably John Dickinson, who have helped in the production of this book and who have shown confidence in my ability to complete this volume.

How to Use This Book

The format for *More Fun and Games* is simple: the text is kept to a minimum and an extensive use of illustrations helps to keep the content user-friendly. This book is broken down into nine chapters and contains 100 activities.

Chapter 1 includes 25 multi-sport games. The subsequent seven chapters include games for use in the following specific sports: basketball and netball (chapter 2), cricket and striking and fielding (chapter 3), hockey (chapter 4), rugby (chapter 5), soccer (chapter 6), tennis and badminton (chapter 7) and volleyball (chapter 8). Chapter 9 includes activities that are suitable for use during cool-down periods.

Keep in mind that although an activity may appear in one of the sport-specific sections, you may be able to modify it for use in other sports as well. Even the activities in the multi-sport and cool-down chapters (chapters 1 and 9, respectively) can be modified for use in other sports. This means that although the cover states that this book contains 100 activities, effectively there are many more. A Variations section in each game outlines how the rules can be adapted or modified in a number of ways. You can vary activities according to the number of participants in your group. You can also adapt games to make them easier for less able participants or more challenging for more able participants.

Each chapter contains a brief introduction to the types of games and activities it addresses, which includes important safety recommendations. Therefore, it is vital that you read these sections before embarking on the activities in the chapter.

In the sport-specific chapters, I tried to include games that anyone could implement. The majority of games do not require you to be a trained physical education teacher or have specific coaching qualifications. However, if you are not coaching or teaching regularly, I advise you to enrol in relevant coaching award courses to gain these qualifications. This should help you to develop your participants' skill levels in addition to providing them with these fun activities.

Game Finder

A breakdown of all the activities is in the game finder found on pages xi to xxii. The activities are listed alphabetically (by chapter) with their page number(s), so you can quickly locate them. The game finder also gives recommended age ranges for each activity, which should help you decide whether a given activity is suitable for the participants you are leading. The game finder also includes a list of equipment needed for each game and the skills and fitness components developed by each activity. When activities can be adapted for use in other sports, the game finder lists these as well.

Game Format

Each activity includes the following sections:

- Ages
- Key Skills and Fitness Components Developed
- Equipment
- Game
- Safety Tips
- Advice
- Variations

Ages

A number of the games and activities in this book can be used with children of any age. However, some are more suited to particular age groups. The age recommendations listed at the beginning of each game should enable you to plan your sessions effectively for a variety of participants. Note that the ages given are only recommendations; you may find that the participants you instruct enjoy playing a particular activity even if they do not fall within the suggested age range. For example, when coaching adults and tutoring coach education courses, I have used a number of the activities in this book and found that children are not the only ones to have fun with them!

Key Skills Developed

Although fun should be the major reason for playing games, it is important that children develop competence when playing games, so they can progress in physical education and sport. If participants become more skilful, they will be more likely to enjoy activities when they get older because they will have enjoyed some success. The Key Skills Developed section at the beginning of each game outlines the abilities, techniques and skills needed to play the game and therefore the skills that can be developed if participants play the game regularly. With younger children it is important to develop fundamental motor skills such as running, jumping and throwing. Many of the activities that are recommended for use with 5- to 11-year-olds are excellent for developing fundamental motor skills. More advanced techniques and sport-specific skills can be developed by regularly playing the games and activities recommended for children aged 11 to 16; however, direct coaching may be required to develop these.

Key Fitness Components Developed

The Fitness Components section at the beginning of each game lists the specific health-related and skill-related components that children can develop by participating regularly in the game. Playing the games and activities included in this book regularly will help children develop and maintain fitness, which will assist them in leading healthy lives. Those who take physical education and sport more seriously will need to develop good fitness to be successful. For example, to be good games players, children need excellent agility (the ability to change direction rapidly, under control). A tennis player needs good agility if the opponent hits the ball to different areas of the court, and a rugby player needs agility to sidestep past an opponent when running with the ball.

Equipment

This section lists the minimal equipment needed to carry out the game or activity. If you do not have enough equipment for a game, consult the Variations section because there may be an alternative way of playing the game that requires less equipment. Most activities in this book require cones for marking out the playing area(s). The number of cones needed is not given, but I suggest you have a stack of approximately 60 to 100. When marking out a playing area, place the cones approximately 3 metres (3.3 yd) apart for younger children because they are more likely to run outside the area when playing. For older children, place cones between 5 and 10 metres (5.5 and 11 yd) apart.

Game

The Game section explains how to set up and run the activity effectively. Some games are played in small groups, whereas others can be 'mass' activities played or performed by all. Normally, group sizes are listed in this section so you can identify the numbers of participants needed to carry out the activity effectively. Group sizes are only suggestions, however. You may be able to modify an activity to suit your group.

Use the information in the Game section to explain to your group how to play the activity. I have provided illustrations where necessary to help you organise the activity successfully. For some games, I provide recommended sizes for the playing areas. For others, I do not specify the size of the playing areas because this depends on the age, ability and numbers of participants in your specific group. The size of the area should allow safe involvement and provide adequate opportunities for success. In some cases you may need to use common sense to determine the size of the playing area needed for the activity. If you lack experience, start the activity as described and monitor how effectively it is running. If it is not working well, stop the game and change the size of the area(s) before continuing.

Quite often the game description will begin with the phrase 'Cone out your playing area'. This means to use the cones to mark out the playing area. For most games, the shape of this area doesn't matter; it could be a square, a rectangle or even a circle. Indeed, quite often the shape of the area is determined by the layout of the sports hall, field or playing area you are using.

Safety Tips

Participation in sport carries an inherent risk of injury, but instructors can minimise this by adequately controlling the group so as not to expose participants to unnecessary dangers. The tips included in this section of each game provide guidance to ensure that activities are carried out safely and effectively. The safety tips listed relate to

- the instructions you give,
- things to be mindful of and
- rule-related information.

Advice

The information I give under this heading helps to ensure that the activity runs smoothly. Advice may include tips on how to best explain the activity, how to group the participants or other related issues.

Variations

The Variations section provides alternative ways of running the activity. This section may suggest a slightly different way of playing, or ways to change the level of difficulty. Sometimes an activity can be carried out with more or fewer participants, and the information here should help you decide whether you can adapt a game to suit the numbers you have. When activities can be adapted for other sports, I list these here as well.

Warming Up and Cooling Down

It is important to start each session by warming up. A warm-up prepares the body and mind for the activity ahead and can also prevent injury. Older children in particular should have a good warm-up to prevent muscle injuries such as tears and strains. Younger children have less of a need for a warm-up to prevent injury, but they should be taught good warm-up habits as early as possible. For further information on warm-up and cool-down exercises, see Harris and Elbourn (2002) or Byl (2004).

A progressive warm-up should include the following:

• Pulse-raising activities should start at a low to moderate intensity. The activities should be progressive and aim to increase muscle temperature. This initial part should last for 3 to 7 minutes depending on the environmental temperature. Examples include jogging and sidestepping.

• Mobility exercises should be used to warm up and loosen the joints. Examples include shoulder and ankle circling.

• Stretching exercises should be incorporated to improve the range of movement at a joint. These can include static or dynamic stretches. Static stretches are when a limb is taken to the end range of movement and held in this position. Static stretches should be held 8 to 10 seconds in a warm-up. Examples of static stretches are hamstring and calf stretches, whereas dynamic stretches involve moving a body part slowly through a full range of motion. Examples include leg swinging and heel flicks.

A number of the activities in this book are suitable for use as part of a progressive warm-up. Most involve pulse-raising activities, so you should incorporate mobility and stretching exercises into them.

Because many of the activities in the book involve ballistic movements, sprinting, or both, it is also important that participants cool down to help recover after playing. Chapter 9 provides a number of activities that are suitable for use in a cool-down. That chapter also explains why it is important to cool down after exercise.

References

Harris, J. and Elbourn, J. 2002. *Warming Up and Cooling Down*. Champaign, IL: Human Kinetics.

Byl, J. 2004. *101 Fun Warm-Up and Cool-Down Games*. Champaign, IL: Human Kinetics.

Game Finder

Name of game	Page number	Age group suitable for	Equipment	Sports suitable for	Skills needed/ developed	Fitness components needed/ developed
Name Game Sprint	22	5 to 16 yrs	Cones	Basketball, hockey, soccer	Decision making, running	Reaction time, speed
Partner Chase	24	5 to 13 yrs	Cones	Cricket, basketball, netball, rugby, soccer	Decision making, dodging, running	Agility, balance, reaction time, speed
Poorly Tag	45	5 to 10 yrs	Bibs and cones	Soccer	Decision making, dodging, running	Agility, balance, reaction time, speed
Quick Cones	26	5 to 13 yrs	Bibs and cones	Soccer, rugby	Decision making, running	Agility, balance, reaction time, speed
Reveal	28	5 to 13 yrs	Cones	Hockey, soccer	Decision making, running	Reaction time, speed
Safety Link Tag	30	5 to 13 yrs	Bibs and cones	Soccer	Decision making, dodging, running	Agility, balance, reaction time, speed
Shark Bait Tag	32	5 to 13 yrs	Bibs and cones	N/A	Decision making, dodging, running	Agility, balance, reaction time, speed
Shower Tag	49	5 to 13 yrs	Bibs and cones	N/A	Decision making, dodging, running	Agility, balance, reaction time, speed
Spots	34	5 to 10 yrs	Coloured spots	Basketball, hockey, soccer	Decision making, running	Agility, balance, coordination, reaction time, speed
Square Court Handball	42	8 to 16 yrs	Bibs, sponge balls and cones	Soccer	Catching, decision making, dodging, throwing, passing	Agility, balance, coordination, reaction time, power, speed
Tactic Tag	46	8 to 16 yrs	Cones	N/A	Decision making, dodging, running	Agility, balance, reaction time, speed

Name of game	Page number	Age group suitable for	Equipment	Sports suitable for	Skills needed/ developed	Fitness components needed/ developed
Team Dodgeball	36	8 to 16 yrs	Benches, cones and sponge balls	N/A	Catching, decision making, dodging, throwing	Agility, balance, coordination, reaction time, power, speed
There and Back	50	8 to 16 yrs	Cones and sponge balls	Soccer	Hitting, catching, decision making, dodging, throwing	Agility, balance, coordination, reaction time, power, speed
Turn Tag	38	5 to 13 yrs	Cones	Basketball, soccer	Decision making, running	Agility, balance, coordination, endurance, reaction time, speed
Video Recorder	40	5 to 10 yrs	Cones	N/A	Decision making, running	Agility, balance, coordination, endurance, reaction time, speed

CHAPTER 2 BASKETBALL AND NETBALL GAMES

Name of game	Page number	Age group suitable for	Equipment	Sports suitable for	Skills needed/ developed	Fitness components needed/ developed
Beat the Ball	58	5 to 8 yrs	Basketballs or netballs	Basketball, cricket, netball, rugby	Catching, running, passing	Coordination, reaction time, speed
Block Shot	60	8 to 16 yrs	Basketballs or netballs, baskets, cones	Basketball, netball	Shooting	Coordination, reaction time, power
Circle Pass Out	62	11 to 16 yrs	Basketballs or netballs, bibs, cones	Basketball, cricket, hockey, netball, rugby, soccer	Attacking, defending, passing, receiving	Agility, balance, coordination, reaction time, power, speed
Copy Shot	64	8 to 16 yrs	Basketballs or netballs, baskets	Basketball	Shooting, layups, dribbling	Dependant on actions chosen by participants
On the Bench	55	8 to 16 yrs	Basketballs or netballs, bibs, cones, benches	Basketball, netball	Attacking, defending, passing, receiving	Agility, balance, coordination, endurance, reaction time, power, speed

(continued)

(continued)

Name of game	Page number	Age group suitable for	Equipment	Sports suitable for	Skills needed/ developed	Fitness components needed/ developed
Outnumbered	66	8 to 16 yrs	Basketballs or netballs, bibs, cones	Basketball, cricket, hockey, netball, rounders, rugby, soccer	Attacking, defending, passing, receiving, support play	Agility, balance, coordination, endurance, reaction time, power, speed
Roll, Go, Pass and Shoot	74	8 to 16 yrs	Basketballs or netballs, bibs, cones, baskets	Basketball, netball	Attacking, defending, shooting, layups, rebounding	Agility, balance, coordination, reaction time, power, speed
Team Ball Tag	68	11 to 16 yrs	Basketballs or netballs, bibs, cones	Basketball, cricket, netball, rugby, rounders	Defending, support play, passing, receiving,	Agility, balance, coordination, reaction time, power, speed
Three-Team Basketball	70	14 to 16 yrs	Basketballs or netballs, bibs	Basketball, hockey, netball, rugby, soccer	All basketball attacking and defending skills	Agility, balance, coordination, reaction time, power, speed
Top Rebounder	72	8 to 16 yrs	Basketballs or netballs, baskets	Basketball, netball	Attacking, defending, shooting, layups, rebounding	Agility, balance, coordination, reaction time, power, speed

CHAPTER 3   CRICKET, STRIKING AND FIELDING GAMES

Name of game	Page number	Age group suitable for	Equipment	Sports suitable for	Skills needed/ developed	Fitness components needed/ developed
Beat the Runner	84	5 to 16 yrs	Cones, cricket bat, tennis ball, chalk and wicket	Cricket, rounders, baseball, softball	Catching, fielding, throwing, running between the wickets, wicketkeeping	Agility, balance, coordination, reaction time, power, speed
Caribbean Cricket	87	8 to 16 yrs	Cricket bats, tennis balls and wickets	Cricket	Batting, catching, fielding, throwing, wicketkeeping	Agility, balance, coordination, reaction time, power, speed

Name of game	Page number	Age group suitable for	Equipment	Sports suitable for	Skills needed/ developed	Fitness components needed/ developed
Collide Catch	90	8 to 16 yrs	Tennis balls	Cricket, rounders, baseball, softball, soccer (goalkeeping)	Catching, throwing	Balance, coordination, reaction time
Decision Run	92	8 to 16 yrs	Cones, cricket bats, tennis balls, chalk and wickets	Cricket, rounders, baseball, softball	Batting, catching, fielding, throwing, wicketkeeping	Agility, balance, coordination, reaction time, power, speed
Four, Two or Out	95	8 to 16 yrs	Cones and tennis balls	Cricket, rounders, baseball, softball	Catching, fielding, throwing	Agility, balance, coordination, reaction time, power
Hit or Score	98	5 to 16 yrs	Cones, tennis balls and wickets	Cricket, rounders, baseball, softball	Catching, fielding, throwing	Agility, balance, coordination, reaction time, power
Knock-Down	100	8 to 16 yrs	Bibs, wickets, tennis balls and cones	Cricket, netball, baseball, rounders, softball, basketball, netball, rugby, soccer	Catching, fielding, throwing	Agility, balance, coordination, endurance, reaction time, power, speed
Leg as Wicket	103	5 to 13 yrs	Cricket bats, soft balls (or tennis balls) and cones	Cricket, basketball or netball (but a softer ball must be used)	Batting, catching, fielding, throwing	Agility, balance, coordination, reaction time, power
One Hand, One Bounce	106	8 to 16 yrs	Cones, cricket bats, tennis balls and wickets	Cricket	Batting, bowling, catching, fielding, throwing	Agility, balance, coordination, reaction time, power, speed

(continued)

(continued)

Name of game	Page number	Age group suitable for	Equipment	Sports suitable for	Skills needed/ developed	Fitness components needed/ developed
Running Two	108	5 to 16 yrs	Cones, chalk, cricket bats, tennis balls and wickets	Cricket, rounders, baseball, softball	Catching, fielding, throwing, running between the wickets	Agility, balance, coordination, reaction time, power, speed
Three-Ball Throw	111	5 to 13 yrs	Cones, hoops and tennis balls	Cricket, rounders, baseball, softball	Catching, fielding, throwing, running	Agility, balance, coordination, reaction time, power, speed
CHAPTER 4 HOCKEY GAMES						
Agility Score	126	5 to 16 yrs	Cones, goals, goalkeeper equipment, hockey balls, hockey sticks	Hockey, basketball, soccer	Attacking and defending skills	Agility, balance, coordination, reaction time, power, speed
Ball Swap	116	5 to 16 yrs	Cones, hockey balls and hockey sticks	Hockey, basketball, soccer	Dribbling	Agility, balance, coordination, reaction time, speed
Collect a Cone	118	5 to 16 yrs	Cones, hockey balls and hockey sticks	Hockey, soccer	Hitting, passing	Balance, coordination
Four Goals	129	8 to 16 yrs	Bibs, cones, hockey balls and hockey sticks	Hockey, soccer	Attacking and defending skills, passing, receiving, support play	Agility, balance, coordination, endurance, reaction time, power, speed
Get There First	120	5 to 13 yrs	Cones, hockey balls and hockey sticks	Hockey, basketball, soccer	Dribbling, running with the ball	Agility, balance, coordination, reaction time, power, speed
Make the Pass	132	8 to 16 yrs	Bibs, cones, hockey balls and hockey sticks	Hockey, basketball, netball, rugby, soccer	Attacking and defending skills, passing, receiving	Agility, balance, coordination, endurance, reaction time, power, speed

Name of game	Page number	Age group suitable for	Equipment	Sports suitable for	Skills needed/ developed	Fitness components needed/ developed
Mines	122	5 to 16 yrs	Cones, hockey balls and hockey sticks	Hockey, soccer	Hitting, passing, receiving	Balance, coordination
Pass Through the Target	124	5 to 16 yrs	Cones, hockey balls and hockey sticks	Hockey, soccer, cricket	Hitting, passing, receiving	Balance, coordination
Shooting From Distance	135	8 to 16 yrs	Bibs, cones, goals, goalkeeper equipment, hockey balls and hockey sticks	Hockey, soccer	Passing, shooting, defending skills, goalkeeping, attacking	Agility, balance, coordination, reaction time, power, speed
Ten Passes	138	8 to 16 yrs	Hockey balls and hockey sticks	Hockey, basketball, netball, rugby, soccer	Passing, receiving, defending skills	Agility, balance, coordination, reaction time, power, speed
CHAPTER 5 RUGBY GAMES						
Cross the Area	152	8 to 16 yrs	Bibs, cones and rugby balls	Rugby, basketball, hockey, netball, soccer	Decision making, passing, receiving, attacking, defending	Agility, balance, coordination, endurance, reaction time, power, speed
Don't Drop It	155	8 to 16 yrs	Rugby balls and cones	Rugby	Catching, kicking	Balance, coordination, reaction time, power, speed
Five Pass and Over	158	14 to 16 yrs	Bibs, cones and rugby balls	Rugby, basketball, cricket, netball, soccer	Attacking, defending, support play, passing, receiving, kicking	Agility, balance, coordination, reaction time, power, speed
Gladiator	161	8 to 16 yrs	Bibs, cones, rugby balls and hoops	Rugby	Attacking, defending	Agility, balance, coordination, endurance, reaction time, power, speed

(continued)

(continued)

Name of game	Page number	Age group suitable for	Equipment	Sports suitable for	Skills needed/ developed	Fitness compo- nents needed/ developed
Invader	164	8 to 16 yrs	Bibs, rugby balls and cones	Rugby	Passing, receiving, decision making, tac- tical aware- ness	Agility, bal- ance, coor- dination, reaction time, power, speed
Pass in Sequence	144	5 to 16 yrs	Rugby balls	Rugby, cricket, basketball, netball, soccer	Passing, receiving, catching	Balance, coor- dination, reac- tion time
Reactor Bounce	146	8 to 16 yrs	Rugby balls and cones	Rugby, soccer, cricket	Kicking, receiving, catching	Agility, bal- ance, coor- dination, reaction time, power, speed
Rugby Golf	167	5 to 16 yrs	Rugby balls, hoops and cones	Rugby, soccer, netball, hockey	Kicking, decision making, catching, passing	Balance, coordination, reaction time, power, speed
Shield Tag	148	8 to 16 yrs	Cones, rugby balls and bibs	Rugby, cricket, basketball, netball	Passing, decision making, receiving, dodging	Agility, bal- ance, coor- dination, reaction time, power, speed
Tadpole Pass	150	5 to 16 yrs	Rugby balls and cones	Rugby, cricket, basketball, netball, soccer	Passing, receiving, running	Balance, coordination, reaction time, speed

CHAPTER 6 SOCCER GAMES

Name of game	Page number	Age group suitable for	Equipment	Sports suitable for	Skills needed/ developed	Fitness compo- nents needed/ developed
Ball Collide	173	8 to 16 yrs	Bibs, cones, soccer balls	Soccer, basketball, netball, rugby	Decision making, passing, receiving	Agility, bal- ance, coor- dination, reaction time, power, speed
Chipping Game	180	11 to 16 yrs	Cones, soccer balls	Soccer, rugby, cricket	Catching, chipping, decision making, receiving	Balance, coordination, reaction time, power, speed
Coconut Shy	183	5 to 10 yrs	Cones, soccer balls	Soccer, hockey, netball, basketball, rugby	Dribbling, passing, receiving	Balance, coor- dination, speed

Name of game	Page number	Age group suitable for	Equipment	Sports suitable for	Skills needed/ developed	Fitness compo- nents needed/ developed
Long-Range Two Touch	186	8 to 16 yrs	Cones, soccer balls	Soccer, hockey	Decision making, passing, receiving, controlling the ball	Balance, coordination, reaction time, power, speed
One Bounce	176	11 to 16 yrs	Cones, soccer balls	Soccer	Decision making, passing	Agility, bal- ance, coor- dination, reaction time, power, speed
Passing Forwards	189	11 to 16 yrs	Bibs, cones, soccer balls	Soccer, hockey	Attacking and defend- ing skills, passing, receiving	Agility, bal- ance, coordi- nation, endur- ance, reaction time, power, speed
Soccer Tennis	192	11 to 16 yrs	Tennis court (or similar), soccer balls	Soccer	Control, passing, heading, vol- leying	Agility, bal- ance, coor- dination, reaction time, power, speed
Throw, Head, Catch	195	11 to 16 yrs	Bibs, cones, soccer balls	Soccer	Decision making, catching, heading, throwing	Agility, bal- ance, coordi- nation, endur- ance, reaction time, power, speed
Volley Game	198	11 to 16 yrs	Goals, soccer balls, cones	Soccer	Goalkeep- ing, throw- ing, volley- ing	Agility, bal- ance, coor- dination, reaction time, power, speed
Weighted Pass	178	5 to 10 yrs	Cones, soccer balls	Soccer, hockey	Passing, receiving	Balance, coor- dination

CHAPTER 7   TENNIS AND BADMINTON GAMES

Name of game	Page number	Age group suitable for	Equipment	Sports suitable for	Skills needed/ developed	Fitness compo- nents needed/ developed
Ball Familiarisation	206	5 to 10 yrs	Tennis balls, rackets	Tennis, badminton	Basic racket control	Dependant on skills chosen
Catching Game	203	8 to 13 yrs	Tennis balls, courts and rackets	Tennis, badminton	Ground strokes, volleying, catching	Balance, coordination, reaction time, power, speed

(continued)

(continued)

Name of game	Page number	Age group suitable for	Equipment	Sports suitable for	Skills needed/ developed	Fitness components needed/ developed
Cooperative-Competitive Rally	210	8 to 16 yrs	Tennis balls, courts and rackets	Tennis, badminton	Ground strokes, volleying, catching	Agility, balance, coordination, power, reaction time, speed, endurance
Lob It	213	11 to 16 yrs	Chalk, tennis balls, courts and rackets	Tennis, badminton	Lobbing, smashing, volleying	Agility, balance, coordination, power, reaction time, speed
Speed Drop	216	5 to 16 yrs	Cones, tennis balls, courts	Tennis, badminton, rugby, soccer	Catching, footwork	Agility, reaction time, speed
Team Catch	219	8 to 16 yrs	Tennis balls, courts and rackets, chalk	Tennis, badminton	Catching, volleying	Balance, coordination, reaction time, speed
Top Square	222	8 to 16 yrs	Chalk, tennis balls, rackets	Tennis, soccer, basketball	Decision making, footwork, basic hitting skills	Agility, balance, coordination, reaction time, speed
Two Shuttle Down	208	8 to 16 yrs	Badminton court, shuttles	Tennis, badminton	Catching, decision making, throwing	Agility, balance, coordination, power, reaction time, speed

CHAPTER 8 VOLLEYBALL GAMES

Name of game	Page number	Age group suitable for	Equipment	Sports suitable for	Skills needed/ developed	Fitness components needed/ developed
Catch and Throw	228	8 to 13 yrs	Volleyballs, volleyball courts	Volleyball	Catching, decision making, digging, throwing	Agility, balance, coordination, power, reaction time, speed
Catch, Pass, Spike	230	11 to 16 yrs	Volleyballs, volleyball courts	Volleyball	Catching, decision making, digging, serving, spiking, throwing, volleying	Agility, balance, coordination, power, reaction time, speed
Dig It, Volley It	232	8 to 16 yrs	Volleyballs	Volleyball, cricket, rugby	Digging, volleying	Balance, coordination, reaction time

Name of game	Page number	Age group suitable for	Equipment	Sports suitable for	Skills needed/ developed	Fitness components needed/ developed
How Many Touches?	234	11 to 16 yrs	Volleyballs, courts	Volleyball	Digging, serving, spiking, volleying	Agility, balance, coordination, power, reaction time, speed
Into the Setter	236	8 to 16 yrs	Volleyballs, courts, rubber spots or chalk	Volleyball	Digging, serving, directional passing, team play, volleying	Agility, balance, coordination, power, reaction time, speed
Line Volley	238	14 to 16 yrs	Volleyballs	Volleyball, soccer	Volleying	Balance, coordination, reaction time, power
Pass in Order	244	11 to 16 yrs	Volleyballs, volleyball courts	Volleyball	Catching, decision making, digging, serving, spiking, throwing, volleying	Agility, balance, coordination, power, reaction time, speed
Skittle Knock-Down	247	11 to 16 yrs	Volleyballs, skittles (or something similar), volleyball courts	Volleyball, tennis	Spiking, volleying	Balance, coordination, power, reaction time
Spike Rally	240	14 to 16 yrs	Volleyballs, a wall	Volleyball	Spiking	Balance, coordination, power, reaction time
Team Keep-Up	242	11 to 16 yrs	Volleyballs	Volleyball, soccer, badminton, tennis	Digging, volleying	Agility, balance, coordination, endurance, reaction time, speed

CHAPTER 9   COOL-DOWN GAMES

Cone Visit	254	5 to 16 yrs	Different-coloured cones	Basketball, hockey, soccer	Decision making, running	Coordination, flexibility (if stretches are added)

(continued)

(continued)

Name of game	Page number	Age group suitable for	Equipment	Sports suitable for	Skills needed/ developed	Fitness components needed/ developed
Count Up	256	8 to 16 yrs	Cones	Any game that involves passing: soccer, netball, hockey, rugby	Decision making, running	Flexibility (if stretches are added)
Down the Gears	257	5 to 8 yrs	Cones	Basketball, hockey, soccer	Running	Flexibility (if stretches are added)
Four Square	258	5 to 16 yrs	Cones, any type of sports ball	Basketball, hockey, netball, soccer, rugby	Decision making, passing receiving, dribbling, running	Coordination, balance, flexibility (if stretches are added)
Inner Circle	262	5 to 16 yrs	Cones, basketballs or soccer balls	Basketball, soccer	Passing, receiving, dribbling, running	Coordination, balance, flexibility (if stretches are added)
Name the Stretch	260	5 to 13 yrs	Cones, chalk	N/A	Decision making	Flexibility (if stretches are added)

one

Multi-Sport Games

The games in this chapter are generic activities. Most involve every participant in the group working on the same task. This increases participant involvement and, therefore, the amount of activity. A number of these games and activities can be used as part of a progressive warm-up. The activities are fun based, and many require minimal equipment. Also included are variations on tag games and team games. Most activities are vigorous and involve running and dodging to encourage activity.

Many of the activities in this chapter are games children have recreated in the playground. In recent years many schools have incorporated programmes to increase exercise and activity during breaktimes. Many of the activities found in this section are ideal for carrying out during breaktimes because they are easy to set up and require minimal equipment. Implementing these games in the playground is an excellent way of making sure that all children meet their recommended daily physical activity requirements.

Bash Ball
Ages 5 to 10

Key Skills and Fitness Components Developed

Skills
- Decision making
- Hitting

Fitness Components
- Coordination
- Reaction time

Equipment
One large sponge ball per 6 to 10 participants

Game
Arrange the participants into groups of 6 to 10 and separate each group into two equal teams. Give one participant in each group a ball. Participants in each group stand in a circle (see the figure on page 3). The participants from one team stand side-by-side, next to each other to make one half of the circle, and participants from the other team do the same to make up the other half of the circle. The circle should be sized so that the participants in the group have their feet approximately 75 centimetres to 1 metre apart. The participants' feet should be touching those standing on either side of them. Participants stand with one hand behind their back and the other hanging in front of them.

To start the game, the participant holding the ball rolls it into the circle. Participants try to stop the ball going through their legs by slapping it away towards their opponents. They must use a flat hand and can use their palms or the backs of their hand, while trying to keep the shot low.

The aim of the game is to hit the ball through the legs of one of the opponents. If a participant hits the ball through an opponent's legs, his team gains a point. The game continues for a set time (e.g., 3 minutes) or until one team has scored a set number of points (e.g., 10).

Safety Tips
- Use soft balls only.
- Participants should not hit the ball too hard or too high.
- Participants should not play the game for too long because they may get sore back muscles from leaning over. By playing this game regularly, participants should strengthen their back muscles and be able to play for longer periods of time.
- Male participants could wear a box, or cup, to protect themselves.
- Participants may hit the ball only when it is front of them. They should not reach across in front of opponents or team-mates to hit a ball.

Advice
- Ensure that all participants have an equal distance between their legs.
- Ensure that participants do not catch or punch the ball.

Variations

- **Easier:** Participants can use two hands.
- **Easier/harder:** Make the circle smaller or bigger so participants have their feet closer together or farther apart to change the level of difficulty.
- **Game variation:** Play in two teams. If the ball is hit through a participant's legs, he is out and must stand up and fold his arms across his body to show the other players that he is out. If a participant hits the ball through the legs of an opponent who is out, then he is also out. When all the participants from one team are out, the opposing team is awarded a point. Play until one team has scored a set number of points (e.g., 5).
- **Game variation:** Play with similar rules to the previous variation but participants play individually. Participants compete against all other members of their group to be the last player in the game.
- **Game variation:** Play the individual version of the game, but use a different point system. All of the participants start with 10 points. They gain a point if they hit a ball though another participant's legs, but lose one if the ball goes through their own legs. The game continues for a set time (e.g., 5 minutes) or until one participant scores a set number of points.
- **Harder:** Add a second ball into the circle.

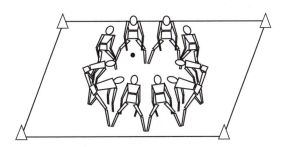

Bean Bag Shift

Ages 5 to 13

Key Skills and Fitness Components Developed

Skills	Fitness Components
· Decision making	· Agility
· Running	· Balance
	· Reaction time
	· Speed

Equipment

- At least one bean bag per participant
- One hoop per three participants
- Cones

There should be an equal number of the different-coloured bean bags and hoops. For example, for 30 participants there would be 10 blue, 10 green and 10 red bean bags and 5 blue, 5 green and 5 red hoops.

Game

Cone out a playing area. Separate the participants into three equal teams, and name the teams the colours of the bean bags and hoops. For example, if you have blue, green and red bean bags, one team is the blue team, another team is the green team and the remaining team is the red team. The participants stand around the outside of the playing area. Scatter the hoops and the bean bags on the floor in the area. Do not place the bean bags in the hoops.

When the game begins, the participants run into the area and try to place the bean bags of the colour corresponding to their teams into their own hoops. For example, the participants in the blue team pick up the blue bean bags and place them in the blue hoops. Participants may carry only one bean bag at a time.

Once teams have placed all of the scattered bean bags in their hoops, they can start taking bean bags from the other teams' hoops. The aim for each team is to have the most correctly coloured bean bags in their own hoops. As opponents take bean bags out of hoops, participants return them to their hoops.

Participants also try to 'mess up' the other teams' bean bags by picking one up and placing it in one of the other coloured hoops. After a set time (e.g., 1 minute) stop the game and count the number of bean bags in each hoop to see which team has the most correctly coloured bean bags in their hoop; this team wins the game.

Safety Tips

- Warn participants to be careful not to crash heads with other players when they are bending over to pick up or put down bean bags.
- Participants should stay on their feet and not slide on the floor on their knees.
- This can be a very tiring game, so remember to give rest periods between games.
- Warn participants to be careful of collisions of any kind.

Advice

- Ensure that participants take only one bean bag at a time.
- Encourage fair play by making sure that participants do not move bean bags after you have stopped the game. If the game is stopped, participants must not pick up any more bean bags, but they can place a bean bag that they have already picked up in one of the hoops.
- Do not allow participants to guard hoops to prevent opponents from picking up bean bags.
- Participants should place, rather than throw, the bean bags into the hoops.

Variations

- **Game variation:** Teams line up on different sides of the area and use a relay system to move the bean bags. Two or three participants from each team run out; they can each move a bean bag and then return to their line so the next team-mate can go.
- **Game variation:** Vary the way the participants can move (e.g., they can only walk, they must skip or they can move only on hands and feet).
- **Small groups:** This game can be played with two teams. Use only two different-coloured bean bags, but three different-coloured hoops. Participants place their own bean bags into their own coloured hoops, but they move opponents' bean bags into the other coloured hoops.
- **Sport-specific:** This game can be modified for use in soccer sessions, but it is important that you have three types or colours of soccer ball (or two if you are playing the variation that precedes this one). Use coloured cones to mark out areas approximately 1.5 by 1.5 metres instead of using hoops. Players must move the balls by dribbling them.
- **Sport-specific:** This game can be modified for use in hockey sessions, using hockey balls instead of bean bags. Players must dribble the ball to the hoop and ensure that the ball is stationary inside of it before moving another ball.

Call and Catch

Key Skills and Fitness Components Developed

Skills

- Throwing
- Catching

Fitness Components

- Coordination
- Reaction time
- Speed

Equipment

- Four cones per four or five participants
- One ball per four or five participants

Game

Arrange the participants into groups of four or five. For each group use cones to set up an area 10 by 10 metres (11 by 11 yd). One participant stands in the centre of the area with the ball, and the remaining participants each stand by one of the corner cones (see figure on page 7).

The participant in the centre of the area calls the name of one of the other participants while at the same time throwing the ball up into the air so that it bounces in the centre of the area. After she has thrown the ball, she moves to the corner of the area where no other participant is standing. The participant who has had her name called must run into the centre of the area to catch the ball before it has bounced twice on the ground. The ball must travel above a specified height (e.g., as high as the tallest person, or at least 2 m into the air) so that the person running in to catch it has a fair chance to do so. The participant who attempts to catch the ball should now stand in the centre of the grid and repeat the process of calling a name, throwing the ball up and moving to an empty corner of the area.

This sequence continues until one participant makes an error such as not catching the ball before it bounces a second time or not throwing it high enough. If a participant makes an error, she loses a point. All participants start with 20 points. Have them play for a set time (e.g., 2 minutes); the participant who has the most points at the end of this time is the winner.

Safety Tips

- Warn participants to avoid collisions when running in and out of the square, especially when there are five players with a player starting beside each of the corner cones.
- Ensure participants have completed a thorough warm-up before carrying out this activity because it involves ballistic movements.
- This can be a very tiring game, so remember to give rest periods between games.

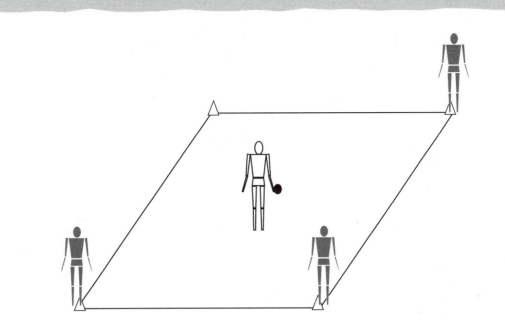

Advice

- Try to group the participants according to speed or quickness.
- Ensure that the ball is well inflated and has enough bounce so it will rebound high enough for the game to be viable.
- Play on firm surfaces because it will not be possible to play if the ball does not bounce high enough.
- Once the participants understand the rules, have them call a name out and throw the ball as soon as they catch it so that the game moves faster.
- Ensure the participant throwing the ball in the air calls the next person's name early.

Variations

- **Easier:** When the participants are in the centre, they cannot call out the name of the person who threw the ball up for them to catch.
- **Game variation:** Play in two teams of three or four. Participants stand in a circle and call out the name of an opponent when they throw the ball into the air. When a participant makes a mistake, the opposing team gains a point. Have them play for a set time (e.g., 3 minutes). At the end of this time, the team with the most points wins.
- **Sport-specific:** This game can be played in netball, rugby and basketball sessions using the relevant ball for each sport.
- **Sport-specific:** This game can be played in cricket sessions using a tennis ball.
- **Sport-specific:** This game can be adapted for use in soccer sessions with older or more advanced participants. The participants must kick the ball to send it into the air. They must also call the name of the next participant before they kick the ball.

Catch to Come Back
Ages 8 to 16

Key Skills and Fitness Components Developed

Skills

- Catching
- Decision making
- Dodging
- Throwing

Fitness Components

- Agility
- Balance
- Coordination
- Power
- Reaction time
- Speed

Equipment

- One bench per six to eight participants
- Cones
- Approximately one large sponge ball per five participants

Game

This game is best played indoors. It is a good activity to play when you have a large group (e.g., 20 to 40 participants) in a small sports hall. The game set-up is shown in the figure on this page. Separate the participants into two teams and number them Team 1 and Team 2. Team 1 stands in one half of the playing area or field while Team 2 stands in the other. Place benches behind each team on the outside of the area. Use cones to mark out a no-man's-land between the two teams. There should be approximately one sponge ball for every five participants and each team should be given half of the balls.

When the game starts, participants throw the balls at opponents trying to hit them directly below the waist. The ball cannot bounce off the floor, a wall or a team-mate before hitting an opponent. If a participant is hit, he is out. Participants try to avoid get-

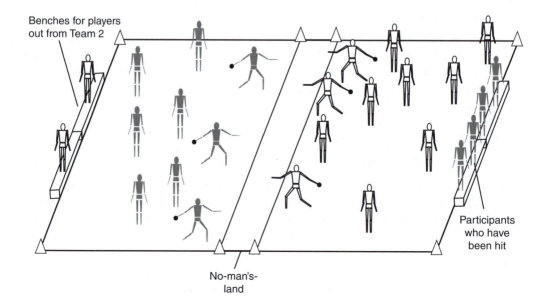

Benches for players out from Team 2

Participants who have been hit

No-man's-land

ting hit by dodging out of the way, or if they have a ball in their hand, using this as a shield. If a player catches a ball thrown by an opponent, the person who threw the ball is out. Participants who are hit (or caught out), stand on the bench *behind the opposing team*. Teams try to win a game by getting a set number of opponents out of the game.

Participants who are out have a chance of rejoining the game. To do this, they must catch a ball that has been thrown to them by a team-mate (usually over the heads of the opponents). For this to be counted as a catch, the person must be standing on the bench when he catches the ball and must not step off until he has full control of it.

When playing with a large group, the game continues until one team gets a set number of opponents out (e.g., 10 for teams of 15 to 20). This team scores a point, the teams swap sides and the fun begins again. When playing with smaller groups (e.g., teams of three to eight), all of the opposing players must be out before a team can win a point. Have participants play until a team has won a set number of points (e.g., 5) or for a set time (e.g., 20 minutes).

Safety Tips

- Ensure participants have completed a thorough warm-up before carrying out this activity because it involves ballistic movements.
- Do not allow participants to go into the no-man's-land to collect any of the sponge balls. Participants who go into this area are out and must stand on the bench behind the opposing team.
- Have participants use low throws to avoid hitting anyone in the face.
- Ensure that the participants do not throw the ball too hard.
- Use soft balls only.
- Place benches at least 2 metres away from walls or other obstructions in case participants fall.

Advice

- This activity is ideally played in a sports hall or gymnasium.
- For this game to run smoothly, participants must play fairly, so encourage honesty.
- Put more balls in to speed up the game.

Variations

- **Easier/harder:** Use wider or narrower distances between the benches and the no-man's-land to increase or decrease difficulty.
- **Game variation:** A participant can attempt to free a team-mate who is out by running through the opposing team's area and tagging the team-mate. Participants who run into the opposing team's area can be hit by a ball thrown at them. The participant running through the opposing team's area can carry a ball with him to use as a shield; he cannot throw this ball at opponents once they have left their own area. If the participant running through manages to tag his team-mate without getting hit by a ball, then both can return to their side freely. This means they cannot be hit by the opponents on their walk back. A team-mate running through the opposing team's area can free only one team-mate at a time. If a participant is hit when running through the opposing team's area, he is out.

Change Chase
Ages 5 to 13

Key Skills and Fitness Components Developed

Skills

- Decision making
- Dodging
- Running

Fitness Components

- Agility
- Balance
- Reaction time
- Speed

Equipment

- One bib (pinnie) per 6 to 10 participants
- Cones
- Balls (if playing game variation)

Game

Cone out your working area. Choose some participants to be chasers; the rest are runners. There should be one chaser for every 6 to 10 participants, and each of them should be given a bib (pinnie). Younger participants should hold bibs in their hands rather than put them on. However, they should fold the bib over in their hand so they do not trip over it when they are running. Older participants can put the bibs on.

When the game begins, the chasers run around trying to tag the runners. When tagged, the participants swap roles, so that the chaser becomes a runner and the runner becomes a chaser. The chaser hands her bib to the runner. The new chaser is not allowed to tag the participant who tagged her. Have the participants play for a set time (e.g., 1 to 2 minutes); any participant who is a chaser at the end of the set time has to perform a fun challenge. The challenge should be something fun—for example, saying something funny or performing an animal impression.

Safety Tips

- Warn participants to be careful of collisions.
- Warn chasers not to tag too hard.
- Chasers should fold their bibs over when they are holding them so they do not trip over them when they are running.

Advice

- Chasers should not hide their bibs; all the participants they are chasing should be able to see it.
- Remind participants that when they become chasers they cannot tag the person who tagged them.
- Chasers should hand their bibs to the runners when they tag them. They should not throw the bibs at them or drop them on the floor.
- The challenges that the chasers perform at the end of the set time should not be seen as a punishment. Make sure that no challenge is too strenuous or severe.

Variations

- **Game variation:** Chasers wear their bibs and continue in this role throughout the game. Any runner who is tagged puts on a bib and becomes a chaser. Have participants continue until there is only one runner not tagged; this participant is the winner.

- **Game variation:** Runners have a few balls that they can pass (throw) among themselves. Chasers cannot tag runners holding balls.

- **Harder:** Instead of tagging, chasers throw sponge balls underarm and try to hit the runners. They should aim to hit the runners on the legs.

- **Sport-specific:** This game can be adapted to soccer. Have one chaser to every 3 to 4 runners. Chasers run around dribbling a soccer ball and try to hit the runners below the knees with the ball to tag them.

Crossover

Ages 8 to 16

Key Skills and Fitness Components Developed

Skills

- Decision making
- Running

Fitness Components

- Agility
- Balance
- Reaction time
- Speed

Equipment

Four cones per group

Game

Arrange the participants into groups of five. For each group use cones to set up an area of 10 by 10 metres (11 by 11 yd). Within each group four participants stand on each of the corner cones. These participants are runners. The remaining participant stands in the centre of the area and is the chaser.

The runners work together against the chaser. The idea is for two of the runners to swap positions. In the figure on this page you can see that the two participants at the top of the area are trying to swap. Each time two runners swap positions, a point is scored against the chaser. The chaser tries to become a runner. To do this, he tries to get to one of the corner cones before a runner does, when two runners are attempting to switch.

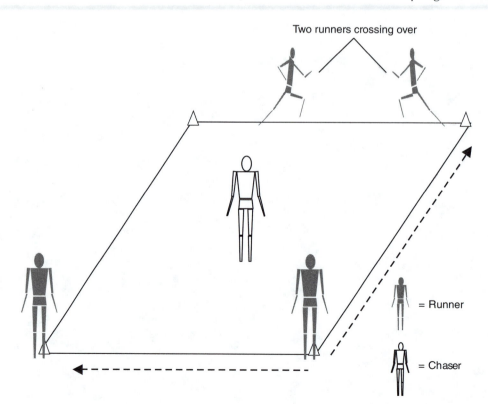

Two runners crossing over

= Runner

= Chaser

If the chaser gets to the corner cone before the runner, they swap roles, and the runner becomes the chaser.

The runners count loudly the number of points they score against the chaser. Each time a new participant becomes a chaser, the runners count up from zero again. Have participants play for a set time, such as 3 minutes. At the end of this time the participants are ranked based on the greatest number of points that were scored against them on a single occasion while they were the chaser. For example, if the greatest number of points that were scored against one of the participants when he/she was a chaser was 5, and all of the other participants had more than that, then the participant with 5 points scored against him wins.

Safety Tips

- Ensure participants have completed a thorough warm-up before carrying out this activity because it involves ballistic movements.
- Warn participants to be careful of collisions.
- Participants should stay on their feet and not slide to get to a cone first.
- Leave suitable gaps between groups.

Advice

- Try to match the participants in each group according to speed or quickness.
- If runners have not switched for approximately 10 seconds, the chaser can count down from 5 to 0. If at the end of the count the runners still haven't swapped places, then the chaser can choose one of the runners to switch with.
- Make sure runners call loudly when they score points.
- Ask participants to remember the greatest number of points scored against them when they are the chaser.

Variations

- **Game variation:** Each participant takes a turn to be a chaser. Runners score a point each time they swap positions. If two runners try to swap and the chaser gets to a cone first, then the chaser takes 3 points off the total. The chaser continues to chase and does not switch with a runner. Again, participants are ranked according to how many points were scored against them when they were the chaser.

Empty It
Ages 5 to 13

Key Skills and Fitness Components Developed

Skills
- Decision making
- Running

Fitness Components
- Agility
- Balance
- Reaction time
- Speed

Equipment
- Four hoops per group
- Twelve bean bags per group (cones, balls, shuttles or other similar objects could be used as an alternative to bean bags)

Game

Arrange the participants into groups of four. Place the hoops on the floor in a square formation, with three bean bags in each. The square should be approximately 10 by 10 metres (11 by 11 yd). Each participant should stand beside a hoop (see figure on this page).

When the game begins, the participants try to empty their hoop of bean bags. Participants pick up *one* of the bean bags, run with it and place it in an opponent's hoop. Participants must place the bean bag in the hoop rather than throw it. They then return to their hoop and take another bean bag so they can once again place it in another participant's hoop.

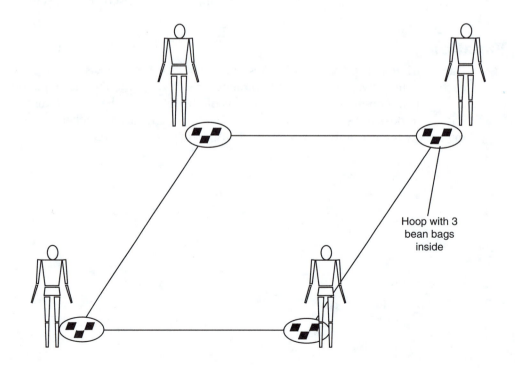

Hoop with 3 bean bags inside

The game continues until one of the participants has emptied her hoop of bean bags. If a participant empties her hoop of bean bags, she returns to her hoop, stands inside of it before putting her hand in the air and shouts 'empty'. If a participant does this, then she wins the game. If none of the participants have won after a set time (e.g., 1 minute), shout 'stop' to halt the game; then count how many bean bags each participant has in her hoop. The participant with the fewest bean bags in her hoop is the winner. Return the bean bags to the hoops, have participants rest and after they have rested, start the fun again.

Safety Tips
- Warn participants to be careful of collisions.
- Warn participants about the tendency to crash heads with others when they are picking up or placing bean bags in the hoops so they can avoid doing this.
- This game is very intense so do not let the participants play for too long, and give them rest periods between games.
- Hoops can slip on some surfaces, so warn the participants not to step on the hoops.

Advice
- Participants may take only one bean bag at a time.
- Participants should keep looking at opponents' hoops in case one of them is close to emptying it.
- Participants should place the bean bags into the hoops and not throw them. They must place the bean bags so that they stay in the hoops.
- Watch for participants moving bean bags after you have shouted 'stop'.
- Choose groups by ability so the game is challenging for all participants.

Variations
- **Game variation:** Place the hoops a few metres further apart. Use cones to form a circle around each hoop with the hoop in the centre. The diameter of the coned circle should be approximately 6 to 8 metres (6.6 to 8.7 yd). Participants must throw a bean bag into an opponent's hoop from outside the coned circle. If they miss with a throw, they pick up the bean bag, move back outside the cones, continuing to do this until the bean bag has landed in the hoop. They can then return to their own hoop to get another bean bag or to win the game if there are no bean bags left to collect.

Exercise Detective

Ages 5 to 10

Equipment

None

Game

Arrange the participants into groups of 10 to 20. Ask the participants to stand in a circle 1 to 2 metres apart. Choose one participant to be a detective and ask him to stand in the centre of the circle. When you have explained the rules of the game, ask the detective to cover his eyes. Now choose one of the other participants to be a criminal by pointing at him, making sure all of the other participants in the circle know who the criminal is. Make sure the detective does not peek so he does not know who the criminal is.

Have the criminal start performing an exercise, such as star jumps, punching the air above his head, jumping from side to side, running on the spot or any other physical exercise that can be done in one place. Once the criminal starts the exercise, the remaining participants copy his action. Every 10 to 20 seconds the criminal must change the exercise, and again, the rest of the participants must copy the new action.

Once the group has started copying the criminal's exercise, the detective can open his eyes. He has to remain in the centre of the circle, but he can turn in any direction. The detective must try to look around to discover who the criminal is and then reveal him. The detective has a set amount of time (e.g., 2 minutes) to make three guesses to discover who the criminal is. If the detective does not identify the criminal within three guesses or by the end of the set time, the criminal becomes the detective for the next round. If the detective correctly identifies the criminal, choose a new detective and criminal for the next round.

Safety Tips

- Space the participants in the circle so they do not bump into each other or hit or kick each other when they are performing the exercises.

- Some exercises may be too vigorous for some participants to carry out for longer than a few seconds. Inform these participants that they can rest or perform the exercise at a lower intensity (e.g., jumping lower during knees-up jumps) if they need to. Participants should try their best to complete each activity.

Advice

- It helps if the participants know a number of physical exercises prior to starting the game, so try to show them approximately 8 to 12 exercises before starting. Ask them to be imaginative if they are the criminal and to try to change the exercise regularly.

- If the criminals are getting caught too easily, tell participants to make sure the detective is turned away from them before changing to a new exercise. It also helps if you tell the other group members not to constantly stare at the criminal because a good detective can see where they are looking.

- If the detective is struggling to work out who the criminal is, suggest that he listen carefully for changes in noise when a new activity is chosen.

Variations

- **Game variation:** Instead of having the participants play in a circle, have them move around inside a coned area. The detective must again stay in the centre of the area, but the other participants can move anywhere they like. The criminal must choose moving exercises—for example, jogging, skipping, running backwards, sidestepping or hopping.

- **Game variation:** Each of the participants takes a turn being the detective and tries to work out the criminal in the fewest guesses. The participant who works out the criminal in the fewest guesses is the winner.

Hide From the Giant
Ages 5 to 8

Key Skills and Fitness Components Developed

Skills	Fitness Components
· Dodging	· Agility
· Running	· Balance
	· Reaction time
	· Speed

Equipment
- One bib (pinnie) per participant
- One cone per participant

Game

This is a game that younger children really enjoy playing. Scatter the cones in the playing area; these are rocks. There should be one cone per participant. Explain how to play the game then choose one participant to be a chaser, or the sleeping giant. The giant should put a bib on. The remaining participants are runners. The giant lies down on her side at the edge of the area, facing away from the cones, and pretends to go to sleep. To add effect the giant can pretend to snore loudly. The runners move close to the giant and try to wake her up by gently tapping her on the back with their hands or shaking her softly. The runners can also try to wake up the giant by saying 'Wake up, giant' or something similar.

After a few moments the sleeping giant jumps up from the ground and tries to tag the runners. The runners run away and stand by one of the cones to hide behind a rock from the giant. There can only be one runner hiding behind each of the cones, or rocks. If the giant tags one of the other runners, that participant puts a bib on and becomes a giant for the next round of the game. Once all of the remaining runners are hiding behind rocks, the giant and any of the participants she tagged return to the location where they were sleeping, lie down and once again pretend to go to sleep. The runners again try to wake the giants, and when the original giant wakes up, the new ones will also awaken. Any of the giants can tag the runners. When the runners are trying to wake the giants, remove some of the cones. You should remove one cone for each participant who has become a giant. Continue the game until there is one participant who has not been tagged; this is the winner. The winner becomes the giant for the next game.

Safety Tips
- Warn participants to be careful of collisions.
- Participants should not tag too hard.
- Participants should be careful when they are trying to stand by a rock if another participant is trying to stand by it, too. They should be careful not to bump into each other or to step on other participants' feet or toes.
- Participants should stay on their feet and not slide to get to a cone first.

Advice

- If the ground is too wet or hard to lie on when the sleeping giants are pretending to be snoozing, then the sleeping giants can crouch down instead of lying down.
- To speed up the game, have fewer cones than the number of runners.
- All runners should go close to the giant to wake her up. They cannot be hiding by the rocks while the other participants wake up the giants.
- Runners should not be too rough or too loud when they try to wake the giants.

Variations

- **Easier/harder:** Make the game more difficult for the giants by adding more cones for the runners to hide behind. Taking more cones away makes it easier for the giants.
- **Game variation:** Children may have more fun if you are the giant to begin with. They certainly will if you pretend to be a giant and make 'giant noises' when you are chasing them.
- **Game variation:** Choose a number of participants to be giants. When a participant is a giant and she tags another participant, then the two of them switch roles for the next round.
- **Sport-specific:** This game can be adapted to sports that involve dribbling, such as hockey or soccer. The giants do not have a ball, but the other participants do, and they must dribble to a cone when the giant wakes up. Instead of tagging the participants, the giant tries to take their ball from them. If she manages to do this, the runner becomes a giant.

Hurdles
Ages 5 to 13

Key Skills and Fitness Components Developed

Skills

- Running
- Jumping

Fitness Components

- Agility
- Balance
- Reaction time
- Speed

Equipment

- Mini-hurdles
- Four cones for every 12 participants

Game

Arrange the participants into groups of 12; then separate each group into two teams of six. The figure on page 21 shows how each group should be set up. Participants line up in their team, with each of them facing an opponent. The teams line up with a distance of approximately 5 metres (5.5 yd) between them. Team-mates stand approximately 2 to 4 metres apart. Participants sit on the floor facing an opponent with their legs flat on the ground. Place a cone on the ground 2 metres away from each of the participants at the end of the rows. Starting at the same end, number the participants in each team 1 to 6. Place a mini-hurdle by the feet of each participant. This means there should be two hurdles between each participant and the opponent they are facing. The hurdles should be placed at least 1 metre from the participants and there should be a gap of at least 1 metre between the hurdles.

Call out one of the numbers—for example, 'number 2'. The participants numbered 2 in each team stand up and run through the gap between the participants, jumping over each of their team's hurdles. Once they get over the end hurdle, they run around the cone at the top of their line, run behind their team-mates to the other end of their team's line. They then run around the cone at the other end of the line and down the middle of the teams, jumping over the remaining hurdles until they get back to their starting positions, where they sit back down. The participant who gets back to her start position first wins a point for her team.

Call out another number to repeat the process. Have them play for a set time (e.g., 5 minutes) with the team scoring the most points at the end of the set time winning. Alternatively play until one team has won a set number of points (e.g., 15). Change participants in one team so they are sitting in a different place and compete against a different opponent and start the fun again.

Safety Tips

- Most mini-hurdles are made to fall over easily when struck. However, this occurs only if the person is jumping over it the correct direction. Ensure that the hurdles are set up facing the same way and that the participants jump over them in the correct direction.

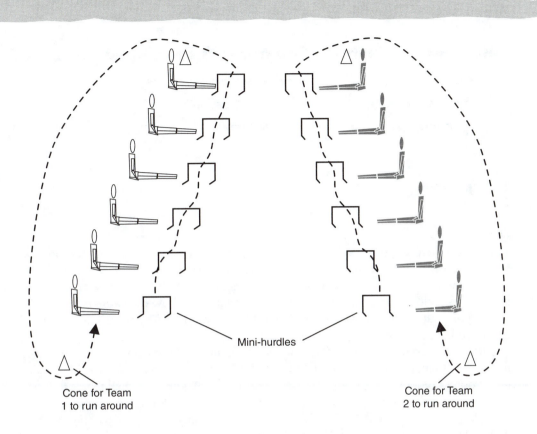

Mini-hurdles

Cone for Team 1 to run around

Cone for Team 2 to run around

- Participants sitting on the floor should not have their hands on the floor behind them because the runners may step on them as they run past.

Advice

- Try to match the participants by ability so all races are competitive.
- Ensure that participants are all seated in the correct position before you call out a number.
- Do not call out the same number too many times in a row to ensure that participants have a rest between sprints.

Variations

- **Game variation:** Participants run a relay starting with one of the end participants. When she has completed her run, the next person in the line runs. The relay continues until all participants have run, and the team finishing first is the winner.
- **Game variation:** Have participants weave in and out of the hurdles instead of jumping over them.
- **Game variation:** This game can be modified for use with sports that involve dribbling (e.g., basketball and soccer). Remove the hurdles and give each participant a ball. Participants have to dribble their balls between the two teams, around the back of their team-mates and back down the middle to their start position when their number has been called out.

Name Game Sprint
Ages 5 to 16

Key Skills and Fitness Components Developed

Skills
- Decision making
- Running

Fitness Components
- Reaction time
- Speed

Equipment
Cones

Game
This activity involves participants competing in a number of sprint races, but there is a twist to how the races are started. Arrange the participants into groups of 5 to 15. Using cones, mark two lines approximately 10 to 20 metres (11 to 22 yd) apart. Have participants line up along one of the lines of cones; then explain how the game is played. The line of cones the participants are standing on is the start line. The other line of cones is the finish line.

Participants compete against the other participants in their group. Choose a category that the participants know something about. For example, if you were coaching soccer to a group of older participants, you may choose the category 'national teams that have won the soccer World Cup'. Call out the name of a country. If the national soccer team from that country has won the World Cup, the participants race to the finish line. If that national team has not won the World Cup, then participants must stay on the line where they are standing and not run. For example, if you call 'Germany' (men's and women's World Cup winners), 'Brazil' or 'England' (men's) or 'USA' (women's), the participants would run, whereas if you called 'Scotland', 'Australia' or 'Canada', the participants would not run. Points are scored for the participants who finish the sprint in the first three positions, as follows:

- 3 points for finishing first
- 2 points for finishing second
- 1 point for finishing third

Participants who make a mistake (e.g., run when they are not supposed to or don't run when they are supposed to) have to perform a fun challenge. Have participants play for a set number of sprints (e.g., 10) and declare the participant with the most points the winner. Alternatively have them play until one participant scores a set number of points (e.g., 15). Start the game again with a new category.

Safety Tips
- Ensure participants are suitably warmed up before playing this activity because it involves ballistic movements.
- Participants should stand with an appropriate space between them. When they race, participants should run straight ahead and not across any other participants' running paths. This is also applicable when they are slowing down after the finish line.

- Leave a suitable gap between the finish line and any obstructions (e.g., the gymnasium or sports hall wall) so participants have enough space to slow down when they have completed the race.

Advice

- Try to use categories that the participants know about. If you are a teacher, you can use categories from the lessons you have been teaching.
- Sample categories for younger participants include titles of nursery rhymes, cartoon characters, names of various sports or colours of the rainbow.
- Sample categories for older participants include names of muscles in the body, sports teams in a certain league (e.g., the English Premier League or the National Football League in the USA), movies featuring a specific actor or actress, sports stars who play for a certain team (e.g., Manchester United Football Club in England or the Chicago Cubs in the USA) or countries in a specific continent.

Variations

- **Game variation:** Vary the starting position of the group. For example, they could face away from the finish line or sit down on the start line.
- **Game variation:** Participants complete a shuttle in which they must run to the other line of cones and back to their original start positions to finish the race.
- **Large groups:** If you have a large number of groups but a small playing area, have the groups take turns to race. The first group lines up at the start line, and the second group waits a few metres behind them. After each sprint the participants walk down the side of the playing area to return to the start. The next group can be started as soon as all the participants from the previous group are out of the way.
- **Small groups:** Participants play in smaller groups, and within each group one participant acts as the leader and chooses the category.
- **Sport-specific:** This activity can be adapted to sports that involve dribbling skills, such as basketball, hockey or soccer. Participants travel to the end line dribbling their balls and must stop when they get to the finish line.

Key Skills and Fitness Components Developed

Skills	Fitness Components
· Decision making	· Agility
· Dodging	· Balance
· Running	· Reaction time
	· Speed

Equipment

Cones

Game

Cone out your playing area. The size of the area should be appropriate for the number of players in your group and their abilities. Arrange the participants in pairs. The participants in each pair compete against each other and should be numbered 1 and 2. Number 1 jogs around the area in various directions. Number 2 follows his partner. The number 1s move at a slow speed so that their partner can stay close behind them. If you call 'change', the participants switch roles so that number 2 is leading. If you call 'go', the participant leading tries to run around the area trying to get as far from his partner as possible. The participant who is following becomes a chaser. The chaser tries to stay as close as possible to the leader, but he is not allowed to touch the leader.

Let the chase go on for between 5 and 10 seconds, and then halt the game by shouting 'stop'. At this point all participants stop and stand still. If the chaser is close enough to tag his partner without stepping forwards, he is awarded a point. If the leader is too far away to be tagged, then he is awarded a point. Participants then move off again working at a slow speed with number 2 leading. Have participants play for a set time (e.g., 3 minutes) or until one of the partners has scored a set number of points, such as 5.

Safety Tips

- Warn participants to be careful of collisions, especially when you call 'go'.
- Chasers should not tag too hard.
- Ensure participants are suitably warmed up before shouting 'go'.
- Let the participants recover suitably by ensuring that they work long enough at the slower speed between calls of 'go'.

Advice

- Watch for participants moving after you call 'stop'.
- Encourage the participants being chased to dodge, change direction quickly and run through the gaps between other pairs to evade their partners.
- The participant who is leading must not move too fast before you call 'go'. If you see a leader moving too quickly , call 'change'.

- Leaders must stay inside the playing area. If they run out of it, their opponent gains the point.
- Remind participants to keep their own scores.
- Change partners after each game to maintain motivation. Partners should start the new game with zero points.
- You may want to match participants by ability.

Variations

- **Easier:** Make the game easier for the chasers by allowing them to have a specific number of steps (e.g., 2) after you have called 'stop'.
- **Game variation:** Pairs move around with the chasers staying between 2 and 4 metres behind their partners. Once you call 'go', the chaser has 10 seconds to tag his partner. He scores a point if he tags his partner, but the partner scores a point if he doesn't.
- **Game variation:** Participants play in groups of three and are numbered 1, 2 and 3. Call out the number of the participant who should lead (instead of calling 'change'). The other two follow the leader until you call 'go'; then the chase starts again, with both of the other participants chasing.
- **Sport-specific:** This game is similar to Dribble Chase in *Fun and Games* on page 150, so it can be adapted for use in soccer sessions.
- **Sport-specific:** This game can be adapted for use in throwing and catching sports, such as rugby, cricket, basketball and netball. Participants are again in pairs, and they move around the area, passing the ball to each other. They should stay between 3 and 5 metres (3.3 and 5.5 yd) apart as they are moving. After the participants have been moving for a few moments, call 'go'; then count down from 5 to zero slowly. The participant with the ball becomes the chaser, and the one without the ball must evade his partner. The chaser must try to tag his partner by touching him with the ball gently; he should not throw it at him. The chaser has to make the tag before you count down to zero. The chaser scores a point if he tags his partner, but the partner scores a point if he doesn't.

Quick Cones

Ages 5 to 13

Key Skills and Fitness Components Developed

Skills

- Decision making
- Running

Fitness Components

- Agility
- Balance
- Reaction time
- Speed

Equipment

- One bib (pinnie) per 6 to 8 participants
- Cones

Game

Arrange the participants in groups of 12 to 16. Cone out a playing area for each group. Choose two of the participants in each group to be chasers and give them bibs (pinnies) to put on. Four participants start as runners and stand at the side of the area. Give each remaining participant a cone. The participants with the cones should find a space in the area, place their cone on the floor and stand next to it.

When the game starts, the chasers count up loudly from 0 to 20 at a rate of approximately one number every second. As soon as the chasers have started counting, the runners move to participants who are standing by cones to switch roles with them; the runners stand beside the cones, and the participants who were standing by the cone become runners. To ensure that the participant at the cone switches with the runner, the runner should touch the participant on the shoulder and say 'switch cone'. Once the chasers have counted up to 20, the runners cannot switch with a participant on one of the cones. The chasers try to tag the runners who are not standing beside cones. The participants at the cones start to count down from 20 to 0. The runners try to avoid being tagged. If the chaser tags a runner, they both move to the side of the playing area while the countdown is completed, but they switch roles for the start of the next game. If a chaser does not tag a runner before the countdown to 0 is completed, then she stays as a chaser for the next game.

Safety Tips

- Warn the participants to be careful of collisions.
- Chasers should not tag too hard.
- When the chasers are trying to tag the runners, neither of them should grab or pull participants who are standing by the cones as they run around them.

Advice

- Have the participants who are runners practise changing with those at the cones to ensure that they are doing this correctly before the chasers start counting up.

- It is advisable to use different cones for marking out the area from those the participants place inside it. For example, you could use a different colour or different type of cone to mark out the area boundary.
- Make the area big enough so that the participants at the cones are well spaced out.
- All participants must stay inside the coned area when the chasers are trying to tag the runners.

Variations

- **Game variation:** Chasers have sponge balls and try to tag the runners by hitting them on the legs with the ball. They should throw the ball using an underarm action.
- **Sport-specific:** This game can be adapted for use in rugby sessions. Assign double the number of chasers and have them work in pairs. Give each pair of chasers a ball. The chasers have to tag the runners by touching them with the ball. The ball must be in the chaser's hand when they tag a runner. The chaser must not throw the ball at a runner to tag them. Chasers are not allowed to move when they are in possession of the ball.
- **Sport-specific:** This game can be adapted for use in soccer sessions. Chasers each have a soccer ball and try to tag the runners by hitting their ball against the runners' lower legs. The chasers try to kick their ball so it gently hits the runners below the knees to tag them. Chasers should not kick the ball too hard, and they should keep their shots low.

Key Skills and Fitness Components Developed

Skills
- Decision making
- Running

Fitness Components
- Reaction time
- Speed

Equipment

Cones

Game

This game incorporates a fun activity based on the rules of the game Rock, Paper, Scissors. In this version, instead of making the required shape (rock, paper or scissor) with their hands, participants choose to be a wizard (pretend to zap their opponent and say a spell, such as 'shazam!'), a giant (reach up with both arms and growl) or a goblin (make a shrieking noise while rubbing fingers and thumbs together with both hands). Similar to the game of Rock, Paper, Scissors, each action can be beaten by one other action. *A wizard action beats a goblin action, a goblin action beats a giant action and a giant action beats a wizard action.*

Arrange the participants in pairs, and allow them to practise the actions so that they become familiar with them. Once they have practised, arrange the participants into two teams with equal numbers of participants in each (a simple way would be to ask the pairs to number themselves 1 and 2). Teams stand in a circle, away from their opponents, and secretly choose the action they will all perform. The participants in each team line up facing an opponent. There should be a gap of approximately 2 metres between opponents and a similar sized gap between the team-mates in line. Place two lines of cones on the ground, one on either side of the participants (see figure on page 29) approximately 7 to 10 metres (7.7 to 11 yd) away.

When the participants are lined up, call out 'reveal!', at which point participants carry out their actions. If the teams perform different actions, the participants in the team that performs the losing action quickly turn and run towards the nearest line of cones. The aim is to get to the cones before the opposing team tags them.

The participants in the team that performs the winning action chase their opponent and try to tag them before they get to the line of cones. If a participant being chased reaches the line before she is tagged, she beats her opponent. However, if the chasing participant tags her opponent before she gets to the line, she wins that round. Add up the number of participants who win to determine which team wins each round. The participants should then go back into their teams to decide the next action they will perform. If teams choose the same action, they return to their circle to decide on the next action they will perform, then line up again at the centre and wait for you to start the game. Continue for a set time (e.g., 5 minutes) or until one team wins a set number of rounds (e.g., 10).

Safety Tips

- Ensure participants have completed a thorough warm-up before carrying out this activity because it involves ballistic movements.

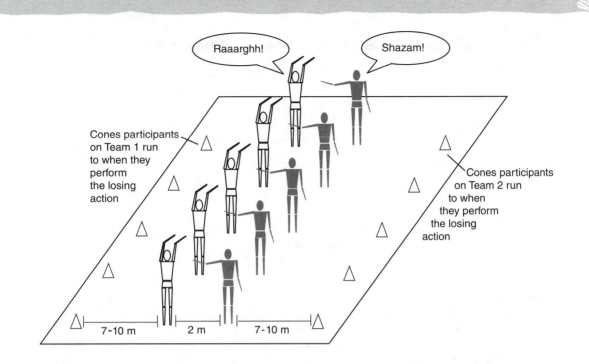

Raaarghh!

Shazam!

Cones participants on Team 1 run to when they perform the losing action

Cones participants on Team 2 run to when they perform the losing action

7-10 m   2 m   7-10 m

- Warn participants to be careful of collisions.
- Participants should not tag too hard.
- Participants should turn and run in a straight line towards the cones and not cut across other participants' paths. It may be useful to use cones to mark out where the participants should stand before 'reveal' is called so they are not standing too close to team-mates.

Advice

- Participants should practise the actions a number of times so that they become familiar with which action beats which other action.
- Change partners regularly.
- If you have a wide range in ability, it may be best to match opponents by speed or ability.

Variations

- **Game variation:** This activity can be played individually. Participants play against an opponent for a set number of turns (e.g., the best out of five or seven) to decide who wins, and then change partners.
- **Game variation:** With older participants (e.g., 11- to 13-year-olds), you may want to use the Rock, Paper, Scissors actions.
- **Sport-specific:** This game can be adapted for use in other sports that involve dribbling, such as soccer and hockey. Participants each have a ball beside them. After they have 'revealed', the losing participant has to dribble the ball to the line before being tagged. The participant who is chasing does not dribble a ball.

Safety Link Tag

Ages 5 to 13

Key Skills and Fitness Components Developed

Skills

- Decision making
- Dodging
- Running

Fitness Components

- Agility
- Balance
- Reaction time
- Speed

Equipment

- One bib (pinnie) per 6 to 10 participants
- Cones

Game

Cone out your playing area. Participants should be set up as shown in the figure on this page. Choose some of the group to become chasers. Each chaser puts a bib (pinnie) on and stands at the side of the area until the game begins. There should be one chaser for every 6 to 10 participants. The remaining participants are either runners or linkers. There should be one runner for every chaser (i.e., if there are four chasers, there should be four runners). The remaining participants are linkers. The linkers are arranged in pairs

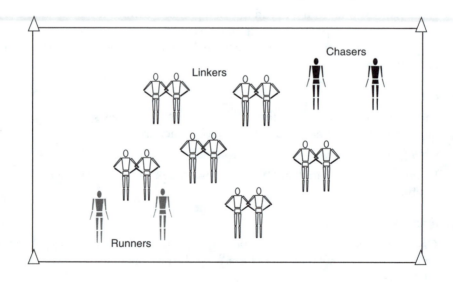

1. Runner becomes linker by joining a pair

2. Linker becomes runner when the runner links with their partner

3. Runner is now linker

4. Linker is now runner

and spread out around the area. The linkers link arms with their partners and place the hand on the arm that is not linked with their partner on their hip.

Once the game starts, the chasers try to tag the runners and the runners try to avoid being tagged. If a chaser tags a runner, the chaser takes the bib off and gives it to the runner and they switch roles. The runners can avoid being tagged (or have a rest) by becoming linkers. They do this by running to a pair of linkers and putting an arm through a linker's spare arm (one of the arms on the outside). *If a runner puts his arm through a linker's arm, the linker's partner unlinks and becomes a runner.* He must release his link and move around the area to avoid being tagged by a chaser. Have them play for a set time (e.g., 3 minutes). Any participant who is a chaser at the end of the game has to perform a fun challenge, such as saying something funny or performing an animal impression.

Safety Tips

- Ensure participants perform a thorough warm-up before carrying out this activity because it involves ballistic movements.
- Warn participants to be careful of collisions.
- Runners should not run from the side towards linkers when they are trying to link with them because they may run into the linker. Tell them to run from behind and to the side of the linkers and to slow down when they get there.
- Runners and chasers should not pull or hold the linkers as they run around them.

Advice

- Ask questions to check understanding after explaining the rules.
- Let the runners practise changing with the linkers so they can do this correctly.
- This can be a very tiring game, so remember to give rest periods between games.
- Challenges should not be seen as a punishment. Make sure that no challenge is too strenuous or severe.

Variations

- **Small groups:** With smaller groups play with hoops on the floor instead of linkers. For example, if you were playing this game with 8 participants you would choose one chaser and two runners. The remaining participants have a hoop each, which they place on the floor and stand in. Runners move to a participant in a hoop, and tap them gently on the shoulder if they want to switch roles.
- **Sport-specific:** This game can be adapted for use in soccer sessions. Choose one or two more chasers. The chasers dribble balls around the area. To tag runners, they try to pass the ball gently at them so it hits them below the knee.

Shark Bait Tag
Ages 5 to 13

Key Skills and Fitness Components Developed

Skills
- Decision making
- Dodging
- Running

Fitness Components
- Agility
- Balance
- Reaction time
- Speed

Equipment
- One bib (pinnie) per 9 to 15 participants
- Cones

Game

This game requires a minimum of 11 participants. Cone out your playing area. Participants are set up as shown in the figure on this page. Choose some of the participants to be chasers and give them bibs (pinnies) to put on. The chasers are sharks, and there should be one shark for every 9 to 15 participants. The remaining participants are arranged in threes. Within each group of three, one participant is the runner (called the shark bait) and the other two make up a net. The participants who are nets stand holding hands around the shark bait (see figure).

Start the game by shouting 'shark bait!' Once you have called this, the participants who are the nets lift their arms up so that each shark bait can leave her net. The shark

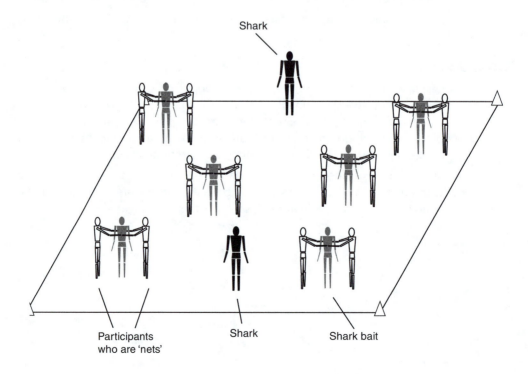

Shark

Participants who are 'nets'

Shark

Shark bait

32

baits must run into different nets. The sharks try to tag the shark baits when they are running between the nets. If a shark tags a shark bait, the two switch roles. The new shark puts on the bib, and the participant who is now a shark bait moves to and stands in an empty net. There can only be one shark bait per net. Once a shark bait gets in a net, the participants who are making the net lower their arms to encircle the shark bait.

If a shark bait leaves a net but finds all of the other nets full, he can return to the net that he left. If two shark baits get to a net at the same time, the participants forming the net decide who has to leave to go to a different one. Have participants play for a set time (e.g., 2 minutes), after which one of the participants who formed a net switches roles with the shark bait. After another couple of minutes, have them rotate so the last net person becomes a shark bait. This should ensure that all participants have a go at being the shark bait.

Safety Tips

- Ensure participants have completed a thorough warm-up before carrying out this activity because it involves ballistic movements.
- Sharks should not tag too hard.
- Warn participants to be careful of collisions.
- Shark baits should be careful to avoid bumping into other shark baits if they try to get into the same net simultaneously.
- Shark baits and sharks should not pull or hold on to the nets as they run around them.

Advice

- Ask questions to check understanding after explaining the rules.
- Let the shark baits practise changing nets before allowing the sharks to chase after them.
- Instruct the shark baits to run out of the net on a side that is away from the sharks so they do not get tagged too easily.

Variations

- **Easier/harder:** Change the number of sharks to make the game easier or harder for the shark baits.
- **Game variation:** The sharks chase for a set period of time and do not change with shark baits that they tag. They keep count of how many tags they make. Each participant takes a turn being a shark, and the one with the most tags is the winner.
- **Small groups:** With smaller groups choose one or two of the group to be chasers. The remaining participants are runners, or shark baits. Each of the shark baits are given a hoop (net), which they place on the floor in the area and stand inside. The shark baits have to run to a different hoop when you call 'shark bait'. Shark baits should be careful not to step on the hoops because they may slide on some surfaces.

Spots

Ages 5 to 10

Key Skills and Fitness Components Developed

Skills

- Decision making
- Running

Fitness Components

- Agility
- Balance
- Coordination
- Reaction time
- Speed

Equipment

At least one spot per participant, ideally in four or five different colours. If you do not have spots, use cones.

Game

This is a good activity for use as part of a progressive warm-up. Scatter the spots randomly on the floor so that they are not too close together. The participants move around the area following your instructions—for example, jogging, hopping, skipping, sidestepping, moving backwards or marching. Start with exercises that are fairly low intensity, but increase this steadily as the game progresses. Shout 'spots' and quickly turn away from the group. The participants must run to a spot and stand on it. There can be only one participant per spot. Turn to face the group to see which participants are standing on spots of the colour that you called. Each of the participants standing on that colour spot are awarded a point. Participants should again move around the area following your instructions until you shout 'spots' again. Continue for a set time (e.g., 3 to 5 minutes), after which the participant with the most points is the winner. Alternatively, you can have them play until one participant has scored a set number of points (e.g., 7 to 10).

Safety Tips

- Warn participants to be careful of collisions.
- Participants should be careful when they are trying to stand on a spot if another participant is also trying to stand on it at the same time. They should be careful not to bump into each other or step on each other's feet or toes.

Advice

- Remind participants to keep their own scores and check regularly to ensure that they are doing this.
- Having a few more spots than participants speeds up the game.

Variations

- **Game variation:** Participants move around in pairs, either holding hands or just moving beside each other. When you call 'spots', they move to a spot together. They score 1 point if they are standing on a spot of the colour that you call out.

- **Game variation:** A different variation of the previous version is that pairs can either separate or stay together when you call 'spots'. They score 2 points if they move to a spot together and you call the colour of that spot. They score 1 point if they separate and go to different colours, and one of those colours is called out.

- **Game variation:** Change the rules so that participants are out of the game if you call the colour of the spot they are standing on. Once a participant is out, she still copies the actions but she does this around the outside of the area and does not find a spot when you call 'spots'. Have them play until all but one of them are out. The one remaining is the winner.

- **Sport-specific:** This game can be adapted for games involving dribbling, such as basketball, hockey and soccer. Participants dribble their balls around the area until you call 'spots'.

Team Dodgeball

Ages 8 to 16

Key Skills and Fitness Components Developed	
Skills	**Fitness Components**
· Catching	· Agility
· Decision making	· Balance
· Dodging	· Coordination
· Throwing	· Power
	· Reaction time
	· Speed

Equipment

- Four benches per group
- Cones
- Large sponge balls, approximately one ball per five participants

Game

This game is best played indoors. It can be a great game to play with a large group (20 to 40 participants) working in a gymnasium or sports hall. The game set-up is shown in the figure on this page. Separate the participants into two teams. One team stands in one half of the playing area and the other team stands in the other. Place benches at the side of the playing area near the halfway point. Cones should be used to mark out a no-man's-land between the two teams and a safety area around the benches that no one who is actively playing the game is allowed to go into.

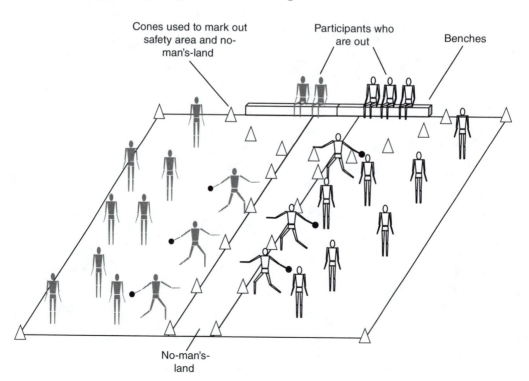

Cones used to mark out safety area and no-man's-land

Participants who are out

Benches

No-man's-land

Teams start with an equal number of sponge balls, which participants throw at opponents to try to hit them below the shoulders. The ball must be a direct hit; it cannot bounce off the floor, a wall or another participant. Participants avoid being hit by dodging out of the way or using a ball as a shield. Participants who are hit are out, and they should sit on the bench on their side of the court. A participant is also out if she throws a ball at an opponent who catches it before it bounces on the floor.

Participants who are out still have a chance of rejoining the game. They should make a mental note of who got them out because if that person is hit or caught out, then all of the people she hit may rejoin the game. The game continues until an entire team is out or, if playing with a large group, until a set number of participants (e.g., 10) are out. At the end of each game, teams swap sides, and the fun can start again. Have participants play for a set time (e.g., 20 minutes) or until one team has scored a set number of points.

Safety Tips

- Use soft balls only. This game can be dangerous if played with hard balls. Volleyballs and other similar balls should not be used.
- Lead participants in a thorough warm-up before carrying out this activity because it involves ballistic movements.
- Participants may not go into no-man's-land to collect any of the sponge balls.
- Participants should use low throws to prevent hitting others in the face.
- Participants should not throw the ball too hard.
- Set up a safety area around the benches to ensure that the participants who are out of the game are not hit by those taking part in the game. No participants are allowed in this area unless they are out of the game.

Advice

- For this game to run smoothly, participants must play fairly, so encourage honesty when participants are hit or caught out.
- This activity is ideally played in a sports hall or gymnasium.
- If a participant is out but has not seen which opponent got her out, she can pick another opponent. She must let you know who she has chosen. Once the chosen participant is out, she may rejoin the game.

Variations

- **Easier:** Participants can be out even if the ball bounces on the ground before it strikes them.
- **Game variation:** If a participant uses a ball as a shield and deflects a ball into the air and this ball is subsequently caught by a team-mate, then the opponent throwing the ball is out.
- **Smaller groups:** This version is good to play when there are fewer than six participants on a team. Participants who are out can only rejoin the game if a team-mate catches a ball. When that happens, the thrower of the ball is out and the catcher can choose one of her team-mates to rejoin the game.
- **Smaller groups:** With groups of fewer than 12 it is best to stipulate that an entire team must be out for the opposing team to win the game.

Turn Tag
Ages 5 to 13

Key Skills and Fitness Components Developed

Skills
- Decision making (tactics)
- Running

Fitness Components
- Agility
- Balance
- Reaction time
- Speed

Equipment
Cones

Game

Ideally there should be 14 or more participants for this activity. Cone out a playing area. Choose one participant to be a chaser and another to be a runner. The remaining participants stand in lines. If there are 16 participants remaining, they stand in four lines of four. Participants hold hands in their lines with their arms extended as shown in the figure on this page. The chaser stands in one corner of the area, and the runner stands in the opposite corner.

When the game begins, the chaser has a set time (e.g., 30 to 60 seconds) to try to tag the runner. Both the runner and the chaser must stay inside the area. They are both allowed to run between the lines of the participants, but they cannot pass under their arms. Within the set time the runner and the chaser are each allowed to call 'change' three times. When 'change' is called, the participants in the lines release holding hands, turn through 90 degrees and hold hands with the participants standing in front of or behind them. If the chaser is close to tagging the runner while running through the lines, the runner may call 'change' so that the chaser is in a different line to the runner. After the chaser has tagged the runner or the time is up, change the runner and chaser and start the fun again.

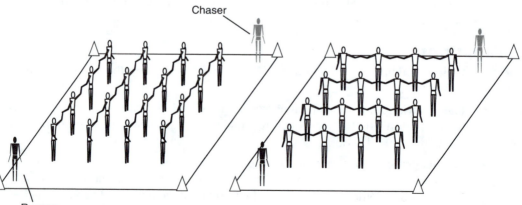

Chaser

Runner

Safety Tips

- Chasers should not tag too hard.
- Warn participants to be careful of collisions.
- Ensure participants have completed a thorough warm-up before carrying out this activity because it involves ballistic movements.
- Runners and chasers should not pull or hold the participants in the lines as they run around them.
- Inform the runner and the chaser to slow down or stop as soon as 'change' is called so that they do not run into the arms of the participants in the lines as they turn around.
- Participants should hold hands at a low level so that they do not hit a runner or a chaser around the neck or head area when 'change' is called.

Advice

- This game is lots of fun, and most participants want to have a turn as the chaser or the runner, so make sure you have enough time for everyone to have a turn in one or both of these roles. It is good to play this game if you have a long session because participants may need time to rest.
- Remind chasers and runners to try to use the change call to outwit their opponent.
- Allow the participants who are in the lines to practise changing on command so they hold hands with the correct other participants. Ensure that they all turn the same way through the 90-degree turn.
- If there are some lines drawn on the court (e.g., tennis court markings), use some of these to guide the participants where to stand.

Variations

- **Larger groups:** With larger groups (e.g., over 25) play with two runners and two chasers or arrange the participants into two games.
- **Sport-specific:** This game can be adapted to soccer or basketball. The chaser and the runner both have balls, which they must dribble in the area.

Video Recorder

Key Skills and Fitness Components Developed

Skills

- Decision making
- Running

Fitness Components

- Agility
- Balance
- Coordination
- Endurance
- Reaction time
- Speed

Equipment

Cones

Game

This activity is good for use as part of a progressive warm-up. Cone out your playing area making sure that the size of the area is large enough for the participants to move around in. Once the participants are moving around, call out one of the following video recorder control buttons, which players must respond to accordingly:

- **Play:** Participants jog around the area.
- **Review:** Participants walk backwards around the area.
- **Fast forward:** Participants sprint around the area.
- **Pause:** Participants jump on the spot.
- **Stop:** Participants freeze on the spot.
- **Rewind:** Participants run backwards around the area.
- **Slow motion:** Participants pretend to walk, jog or sprint in slow motion.
- **Eject:** Participants jump in the air.

If you are using this game as a warm-up, slowly build up the speed of the movements.

Safety Tips

- If you are using this game as part of a warm-up, ensure that movements are progressive in intensity. Begin with less intense movements (e.g., review and play) and add more vigorous actions (e.g., eject and fast forward) towards the end.
- Warn participants to be careful of collisions.

Advice

- Add one video control command at a time, because the participants may not remember all of the actions if you say them all at the start.
- With some groups you can make the game more fun by asking them to make the sound effects of the various actions of a video recorder. This may depend on whether they have used a video recorder before.

40

Variations

- **Game variation:** Add different instructions for the participants to follow that could refer to a subject on the video or DVD. For example, if you say 'martial arts movie', the group could pretend to be in the film and carry out mock martial arts actions, or if you say 'aerobics video', the participants could pretend they are instructors of an aerobics video.

Square Court Handball
Ages 8 to 16

Key Skills and Fitness Components Developed

Skills	Fitness Components
· Catching	· Agility
· Decision making	· Balance
· Dodging	· Coordination
· Passing	· Power
· Throwing	· Reaction time
	· Speed

Equipment

- One bib (pinnie) per two participants
- One sponge ball (or similar) per 20 participants
- Cones

Game

For the set-up of this activity, see figure on page 43. Arrange the participants into groups of 20; then separate the groups into two teams of 10. Number the teams 1 and 2, and give bibs (pinnies) to the participants from one team. Cone out a playing area of approximately 10 by 10 metres (11 by 11 yd) for each group of 20. The participants in each team should be numbered 1 to 10. Numbers 1 to 5 from team 1 stand on one side of the area; this is a goal, as are all of the other sides of the area once the game begins. Participants defend the goal they are standing in. The remaining participants from Team 1 stand on the opposite side of the area; this is their goal. Participants from Team 2 repeat this process on the other two sides. This means that each team defends two goals.

Place the sponge ball in the centre of the area. Call out two numbers—one between numbers 1 and 5 and the other between numbers 6 and 10 (e.g., '3 and 7'). The participants who have been given these numbers run in to the area to get the ball. The team-mates who get the ball must make a set number of passes (e.g., 3 to 5). The two opponents who do not gain possession of the ball try to prevent the team in possession from making the set number of passes. If they manage to gain possession, by intercepting a pass or picking up a ball that has been dropped by an opponent, then they must also make the set number of passes. Participants can pass using any techniques they desire. They are allowed to move when they have possession of the ball, but passes must be over a distance of at least 2 metres. When a participant has possession of the ball, she can hold on to it for only 5 seconds; if she holds on to it for longer than 5 seconds, possession is given to the opponents. Defenders are not allowed to make any contact with the participants from the opposing team, but they can knock the ball out of the opponents' hands.

Once the team with the ball has made the set number passes, they can score a point by throwing the ball through one of the opposing team's goals. Shots at the goals must be taken from a distance of at least 5 metres (5.5 yd). To score a goal, a participant must throw the ball through the goal but below a specified height (e.g., waist or head height). After a shot, if the ball is saved and it comes back into play, any of the participants in

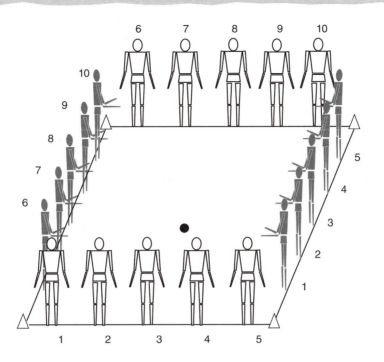

the centre can pick it up and try to throw it through one of the opposing team's goals; they do not have to make the set number of passes before shooting. A goal can only be scored by the participants in the centre, so if it is saved or rebounds off a goalkeeper and goes directly into the opposing team's goal without being touched by a participant in the centre, no points are scored and the participants move back to their starting positions. After a goal has been scored or the ball goes out of play, all of the participants return to their start positions ready for you to call out another two numbers. Have participants play for a set time (e.g., 10 minutes) or until one team has scored a set number of points (e.g., 10).

Safety Tips

- Warn participants to be careful of collisions.
- Warn participants to be careful when they are running into the area to get the ball. They should stay on their feet and be careful not to crash heads with opponents.
- To prevent all four participants running to the ball and possibly colliding, delay calling the second number for a second or two, so only those who have the first number run to get the ball.
- Use a soft ball only.
- Participants who are on the goal line should not dive when trying to save throws at the goal. This is to prevent team-mates colliding while diving.

Advice

- Try to arrange the participants so that they are paired against opponents of similar ability.
- Wait until all participants are set up before calling a number.
- Encourage participants to listen carefully for their numbers being called out.

(continued)

Variations

- **Easier/harder:** Vary the set number of passes team-mates must make before shooting to change the level of difficulty.

- **Easier/harder:** Change the size of the area to change the level of difficulty. A larger area gives the participants more space when they are in the middle and makes it easier to score because the goalkeepers have more space to cover.

- **Game variation:** Call out only one number, and allow participants to throw the ball through either of the opponents' goals straightaway when they have possession.

- **Sport-specific:** This game can be adapted for use during soccer sessions. Have participants use a soccer ball and do not allow them to contact the ball using their hands; they must score by shooting through the goal so that the ball passes below waist height. Goalkeepers can or cannot use their hands as another variation.

Poorly Tag
Ages 5 to 10

Key Skills and Fitness Components Developed

Skills
- Decision making
- Dodging
- Running

Fitness Components
- Agility
- Balance
- Reaction time
- Speed

Equipment
- One bib (pinnie) per 8 to 10 participants
- Cones

Game
Cone out your playing area. Choose some of the participants to be chasers. Each chaser puts a bib (pinnie) on. There should be one chaser for every 6 to 10 participants. The rest of the participants are runners.

When the game begins, the chasers run around trying try to tag the runners. If a runner is tagged, she stands on the spot and pretends to be 'ill'. Ill runners are healed or restored to health when two of the other runners make a ring around them with their arms and hold hands. Once a runner has been healed, she may rejoin the game. The runners who healed the ill runner also continue to run around the area, trying to avoid being tagged. Continue the game for a set time (e.g., 45 to 60 seconds) or until all of the participants have been tagged; then change the chasers and start the fun again.

Safety Tips
- Warn participants to be careful of collisions.
- Ensure that the chasers do not tag too hard.

Advice
- Choose only one chaser per 8 to 10 participants to keep the game going.
- The number of chasers should also be relative to the size of the area.
- During the game you can help to free participants who are ill (or tagged) if too many of them are static.

Variations
- **Harder:** Have participants play the game on all fours rather than running (but only on a suitable surface).
- **Harder:** Instead of tagging, the chasers could each have a sponge ball that they throw underarm at the runners. They should aim to hit the runners on the legs to make them ill.
- **Sport-specific:** This game can be adapted to soccer. Each chaser runs around dribbling a soccer ball and tries to hit the runners below the knees with the ball.

Tactic Tag
Ages 8 to 16

Key Skills and Fitness Components Developed

Skills
- Decision making (tactics)
- Dodging
- Running

Fitness Components
- Agility
- Balance
- Reaction time
- Speed

Equipment
Eight cones per group of four

Game
This activity is good for introducing the concepts of tactics and strategies in games. Arrange the participants into groups of four; then separate each group into teams of two. For each group of four use cones to mark out two 10-by-10-metre (11-by-11-yd) playing areas approximately 15 to 20 metres (16 to 22 yd) apart. Number the teams 1 and 2, and have Team 1 stand in one playing area and Team 2 stand in the other playing area (see figure on page 47).

When the game begins, one participant from Team 1 becomes an attacker while both participants from Team 2 are defenders. The attacker from Team 1 begins to move across the area between the two teams, towards Team 2's playing area. Once the attacker from Team 1 has left his area, the participants from Team 2 count down slowly from 20 to 0. They should call out the numbers at a rate of approximately one every second, so the attacker has 20 seconds to attack. The attacker must have tagged an opponent before the countdown has finished. The attacker's aim is to tag one of the defenders and then run back to his own area without being tagged by the other defender. Therefore, when one of the defenders from Team 2 has been tagged, his team-mate must try to tag the attacker from Team 1 before he gets back to his own area.

The defenders can move anywhere they like inside their area, but they must stay inside until one of them has been tagged. At that point the defender who is chasing the attacker can leave his area. The attacking team scores a point if the attacker successfully tags a defender and gets back to his own area without being tagged. The defending team scores a point if the chasing defender tags the attacker before he returns to his area. Once a team has counted down to zero, the attack is over and the attacker cannot tag an opponent. In this instance the defending team is awarded a point. The attacker should return to his area where he and his team-mate are now defenders when a participant from the opposing team attacks.

After the attack by Team 1, the teams switch roles so that Team 2 attacks. Again, only one participant from Team 2 attacks. Teams then alternate between attacking and defending, and within each team, team-mates take turns to attack. Have participants play for a set time (e.g., 5 minutes), until everyone has had a set number of turns attacking (e.g., 3 each) or until one team has scored a set number of points (e.g., 7).

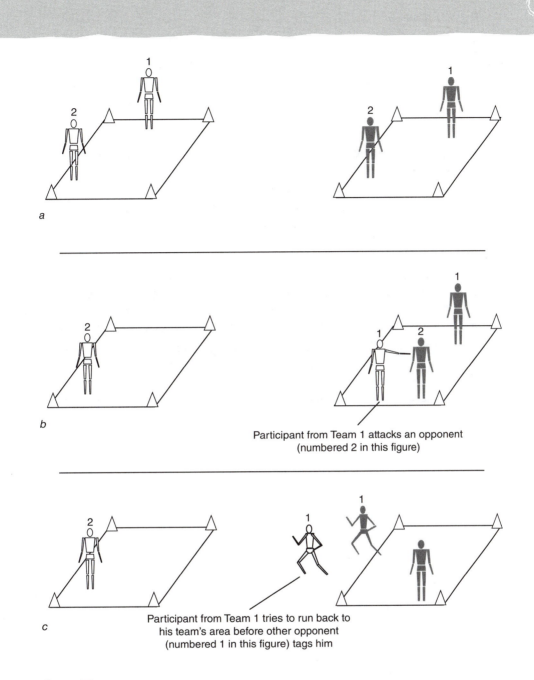

a

b

Participant from Team 1 attacks an opponent
(numbered 2 in this figure)

c

Participant from Team 1 tries to run back to
his team's area before other opponent
(numbered 1 in this figure) tags him

Safety Tips

- Participants should not tag too hard.
- Warn participants to be careful of collisions.
- Lead participants in a suitable warm-up before carrying out this game.

(continued)

47

Advice

- Try to be very clear when you explain the rule about the defender who is not tagged chasing the attacker after a tag. It also helps to demonstrate this rule before playing the game.

- Teams should count down slowly from 20 to 0; they should not count too slowly or too fast. You may want to count down for all the groups using a stopwatch or timer for guidance.

- The size of the areas and the distance between them depends on the age or ability of the participants. Smaller areas and a shorter distance between the areas are preferable for younger or less able ones.

Variations

- **Game variation:** The defenders have a sponge ball, which they can pass to each other. The attacker has to tag the opponent who does not have possession of the ball. When the attacker has tagged an opponent, his team-mate must try to hit the attacker with the sponge ball before the attacker gets back to his area.

- **Game variation:** Create groups of three or bigger teams. If playing with bigger teams, have more than one attacker going at a time. However, do not have more than half of the team attacking at the same time.

Shower Tag
Ages 5 to 13

Key Skills and Fitness Components Developed

Skills	Fitness Components
· Decision making	· Agility
· Dodging	· Balance
· Running	· Reaction time
	· Speed

Equipment
- One bib (pinnie) per 6 to 10 participants
- Cones

Game
Cone out your playing area. Choose some of the group to be chasers and have each of them put a bib (pinnie) on. There should be one chaser for every 6 to 10 participants. The remaining participants are runners, and they run around the area trying to avoid being tagged. When the game begins, the chasers try to tag the runners. When they are tagged, runners hold one hand in the air pretending to be a shower. The runner cannot move from this caught position unless they are freed by another runner. To free a runner, another runner has to stand under the shower and pretend to wash her face or body for 2 or 3 seconds. Then both runners can run off. Have the game continue for a set time (e.g., 45 to 60 seconds) or until all of the runners have been tagged; then change the chasers.

Safety Tips
- Warn the participants to be careful of collisions.
- Chasers should not tag too hard.

Advice
- To increase activity and reduce the amount of time spent in the shower position, choose fewer chasers per runners. For example, if there are 30 participants in your group choose 3 chasers (1 chaser per 9 runners) rather than 4.
- The number of people chasing should also be relative to the size of the coned area; choose fewer chasers if your playing area is small.
- During the game, you can help free participants if too many are in the shower position.

Variations
- **Game variation:** Have participants play in pairs. The chasers and the runners run around linking wrists or holding hands with partners. When a pair of runners is tagged, both partners hold up their free arm (the one they are not linking to their partner with) to pretend to be showers. Another pair must go into to the shower and pretend to wash themselves, with their free hand, to free the caught runners.
- **Harder:** Have participants play the game on all fours rather than running (but only on a suitable surface).

Key Skills and Fitness Components Developed

Skills	Fitness Components
· Catching	· Agility
· Decision making	· Balance
· Dodging	· Coordination
· Hitting	· Power
· Throwing	· Reaction time
	· Speed

Equipment

- Cones
- Large sponge balls

Game

This game is good for introducing and developing the use of tactics and strategies in team games. Although this game can be played outdoors, it is best played in a sports hall or similar indoor facility. The set-up for this game is shown in the figure on page 51. Use cones to mark out a hitting area, safety area and score line. Arrange the participants into two teams. Nominate one team to field and one team to hit. The fielding team chooses one participant to bowl and one to be a backstop (they have a similar role to a wicket-keeper in cricket). The bowler stands with the ball approximately 7 metres (7.7 yd) from the hitting area. The backstop stands behind hitting area, and for safety reasons, must be at least 2 metres away from the hitting area. The rest of the fielding team spreads out in the outfield.

One of the hitters starts as the striking hitter and stands in the hitting area. The remaining participants on the hitting team line up behind and to the side of the hitting area to wait for their turn to be the striking hitter. The hitters take turns hitting a ball that the bowler on the opposing team bowls or throws underarm to them. Striking hitters aim to hit the ball with the palm of a flat hand or with the inside of a clenched fist so the ball is not caught by the fielding team before it bounces; then they run to the safety area and back over the score line.

The striking hitter does not have to run straight back when she has reached the safety area. Once she is in this area, she cannot be hit by a ball thrown at her by an opponent (see more on this later in the game description). The hitter may wait in the safety area until another hitter has become the striking hitter. Indeed, the hitting team is allowed to have up to five participants in the safety area at any one time. Hitters can score either 1 or 3 points:

- Hitters score 3 points if they run to the safety area and return back over the score line straightaway.
- Hitters score 1 point if they get back over the score line but wait in the safety area for one or more of their team-mates to take their turn as the striking hitter.

The objective of the fielding team is to catch a ball hit by the striking hitter before it bounces. Also, they must try to tag hitters out by throwing the ball at them to strike the hitter below the waist. For example, if the striking hitter hits the ball back to the bowler, there is a good chance that the bowler could hit the striking hitter as she ran past them. Hitters can only be struck with the ball when they are running to the safety area or back to the score line. They cannot be hit when they are standing in the safety area. Hitters tagged out then rejoin the back of their line, where they await their chance to be the striking hitter again. However, 1 point is taken from their team's score. Once the hitters have had a set time hitting (e.g., 10 minutes), or once they have all had a set number of turns as the striking hitter (e.g., three hits each), the teams swap roles. The team scoring the most points after each team has hit wins the game.

Safety Tips

- Use soft balls only.
- Warn participants to be careful of collisions.
- Lead participants in a thorough warm-up before carrying out this activity because it involves ballistic movements.
- Participants should use low throws to avoid hitting anyone in the face.
- Participants should not throw the ball too hard.
- Remind the hitters who are waiting their turn to be the striking hitter to keep watching the game in case a ball is hit towards them.

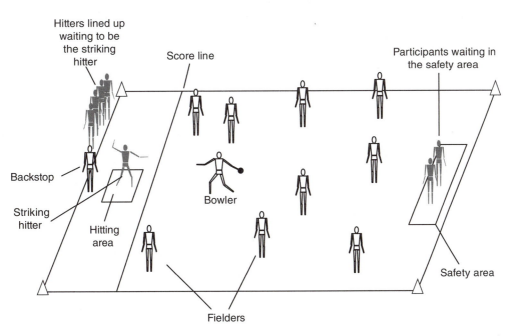

(continued)

Advice

- Remind the participants that the striking hitter must hit the ball away with the palm of a flat hand or with the inside of a clenched fist. They may not punch the ball.

- Hitters must use tactics and good decision making to determine when they can return from the safety area to the score line.

- Ask questions to check understanding after explaining the rules.

Variations

- **Easier/harder:** To make the game easier for the hitters and harder for the fielders, allow participants who field the ball to run with it. Fielders must work together by passing the ball to each other to get a close shot at a running hitter.

- **Game variation:** Add a hitting boundary. For example, if the striking hitter hits the ball all the way to the back wall of the sports hall, her team is awarded a bonus of 5 points.

- **Game variation:** If a hitter is out, then she does not take another turn to be the striking hitter in that inning. The fielders must get a set number of hitters out (e.g., five) before the teams swap roles.

- **Sport-specific:** This game can be adapted for use in soccer sessions. The bowler, or pitcher, kicks the ball to the striking hitter, who must kick the ball away. The fielders can still catch the ball before it bounces to get the striking hitter out; but if the ball bounces or rolls along the floor, they cannot touch it with their hands. In this instance they must try to kick, or pass, the ball at the hitters who are running to or from the safety area. The ball has to hit the runners below the knees to count as a hit, and fielders must not kick the ball too hard.

two

Basketball and Netball Games

The activities in this chapter relate to basketball and netball. The activities

- include a mixture of games, warm-up activities and skill practices;
- can be used to develop passing, dribbling and shooting skills; and
- are written for use in basketball sessions, but you can adapt the passing and shooting activities for netball sessions.

In most activities the rules for playing the game in a netball session will be similar, but you may need to make a few modifications. To find out whether an activity is suitable for netball, consult the Variations section.

When using the games in basketball sessions, ensure that basketballs and basket sizes are appropriate to participants' ages and abilities. England Basketball recommends the following basketball sizes for various age groups:

- Size 7 for boys who are over 15 years of age and girls who are over 16 years of age
- Size 6 for boys who are 13 to 15 years of age and girls who are 14 to 16 years of age
- Size 5 for boys who are under 13 years of age and girls who are under 14 years of age
- Size 3 for very young children

Hoop heights for children under the age of 10 should be 2.6 metres (2.8 yd) from the floor. Those aged 10 and 11 years of age should play with a hoop 3 metres (3.3 yd) from the floor, and children over age 11 should use hoops that are the full, standard height from the floor.

The most important thing to consider when choosing the size of a basketball and the height of the hoop is to ensure that participants experience some success, but are also challenged (so it is not too easy for them). You should use your own judgment when deciding what equipment to use.

On the Bench
Ages 8 to 16

Key Skills and Fitness Components Developed

Skills

· Attacking
· Defending
· Passing
· Receiving

Fitness Components

· Agility
· Balance
· Coordination
· Endurance
· Power
· Reaction time
· Speed

Equipment

- One netball and two benches per 8 to 14 participants
- One bib (pinnie) per two participants
- Cones

Game

For the set-up of this activity, see figure on page 56. Arrange the participants into groups of 8 to 14; then separate each group into two teams. Participants from one of the teams put bibs (pinnies) on. For each group, cone out a large rectangular area. At each of the two shorter sides of the rectangle, place a bench. Teams attack ends, towards one of the benches, and you should tell each team which bench it is attacking. A target player from each team stands on the bench at the end that the team is attacking.

When the teams are set up, throw the ball into the area. The team that gains possession of the ball tries to make a set number of passes (e.g., five). Once they do, they try to pass the ball to their target player. If this is achieved, the participant who passed the ball to the target player joins that player on the bench. Players are not allowed to dribble the ball, travel (basketball rule) or violate the footwork rule (netball).

The opposing team works to stop the set number of passes from being made by trying to intercept a ball passed between participants from the other team. If the team in possession of the ball has made the set number of passes, the opposing team tries to stop the ball from being passed to the target player. If team members gain possession of the ball from their opponents, they must try to make the set number of passes and then pass the ball to their own target player. If a pass is made to the target player, the game is stopped until the passer moves onto the bench to become another target player. The game is restarted by the target player (who caught the ball) giving it to a member of the opposing team. The opposing team's player should be given the ball next to the bench that the target player is standing on.

The game continues until all of the members of one team are on the bench. When one participant is left on the field, she must bounce the ball five times continuously on the floor (i.e., dribble the ball) before she can pass it to one of the target players. Once

(continued)

all of its participants are on the bench, the team wins a point. Have them play for a set time (e.g., 10 minutes) or until one team has scored a set number of points (e.g., 5)

Safety Tips

- Ensure participants have completed a thorough warm-up before carrying out this activity because it involves ballistic movements.
- Warn participants to be careful of collisions.
- Place benches at least 2 metres away from walls or other obstructions in case target players fall off benches.

Advice

- Encourage the target player to move along the bench to make it easier for her team-mates to pass to her.
- At the start of each new game, change the target player on each bench.
- This is a good activity to use to teach participants about the tactics of defending and attacking.

Variations

- **Easier/harder:** Change the number of passes teams must make before passing the ball to the target player depending on the age or ability of the participants or the number on each team.

- **Game variation:** Instead of becoming an extra target player, when a participant has passed to her team-mate on the bench, she switches roles so she now becomes the target player. A point is scored each time the ball is passed to a target player. Teams play for a set time (e.g., 3 to 5 minutes) or until one team scores a set number of points (e.g., 11).

- **Large groups:** It is possible to play the game with larger groups or teams. However, it is best to put two benches at each end, in the corners of the court, so teams can attack two areas rather than one (see the figure on this page).

- This game can be adapted for use in netball sessions using similar rules.

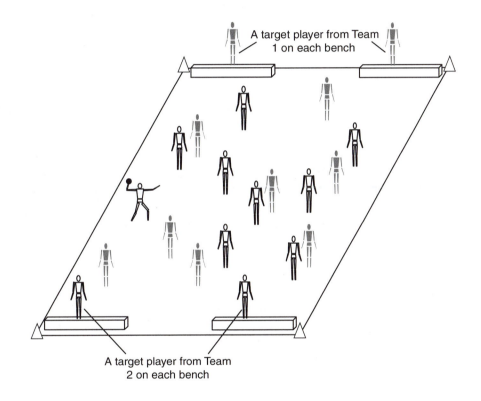

A target player from Team 1 on each bench

A target player from Team 2 on each bench

Beat the Ball

Ages 5 to 8

Key Skills and Fitness Components Developed

Skills	Fitness Components
· Catching	· Coordination
· Passing	· Reaction time
· Running	· Speed

Equipment

One basketball or netball per 8 to 10 participants

Game

Arrange the participants into groups of 8 to 10, and give each group a ball. The participants stand in a circle. Each participant should stand so there is a distance of 2 to 5 metres (2 to 5.5 yd) between them and the participants on either side of them. One participant starts with the ball and passes it to the person standing to her left. This is repeated so that the ball is passed clockwise around the circle.

The participants continue to pass the ball around the circle until one of them drops the ball. That player becomes a runner and runs around the outside of the circle. The participant tries to run around the circle and back to their start position before the other participants can pick up the ball and pass it around the circle. If a participant drops the ball, the participant standing to their left picks the ball up and resumes passing it around the circle. If the participant picking up the ball has to move to pick up the ball, she should return to her starting position before passing the ball. The participants in the circle try to pass the ball around the circle before the runner gets back to her place. If they manage to do this, the runner performs a fun challenge. The challenge should be something fun and not a punishment—for example, saying something funny or performing an animal impression. If the runner gets back to her place before the ball, then the other partici-pants perform the challenge. If the ball is dropped while the runner is completing the lap and the runner beats the ball, then the participant who dropped the ball performs the fun challenge.

Safety Tips

- Ensure participants have completed a thorough warm-up before carrying out this activity because it involves ballistic movements.
- Only play this game on a non-slippery surface.
- Runners should not pull or hold on to other participants when they are running around them.

Advice

- Ask questions to check understanding after explaining the rules.
- Increase the distance between the participants in the circle as they become more able, but if it becomes too hard for the runner to get back before the ball, play one of the variations.

- Ensure all participants catch then pass the ball when they are passing the ball around the circle to beat the runner. No participants should be skipped in the passing sequence.

- Challenges should not be seen as a punishment. Make sure that no challenge is too strenuous or severe.

Variations

- **Game variation:** Change the technique the participants must use to pass the ball—for example, have them use a bounce pass or an overhead pass.

- **Game variation:** The participants in the circle have to pass the ball around the circle twice, and the runner must complete two laps.

- **Harder:** Make the game harder for the passers by having them perform a challenge before passing the ball on. For example, they could circle the ball around their waist or bounce it before passing.

- **Harder:** Make the game harder for the passers by having them clap their hands together before catching the ball. The clap must happen after the person passing the ball has released the ball. They cannot clap before the ball has left the passer's hand and is in the air.

- **Sport-specific:** This game can be adapted for use in other passing and receiving and throwing and catching activities, such as cricket or rugby. Use the same rules but relevant sports balls.

Block Shot
Ages 8 to 16

Key Skill and Fitness Components Developed

Skill
Shooting

Fitness Components
- Coordination
- Power
- Reaction time

Equipment
- One basketball per two participants
- One basket per four participants
- Cones

Game

Arrange the participants into groups of four; then separate the groups into teams of two. There should be one group per basket. See the figure on this page for the set-up of this activity. Number the teams 1 and 2. Team 1 starts as the shooting team, and team-mates line up behind the free-throw line. The shooter at the front of the line has a basketball. Team 2 starts as the blocking team. One blocker stands to the side of the basket, outside of the key, with a ball, and his partner stands on the other side of the basket (without a ball).

The shooter with the ball takes a shot. The first blocker shoots his ball at the shooter's ball to try to hit it to prevent a basket being scored. The blocker should throw the ball so it hits the shooter's ball late in the shot, just before it goes into the hoop. If the shooter

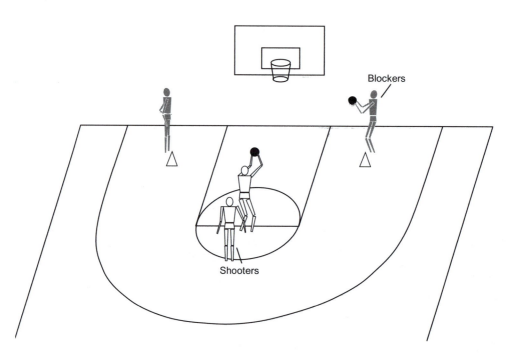

Blockers

Shooters

scores, he gains a point for his team, and he shoots again. If he misses the shot or the ball is deflected by the blocker's ball, the shooter moves to the back of the line. After a shot, the shooter should rebound or collect the ball and give it to his partner. The shooter can score only two baskets in a row, after which he passes the ball to his partner, who takes the next shot. The blocker passes the ball to his team-mate regardless of whether the shooter's shot goes in, so blockers always alternate shooting. Shooters try to score as many baskets as they can in a set time (e.g., 2 minutes). The teams then swap roles. When both teams have shot, the team with the most points wins.

Safety Tips
- Blockers should not shoot the ball too early; they should wait until the shooter's ball is close to the basket.
- Participants should try hard to stop balls from bouncing into other groups' areas.

Advice
The shooter can fake a shot to try to get the blocker to throw his ball. He can then take the shot safely.

Variations
- **Easier/harder:** Change the level of difficulty of the game by varying the distances the blockers and shooters have to shoot from.
- **Game variation:** Participants play individually against the other members in their groups. They all have a ball and rotate positions to take turns as shooters. When they are not shooting, participants are blockers. The first participant to score a set number of points (e.g., 5) wins the game.
- **Game variation:** Participants play individually against the other members in their groups. The participants all start as shooters and try to score three baskets. Four points are awarded for scoring the set number of baskets first. Three points are awarded for finishing second, two for finishing third and one point is awarded to the participant who does not score three baskets. Once they have scored three baskets, participants can be blockers. The first participant to score a set number of points (e.g., 20) wins the game.
- **Netball:** Play with the same rules as basketball, but use cones to mark the shooting position in front of the hoop.

Circle Pass Out
Ages 11 to 16

Key Skills and Fitness Components Developed

Skills

- Attacking
- Defending
- Passing
- Receiving

Fitness Components

- Agility
- Balance
- Coordination
- Power
- Reaction time
- Speed

Equipment

- One basketball per 12 participants
- One bib (pinnie) per two participants
- Cones

Game

Arrange the participants into groups of 12; then separate each group into two teams of six. Number the teams 1 and 2. Cone out a playing area. This should be a small circle surrounded by a larger circle (see the figure on page 63). If possible, use the centre circle of a basketball court or the circle at the top of each shooting area, or key, for the smaller (inner) circle. One participant from Team 1 stands in the small circle, while her team-mates stand outside the larger one. The participant who is standing in the inner circle has the ball. Participants from Team 2 stand inside the larger circle, but they are not allowed to stand in the smaller circle.

When the game begins, the participant with the ball tries to pass it to one of her team-mates. When in possession of the ball, participants cannot move (except for pivoting), but they can move when they are not in possession. The passer must send the ball so it travels below a specified height (e.g., lower than the height of the tallest player). If she manages to pass the ball to a team-mate standing outside the outer circle, she scores a point. The participant who receives the pass can pass it back to the centre participant or to other team-mates around the outer circle. If the ball is passed back to the participant in the smaller (inner) circle, then a point is scored. Team 2 tries to prevent passes going from the outer to the inner circle, or vice versa. If Team 2 manages to do this, Team 1 loses a point. After intercepting the ball, the participant from Team 2 passes it back to the opponent standing in the inner circle to continue the game.

Have participants play for a set time (e.g., 2 minutes); then swap roles so that Team 2 is trying to score points by passing into and out of the inner circle and Team 1 is trying to stop them. Once both teams have taken a turn scoring points, the team with the most points wins the game.

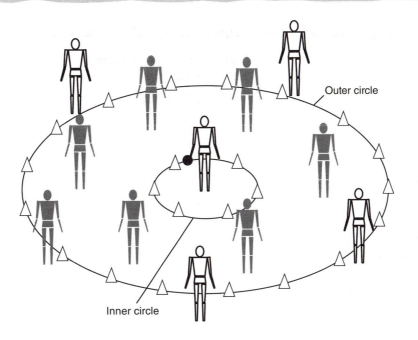

Outer circle

Inner circle

Safety Tips

- Warn participants to be careful of collisions.
- Inform participants to keep their eyes on the ball to prevent being hit by stray shots.

Advice

- The passing team should move quickly into a position where they can receive a pass.
- If the passing team is struggling to pass the ball back to the inner circle, tell them to pass the ball quickly around the outer circle until there is a space to pass the ball through.
- Do not allow the defending team to guard the inner circle. Defenders must not all stand too close to this circle. A minimum distance of 1 metre is recommended.

Variations

- **Easier:** Reduce the number of participants who are defending. The defenders take turns to stop the opposing team passing into and out of the inner circle. For example, three participants defend for the first minute, then their team-mates defend for the second minute.
- **Game variation:** If the defending team intercepts the ball, the two teams switch roles. After a set time, the team with the most points wins the game.
- **Harder:** Participants must pass the ball using a certain passing technique (e.g., bounce pass).
- **Sport-specific:** This game can be adapted for use in other passing and receiving sports using relevant rules (e.g., soccer, hockey, cricket, netball, rugby).

Copy Shot
Ages 8 to 16

Key Skills and Fitness Components Developed

Skills
- Dribbling
- Layups
- Shooting

Fitness Components
Dependent on actions chosen by participants

Equipment
One basketball and basket per two participants

Game
Arrange the participants into pairs, with each pair shooting into one of the baskets. Number the participants 1 and 2. Number 1 starts with the basketball and decides on a method of scoring a basket. This can be an easy shot or layup, or something more difficult (e.g., shooting with their non-dominant hand). Participants may consider the following before deciding how to score:

- Type of shot or layup
- Which hand they will shoot with
- Location from which to take the shot
- How the ball must travel or how it will go in
- How they will dribble the ball before they take the shot or layup

The participant shooting can choose an easy shot, using his preferred shooting hand, from a distance of 2 metres from the basket, or a layup in which he must circle the ball around his waist while taking the steps of the layup. Number 1 should let his opponent know how he is attempting to score before making his attempt. Whether number 1 scores or not, number 2 must also attempt to score using the same method. Participants gain a point if they score, but this must be by using the correct shot or layup. For example, if the ball must go through the basket without hitting the backboard, then no point is awarded if either of the shots hits the backboard, regardless of whether the participants scored. Number 2 then decides how the next shot or layup will be taken. Again, both participants try to score using this method. The game continues for a set time (e.g., 5 to 10 minutes), and the participant who scores the most points is the winner. You may also have them play until one participant has scored a set number of points (e.g., 10).

Safety Tips
- If you have more than one pair per basket, instruct pairs to take turns shooting so they do not collide with each other or get hit by basketballs shot from other pairs.
- Participants should not try to score from too far away from the basket. Long shots are frequently off-target, and if they hit another participant, they are likely to cause harm because the ball will likely be travelling at a high speed.
- Participants should rebound their shots to prevent their balls bouncing in the way of other pairs.

Advice

- Try to match participants by ability so each game is competitive.

- Choose basketballs and basket heights that are appropriate for the participants' ages and experience level.

- With larger groups have two or three pairs working at the same basket (however, see Safety Tips).

Variations

- **Game variation:** Use basketball scoring rules. Players earn 1 point for scoring from the free-throw line, 2 points for scoring from inside the 3-point line and 3 points for scoring from outside the 3-point line.

- **Game variation:** If the participant who decides how the shot or layup must be taken scores but his opponent doesn't, he continues deciding how the next shot or layup will be taken.

- **Large groups:** This game can be played in groups of three or four.

- **Large groups:** Participants are in groups of four and play against each other in pairs. Participants take turns to decide how the shot or layup must be taken. All participants try to score using the selected method, with a point being scored for the team if they are successful.

- **Small groups:** With smaller groups (e.g., fewer than six participants), participants take turns to decide the shot or layup, and all participants in the game must attempt to score using this technique or method.

- **Netball:** This game can be adapted for use in netball but use relevant netball rules when playing the game (e.g., no dribbling or layups are allowed).

Outnumbered
Ages 8 to 16

Key Skills and Fitness Components Developed

Skills	Fitness Components
· Attacking	· Agility
· Defending	· Balance
· Passing	· Coordination
· Receiving	· Endurance
· Support play	· Power
	· Reaction time
	· Speed

Equipment
- Bibs (pinnies) in three colours
- One basketball per 12 participants
- Cones

Game

Arrange the participants into groups of 12; then separate them into three teams of four. Each team should put a different-coloured bib (pinnie) on. For example, you may have one team wearing blue bibs, one wearing red and one wearing yellow. Cone out a playing area of approximately 20 by 20 metres (22 by 22 yd) for each group.

Once you have set up the game, choose one team to be the defenders. The two other teams work together as attackers. The attackers try to make a set number of passes to score a point (e.g., six). For example, if the team wearing the blue bibs is defending, the reds and yellows work together to make the set number of passes. Participants cannot move when they are in possession of the ball, but they are allowed to move around the area when they are not in possession. Both of the teams in possession of the ball gain a point if they make the set number of passes. The defending team tries to stop the other teams from making the set number of passes by intercepting the ball. If the defenders gain possession of the ball, they score a point for their team. After intercepting, the defenders give the ball back to the attackers to restart the game.

The attackers work together for a set time (e.g., 2 to 4 minutes) trying to score as many points as possible. After the set time the defending team becomes an attacking team, switching roles with one of the other teams. Have them play for the same amount of time; then switch so the team that has attacked twice becomes the defending team. After all the teams have taken a turn defending, the team with the most points wins.

Safety Tips
- Warn participants to be careful of collisions.
- Ensure that teams aren't defending for too long because this game is very intense when playing in this role.

Advice

- Ask questions to check understanding after explaining the rules.
- Try to match the teams by ability so all participants are challenged.
- Remind participants of the correct footwork or travel rules when in possession of the ball.

Variations

- **Easier/harder:** Change the size of the area to change the level of difficulty. Smaller areas make it harder for the attackers. Larger areas make it harder for the defenders.
- **Harder:** Specify the type of passing technique the participants have to use (e.g., only bounce passes).
- **Harder:** Participants cannot pass the ball above head height.
- **Game variation:** If playing in a basketball session, allow the participants to dribble the ball when they are in possession.
- **Game variation:** The members of the attacking teams all have balls, which they are allowed to dribble around the area. The defenders try to knock all of the balls out of the area. If a participant's ball is hit out of the area, he ensures that the ball is placed safely out of the game and then helps the other attackers keep the balls inside the area. Attackers can pass their balls to other attackers who do not have balls, to keep them away from the defenders.

  Time how long it takes the defenders to knock all of the balls outside the area. If the defenders have not knocked all of the balls out of the area after a set time (e.g., 2 minutes), count how many they have knocked out. A point is scored for each ball knocked out. The team knocking all the balls out in the fastest time wins the game, but if none of the teams manage to do this, the team with the most points win.

- **Game variation:** If a defender intercepts a ball passed by the attackers, his team becomes an attacking team. The participant who threw the pass that was intercepted becomes a defender, as does his team. Both teams in possession of the ball score a point when they make the set number of passes. Have teams play for a set time. The team with the most points at the end of this time wins the game.
- **Sport-specific:** Play with same rules as basketball.
- **Sport-specific:** This game is suitable for use in a netball session because dribbling is not allowed. This game can be adapted for other sports that involve passing and receiving skills (e.g., soccer, rugby or hockey) or throwing and catching (e.g., cricket or rounders).

Team Ball Tag
Ages 11 to 16

Key Skills and Fitness Components Developed

Skills
- Defending
- Support play
- Passing
- Receiving

Fitness Components
- Agility
- Balance
- Coordination
- Power
- Reaction time
- Speed

Equipment
- One bib (pinnie) per two participants
- One basketball per 14 participants
- Cones

Game

Arrange the participants into groups of 14; then separate each group into teams of seven. Number the teams 1 and 2, and have one team put bibs (pinnies) on. Cone out an area approximately 20 by 20 metres (22 by 22 yd) for each group. Team 1 start as chasers; give one team member of this team a basketball.

When the game begins, the participants from Team 1 work together to try to tag all of the participants from team 2. To tag an opponent, chasers touch them with the basketball while they are holding it. A tag counts only if a chaser tags an opponent with the ball on her back or arms. It should not be pushed into the front of the body, at an opponent's head or in her face. Participants who are tagged out stand on the perimeter of the area. Chasers are not allowed to move if they have possession of the basketball. They can move if they do not have the ball, so they should support their team-mates by moving next to opponents.

Team 2 can intercept a pass to gain possession of the ball, at which point they become chasers and try to tag all of the participants from Team 1. However, if they drop the ball when they are trying to intercept it, they are out. Participants can pass to the team-mates who are out, but these participants are not allowed to tag opponents. Tagged participants must also stand in the same place and cannot move around the outside of the perimeter. The game continues until one team has tagged all of its opponents. If the game hasn't finished after a set time (e.g., 5 minutes), the team that has the fewest participants out wins.

Safety Tips
- Leave a 2-metre gap between playing areas. This should reduce the risk of dropped basketballs rolling into another group's area.
- Warn participants to be careful of collisions.
- Chasers should not tag too hard with the basketball.

- Chasers may tag an opponent only on the arms or back.
- Chasers may not throw the basketball to make a tag. The ball must be in the chaser's hand to touch an opponent.

Advice

- Ask questions to check understanding after explaining the rules.
- Once the participants have grasped the game, you may notice that they use different types of passing techniques. Encourage them to use correct basketball passing techniques, such as chest, bounce and overhead passes.
- Remind participants that they must move to the perimeter and are out if they drop the ball while trying to intercept it.

Variations

- **Game variation:** Allow participants to dribble the basketball.
- **Game variation:** Participants who are out can rejoin the game if they are tagged by a team-mate who is not out. To tag a team-mate who is out, a participant must first receive the pass from another participant who is still in the game. He may not pass the ball to a team-mate who is out and then receive the ball from that team-mate close enough to tag him.
- **Game variation:** Participants who are out are not allowed to receive the ball to help their team when the game is going on, but they can rejoin the game if they are tagged by a team-mate.
- **Sport-specific:** This game is suitable for use in a netball session because no dribbling is allowed. Play with the same rules as basketball.
- **Sport-specific:** This game can be adapted for other sports that involve passing and receiving skills (e.g., soccer or rugby) or throwing and catching (e.g., cricket or rounders). If playing in cricket or rounders sessions use a tennis ball as a cricket or rounders ball is too hard to be tagging with.

Three-Team Basketball

Ages 14 to 16

Equipment

- One bib each. (There should be five bibs [pinnies] in three different colours per group)
- One basketball per 15 participants

Game

This is a team version of basketball that can be good to play when you have a large group and few basketball courts. Arrange the participants into groups of 15; then separate each group into three teams of five. Each group plays on a basketball court. Number the teams 1, 2 and 3, and have each team put on a different-coloured bib (pinnie). For example, Team 1 could put on blue bibs, Team 2 could put on red bibs and Team 3 could put on yellow bibs. Team 1 starts on the halfway, or half-court, line, Team 2 stands in one half of the court, and Team 3 stands in the other half of the court.

Give one of the participants from Team 1 a ball. Team 1 becomes the attacking team and tries to score into the basket that Team 2 is defending. Team 2 defends its basket, trying to stop Team 1 from scoring. After scoring, Team 1 moves back to the centre of the court and then attacks the other basket where Team 3 is defending. If Team 2 gains possession, the players move to the halfway line and attack against Team 3. In this instance Team 1 switches roles and becomes a defending team in the half where Team 2 started. This continues with teams swapping between attacking and defending when possession changes over. Have teams play for a set time (e.g., 10 to 15 minutes) or until one team has scored a set number of points (e.g., 20).

Safety Tips

- Warn participants to be careful of collisions.
- Ensure participants have completed a thorough warm-up before this activity because it involves ballistic movements.

Advice

- Ask questions to check understanding after explaining the rules.
- The continuous variation of this game (see the Variations section) is quicker and has more involvement, so is recommended. However, with most groups, it is best to play the version described earlier first because it is easier to understand and play.

Variations

- **Game variation:** Participants are not allowed to dribble the basketball. This variation places more emphasis on passing and receiving and support play.

- **Game variation:** Have teams play a continuous version of this game. After scoring, the team has to attack the other basket, but players must first pass or dribble the ball out of the half in which they were attacking. They start with an in-bound pass (throw-in) from under the basket where they just scored, and after the ball is in play, they try to pass or dribble the ball into the other half. The team that has just conceded its basket continues to defend, but this time as though the players were defending the other basket. If the team that scored the basket gets past the halfway line, the players attack against the other team. If the defending team regains possession, the players try to score in the basket they were just defending.

- **Netball:** Play with the same rules as basketball.

- **Sport-specific:** This game can be adapted for use in other invasion sports such as hockey, rugby and soccer using similar rules but relevant scoring methods.

Top Rebounder
Ages 8 to 16

Key Skills and Fitness Components Developed

Skills	Fitness Components
· Attacking	· Agility
· Defending	· Balance
· Layups	· Coordination
· Rebounding	· Power
· Shooting	· Reaction time
	· Speed

Equipment
One basketball and basket per two players

Game
This activity develops attacking and defending skills, but it is particularly good for improving the ability to shoot from close range and to rebound. A rebound is when a participant jumps to catch the ball after a missed shot. Arrange the participants into pairs. Each pair should move to its own basket. The participants play against each other, trying to score into the basket. Any time a participant is in possession of the ball, they should try to score. Participants who are not in possession of the ball should defend, trying to stop their opponent scoring. After a shot, whether it goes in or not, the participants try to rebound the ball. Whichever participant wins the rebound tries to take the next shot. Because the players are taking lots of rebounds close to the basket, there should be lots of opportunities to shoot, and lots of baskets will be scored.

Use regular basketball scoring rules, awarding 2 points for shots scored from close range and 3 points for shots scored from outside the 3-point line. If the shooter is fouled during a shot, she is allowed to take a free-throw. The fouling player is not allowed to rebound the free-throw, but the game continues as soon as the shooter has touched the ball after the shot. Participants lose a point if they foul an opponent three times. Participants play for a set time (e.g., 2 minutes); the one scoring the most points wins. Change the pairs and start the game again.

Safety Tips
- Allow rest periods between games to give participants time to recover.
- Warn participants to be careful of collisions.

Advice
- Try to match participants by ability and height.
- Encourage participants to box out after a shot. *Boxing out* means getting between the opponent and the basket after a shot.

- Taller participants have a distinct advantage in this game, so it is important that smaller participants box out after a shot. If smaller participants can box out, they should be able to take any balls that bounce in front of the pair after a shot.

- Have participants call fouls during the game. Encourage them to be honest when calling fouls.

- To rebound effectively, participants should extend their arms fully, jump as high as they can and catch the ball at the highest part of their jump. If they are struggling to catch the ball with two hands and can only contact it with one, they should try to tap it away from their opponent but so they can catch it themselves.

- Teach the group how to use fake shots, fade-away jump shots and other techniques to get a shot away without it being blocked.

Variations

- **Game variation:** Participants play in pairs and compete against another pair, using the same rules.

- **Harder:** Participants are not allowed to dribble the ball if they are within 10 metres (11 yd) of the basket. This should develop long range shooting techniques as well as the ability to use fakes to create space to shoot.

- **Large groups:** Participants can play in groups of three. The participants compete against each other and all play at the same time; the one who scores the most points at the end of the set time wins

- **Sport-specific:** Play the pairs game variation outlined earlier.

Roll, Go, Pass and Shoot
Ages 8 to 16

Key Skills and Fitness Components Developed

Skills
- Attacking
- Defending
- Layups
- Rebounding
- Shooting

Fitness Components
- Agility
- Balance
- Coordination
- Power
- Reaction time
- Speed

Equipment
- One bib (pinnie) per two participants
- Two baskets and two basketballs per 10 participants
- Two cones per 10 participants

Game

For the set-up of this activity, see the figure on page 75. Arrange the participants into groups of 10; then separate each group into teams of five. Each group plays on their own basketball court. Number the teams 1 and 2, and have one team put bibs (pinnies) on. Have teams line up at the half-court line of the basketball court they are using, and give the front participant in each team a ball. Team 1 lines up in one half of the court behind the half-court line, facing one direction, and Team 2 lines up facing the other direction, standing in the other half of the court behind the half-court line. Place cones on the floor approximately 10 metres (11 yd) from the first participant in each line.

When the game begins, the teams try to score in the basket that is in the half of the court where they are standing (but facing away from). The game starts with the participants rolling their balls in front of them. They should roll them gently along the floor. Once the team's ball has rolled past the cone, the front participant chases after it, picks it up and passes it to his team-mates, who continue passing it until each team member has touched it. At this point, the team members try to score in their basket (the one they started the game facing away from). The first team to score a basket is awarded a point.

Participants can work together to score or they can work defensively to stop the opposing team from scoring. After gaining possession of the opponents' ball, a team can make five passes and then try to score in their basket. After a basket has been scored, participants line up at the halfway line ready to start the game again. They should line up in the same order, but the participant who started the last round moves to the back so a new team-mate can roll the ball. Have them play for a set time (e.g., 5 to 10 minutes) or until one team has scored a set number of points (e.g., 10).

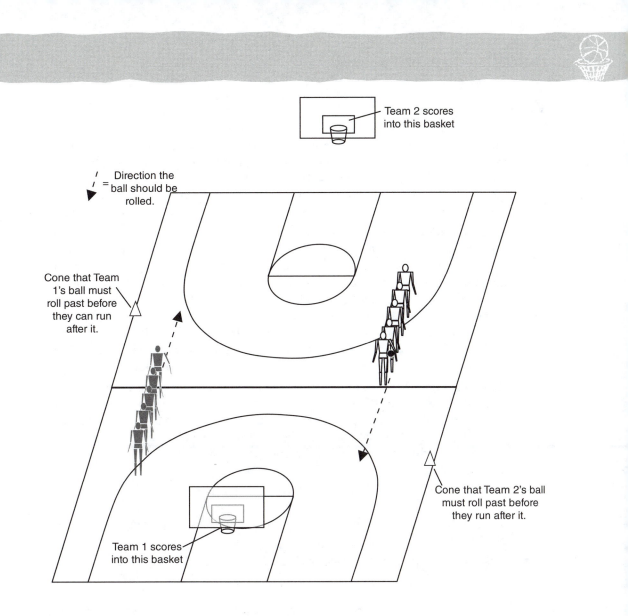

Team 2 scores into this basket

/ = Direction the ball should be rolled.

Cone that Team 1's ball must roll past before they can run after it.

Cone that Team 2's ball must roll past before they run after it.

Team 1 scores into this basket

Safety Tips

- Warn participants to be careful of collisions.
- Ensure participants have completed a thorough warm-up before carrying out this activity because it involves ballistic actions.

Advice

- Participants may not run after their ball until the ball has passed the cone.
- Ask questions to check understanding after explaining the rules.
- Participants can use a variety of tactics to outwit their opponents. Ask them to experiment with the number of participants in their team who defend, and which members of their team should defend. For example, once they have passed the ball, the team may choose two participants to defend. The other three participants attack and try to score in their own basket. Remind participants that everyone on their team must touch the ball before they can score.

(continued)

Variations

- **Game variation:** The teams continue playing until both balls have been shot through the basket. The participant who scores with the first ball places the ball to the side of the court so it will not roll back onto it and then helps his team score with the second ball. Two points are awarded for scoring first, and one point is awarded for scoring second. Therefore, a team that scores with its own ball and then gains possession of its opponents' ball and scores with this, gains 3 points.

- **Game variation:** Create three teams of three or four participants. The teams line up at the halfway line (similar to the original version), but face the same direction. They roll their balls away from the basket, and all the teams will try to score in, after making the set number of passes. The first team to score and move off the court are awarded 2 points (for scoring the first basket). The two teams who remain on court try to score in the other basket first, so they must stop trying to score in the original basket and pass the ball down to the other basket. After the second basket has been scored the teams set up at the centre to start the game again. Play for a set time (e.g., 5 minutes) with the team scoring the most points winning.

- **Game variation:** This is a modified way of playing the preceding variation. Start with the same set-up. The teams try to make the set number of passes and then score in the first basket to gain 2 points. However, the team that scores into this basket is allowed to score into the other basket too, so all three teams compete to score into the second basket. Two points are also awarded for scoring the second basket.

- **Large groups:** It is possible to play this game into one basket. The teams shoot into the same basket and start the game in their lines, beside the basket. The balls are rolled out, and when they are past the free-throw line, participants can run after them.

- **Netball:** Play with the same rules as basketball.

three

Cricket, Striking and Fielding Games

The games in this chapter relate to cricket. Collectively, the activities develop batting, bowling and fielding skills. You can also adapt some of the activities for use in other striking and fielding activities; for example when coaching or teaching rounders, baseball or softball. To find out whether an activity is suitable for these sports and other sports, consult the Variations section of that activity. It is not practical to explain all of the rules of the various striking and fielding activities here for those who are not familiar with them (e.g., many coaches and teachers in the USA will not be familiar with rounders, but the same is true for teachers and coaches in the UK who may not be familiar with the rules for softball or baseball). However, many other coaching manuals or texts are suitable for learning more about any of these sports, such as *Coaching Youth Cricket* by the Australian Cricket Board (2000) or *Coaching Youth Softball* (4th edition) by the American Sport Education Program (2007).

The majority of the activities in this chapter are skill-based practices. However, they all have an element of competition to make them more challenging. Although all the games and activities in this chapter are enjoyable, a few have been really popular with the children I have taught or coached, especially Caribbean Cricket, Hit or Score and Knock-Down. Some children find the full game of cricket boring because often only a few players are involved in the game at any one time. For this reason the activities in this chapter require more participant involvement than the traditional game of cricket. This increases participants' enjoyment of this sport and is more conducive to learning.

In a cricket match, batters continue batting until they are out. This means that the rest of the team can experience long periods of inactivity. Also, once a batter is out, he does not get another chance to bat, which means that if he is out after only a few bowls, he can be sitting around for over an hour waiting for his team to field (if his team has batted first) or for the game to end (if his team has batted second). To resolve these issues, in the games in this chapter the batters take turns to bat, or have short batting times before switching with team-mates. Also, batters may be out in the games, but they still have a chance to bat again, although their team often loses a few runs from the score. Finally, all the games in this chapter have small group sizes to ensure maximum participation, learning and enjoyment.

When you use activities in this chapter in cricket sessions, use tennis balls with beginners or younger participants. For more able participants, you can use a cricket ball, but ensure that batters and wicketkeepers wear appropriate safety equipment. *However, it is not appropriate to use cricket balls when playing Leg as Wicket.*

When playing the games in this chapter, fielders should not stand too close to the batter. This gives the fielders a chance to get their hands to a ball or move their head out of the way if the ball has been hit towards them powerfully. As a general rule, when using tennis balls, fielders should not stand closer than 10 metres (11 yd) from the batter. The wicketkeeper can stand closer to the wickets, but if she is standing up to the wickets, she should wear a protective helmet, especially if the bowler is bowling the ball powerfully. Bats should be a suitable size and weight for your participants.

Because this chapter includes a lot of cricket-specific terms, you should have some understanding of these terms and the rules of cricket if you are to implement the games correctly. The most frequently used terms and rules are described in the following sections, but if you require more information, you can visit the laws of cricket section of the Marylebone Cricket Club (MCC) Web site (www.lords.org/laws-and-spirit/laws-of-cricket/laws). Alternatively, you can enrol in relevant cricket coaching awards or qualifications to gain a greater knowledge of the rules and the key techniques and skills.

Cricket Basics

The game of cricket is similar to other striking and fielding games in that teams take turns to bat and score points (in cricket, points are called runs). At the end of the match, the team with the most runs wins. There are 11 players on a cricket team. An inning is when one team gets a chance to bat. A team that is not batting is said to be fielding, although this includes bowling as part of this role. In a game of cricket, a team gets either one or two innings depending on the competition rules, although in junior cricket matches, competing teams get only one batting inning each. When a team is batting, two of the team-mates bat, although only one faces a bowl. Batters continue to bat until they are out. The aim of their opponents is to get 10 of the batters out, because the last batter cannot bat on his own.

Following are some basic terms to keep in mind while reading through the activities in this chapter:

• **Wicket, stumps, pitch, outfield and boundary:** These terms describe the area where a cricket match takes place. The outer edge of the playing area is called the **boundary** and balls that travel over the boundary will score 4 or 6 runs, depending on whether the ball bounced before travelling over the boundary. If a batter hits the ball over the boundary, she scores 4 runs if the ball bounces or rolls before reaching the boundary and 6 runs if the ball goes over the boundary before bouncing. It is possible to have 4 or 6 runs from a bye or wide (see later sections). In the centre of the playing area is the **pitch**, a rectangular shape 20 metres (22 yd) long and 3 metres (3.3 yd) wide. This is where the bowler delivers, or bowls, the ball to a batter. The pitch has two sets of **wickets** placed 20 metres (22 yd) apart (19 m [21 yd] for under-thirteens and 18 m [20 yd] for under-twelves). The term *wicket* is used to describe the three **stumps** (see the example in figure on page 85). The bowler bowls beside one set of wickets and tries to hit the other set to get a batter out (although there can be other tactics for bowling to get an opponent out).

• **Batters, striking batter, non-striking batter:** Two **batters** bat at the same time, although this does not mean they both receive a bowl at the same time. The batter who is receiving the bowl is the **striking batter,** and he stands at the wickets towards which the bowler is bowling. His team-mate is the **non-striking batter,** and he stands by the other wickets. If the batter runs a single (1 run), the two batters switch ends and roles for the next delivery.

• **Batting crease (popping crease):** The **batting crease** is a line drawn or painted on the pitch. There is one batting crease drawn on the pitch 1.2 metres in front of each of the wickets. The batting creases are significant for the rules of the game and are involved in many of the batting and bowling rules—for example, when batters are running between the wickets, when there is a run-out to be decided or when a stumping occurs. Wherever possible, add creases to your games to increase the realism and to develop correct understanding of the rules. If the surface is suitable, use chalk to mark out the batting creases. See figure on page 85 for the set-up of a cricket pitch and the batting creases.

• **Bowler, bowls, delivery:** Bowling in cricket is the equivalent way of sending the ball to a batter in other striking and fielding games (e.g., bowling in rounders or pitching in baseball or softball). In cricket, one of the fielding teams **bowls** the ball at the batter. The act of bowling a ball towards the batter can also be called a bowl, a ball or a **delivery**. The player bowling is the **bowler**. The bowler bowls beside one of the wickets and aims to get a batter out by hitting these wickets. A bowler is the equivalent of a baseball or softball pitcher, although the technique is very different. Bowlers usually have a run-up before delivering the ball, and the rules of cricket state that the arm must be straight when the bowler releases the ball. If a bowler does not bowl the ball correctly or if it does not fly to the batter correctly, then a no-ball or wide is given (these are discussed later).

• **Overs:** When a fielder is bowling during a cricket match, she is required to bowl one **over**, which is six consecutive deliveries, or bowls. At the end of an over, another bowler bowls, and this is usually from the opposite wicket. Many of the games in this chapter require the bowlers to bowl an over (six consecutive bowls) to familiarise the players with this concept. Many cricket competitions are structured for teams to compete against each other in a specific number of overs. For example, teams each bat for 20 overs in 20-20 cricket, or for 50 overs in one-day matches.

•   **Wicketkeeper:** The **wicketkeeper** is a specialised fielding position that is the cricketing equivalent of a baseball or softball catcher. When a bowler is bowling at a set of wickets, the wicketkeeper stands behind this set of wickets to stop any ball that the striking batter has missed, and that has also missed the wickets. When playing a match using a (hard) cricket ball the wicketkeeper wears protective pads on the legs, a box (cup), thick gloves and a helmet (if he is standing very close to the wickets) to help prevent injuries. In the games in this chapter participants do not need to wear this protective gear if they are wicketkeeping, because we recommend that you use only tennis balls. If you do play games using cricket balls, wicketkeepers should wear the protective gear.

•   **Fielders, slip fielders:** Fielding in cricket is similar to other striking and fielding games. **Fielders** try to catch or run out batters to get them out. Similar to baseball and softball, the cricket fielding positions are given specific names. Advanced players know the locations of the fielding positions and can quickly move to the correct position if their captain or the bowler tells them to move to a named position. This speeds up the game considerably when moving during an over or between overs. There are too many positions to mention here; however, Collide Catch (page 90) requires some participants to stand like **slip fielders**, so a brief description of this position is included here. Once again, if you would like more information regarding fielding positions, refer to specific coaching resources to develop your knowledge. The fielder is said to be in a slip position or to be a slip fielder if he is standing next to the wicketkeeper to his immediate right or left. It is possible to have more than one slip fielder (indeed, it is not unusual for elite teams to have five or six fielders in the slips if a fast bowler is bowling well).

•   **Runs, running between the wickets:** As mentioned previously, a **run** is the name for a point in cricket. The batting team is awarded runs in a number of ways during a match (e.g., wide, no-ball, byes). Batters who hit the ball over the boundary score a 4 or a 6, but the majority of runs scored in a match come from batters **running between the wickets**. For example, if a batter hits the ball into the outfield and the batters switch positions, they score 1 run. It is possible for batters to score more than 1 run. Runners frequently score 2 runs if a batter hits the ball hard over the top of a fielder so it travels close to the boundary. The batters run once to switch ends, but then touch their bats over the batting crease (at the end they are running to) and then return to their start positions. Unlike in softball or baseball, a batter in cricket carries the bat with him. When running two or more, batters touch the ends of their bats over the batting crease when they turn. Doing this gives them extra reach so they can turn without actually running the full distance between the two batting creases. Also, if a batter is close to being run out at the wickets he is running to, he should slide his bat along the floor starting a few metres before the batting crease. This again gives him a slightly greater reach that could prevent him from being run out. In some of the games in this chapter (e.g., Running Two) batters do not hit the ball, but they carry a bat. This is so they get used to running between the wickets with a bat, they learn how to turn when running more than one run, and they learn to slide the bat in if they are close to being run out.

- **Wide:** Bowls must be within a reasonable distance of the batter. If the bowl is delivered too wide, it is not playable, which is unfair for the batter. In a cricket match if the bowler bowls a wide, the batting team is awarded 1 run and the bowler has to bowl the delivery again. However, when coaching or teaching beginners, I usually change this rule to speed up the game by awarding the batting team 2 runs for a wide but not making the bowler bowl the extra delivery. An alternative rule that can also be used instead of my variation is to allow the batter a free hit on the delivery following a wide. This means that the batter cannot be caught, bowled out or given out leg before wicket (LBW; discussed later) on this subsequent delivery, which means that she can play an attacking shot without the risk of being out by these means.

- **No-ball:** A cricket umpire may call a **no-ball** against the bowler or his team for a number of reasons, including the following:

    - The bowler bowls a ball that bounces more than twice, or rolls along the floor, and so is difficult for the batter to hit away.

    - The bowler bowls a dangerous ball. For a fast bowler a dangerous ball is one that travels to the batter without bouncing and reaches him above waist height. For a slower bowler a dangerous ball is one that travels to the batter without bouncing and reaches him above shoulder height.

    - The bowler throws the ball (i.e., does not deliver with a straight arm).

    - The bowler does not deliver from the correct place. With beginners this is usually bowling too close to the batter. The bowler usually runs up to the pitch and bowls from beside the wickets at her end. Before releasing the ball, the bowler must have her front foot on or behind the batting crease. If she steps past the line with her front foot before releasing the ball, this is a no-ball.

The batter can hit a no-ball, in which case he can only be out; if he handles the ball, hits the ball twice, obstructs the field or is run out. This means that he can strike the ball without the risk of being caught out and can swing without worrying about being bowled, stumped or given out LBW (discussed later). Similar to a wide, the batting team is awarded 1 run when a bowler bowls a no-ball, and the bowler has to bowl the ball again.

- **Byes:** A bye is a run taken after the striking batter has missed a delivery, or bowl. If the striking batter misses the ball, the batters can still run. This occurs regularly when the wicketkeeper misses the ball. Beginners frequently do not run a bye even if the wicketkeeper has missed the ball and it has travelled a considerable distance past them, so you should remind batters what a bye is and that they are allowed to run even if they miss the ball.

- **Leg byes:** Batters can still score runs if the ball hits their legs or other parts of their bodies. For example, the ball may hit the batter's leg and be deflected past the wicketkeeper and her nearest team-mate. For leg-bye runs to be awarded, the batter must have attempted to play the ball with her bat; she cannot just kick the ball away without making an attempt to hit it.

Ten Ways to Be Out in Cricket

There are 10 ways a batter can be given out (this is sometimes referred to by the fielding team as 'taking their wicket'). Some of these occur frequently, whereas others occur rarely. This section provides a description of each way of being out so you can start to introduce these to your participants (Australian Cricket Board 2000).

1. Bowled: If a bowler delivers the ball so it hits the wickets, the batter is out. This can be a direct hit or it can deflect off the striking batter's bat, pads or body before hitting the wickets.

2. Caught: If a batter hits the ball into the air or it skims or clips the edge of his bat, the bowler, a fielder or the wicketkeeper can catch it. The catch must be taken before the ball bounces. A batter can also be out if the ball is caught after it has hit the batter's hand (or glove if she is wearing one), as long as the hand was in contact with the bat when the ball made contact with the batter.

3. Run out: As mentioned previously, batters can score runs by running between the wickets. This can be a single run or more depending on how far the ball has been hit and how close the opponents are to it. If the striking batter hits the ball and runs to the other wickets, his team-mate must also run (switching to the striking batter's end). If the batters are running and one or both of them are not on or over the batting crease the fielding team (fielders, bowler and wicketkeeper) can **run out** one of the batters by 'breaking the wicket'. The term *breaking the wickets* means hitting the wickets with the ball or with the hand if it is holding the ball. For example, a run out can occur if a fielder throws the ball at the wickets or the fielder throws the ball to the wicketkeeper or another team-mate, who is standing next to a set of wickets, for them to hit the wickets with the ball. To avoid being run out, a batter needs to have part of her bat or a part of her body (usually one or both feet) over the batting crease before the fielding team breaks the wickets. A run-out also occurs if a batter starts to run but returns to the wicket she was standing at if the fielding team break the wickets before she gets back to the batting crease.

4. Stumped: Being **stumped** is similar to being run out, except that a stumping occurs straight after the batter has missed the ball. If the batter moves towards the bowler and he is standing out of the batting crease or he lifts his foot up and does not have a part of his body touching the ground behind the batting crease, there is a good chance the wicketkeeper will catch the ball and throw this at the wickets. If the wicketkeeper hits the wickets when the batter does not have his bat or a part of his body touching the floor on or behind the batting crease, the batter is stumped out.

5. Hit wicket: If the striking batter hits the wickets with her bat or steps onto them when playing a ball bowled at her, she is out. Younger and novice batters are quite often out **hit wicket** because they stand too close to the wickets. Tell participants to stand with one foot on either side of the batting crease when they are facing a delivery. However, they must be careful because if they lift their back foot off the floor and miss the ball when playing a shot, there is a chance they can be stumped.

6. LBW (leg before wicket): If a bowler delivers a ball that would have hit the wickets but the striking batter stops it from doing so using any part of his body (not just his legs), then he is given out **LBW**.

7. Obstructing the field: Batters are not allowed to 'put off' fielders or deliberately interfere with their efforts to field or catch a ball. For example, if a batter shouts at a fielder when she was about to catch a ball, or if she were the non-striking batter and deflected a ball with her bat away from a fielder, then she would be given out **obstructing the field**. Another example of inappropriate play that would result in being given out is if a runner deliberately changes the direction of her run (when scoring a run) so that she runs across a fielder's path to prevent her from getting to the ball.

8. Handling the ball: Batters are not allowed to deliberately touch the ball with their hands and are given out if they do so. The only exceptions to this rule are if the batter's hand is gripping or holding the bat when the ball strikes his hand and if the batter has asked an opponent's permission to touch the ball. The latter event occurs if a batter has played a defensive shot and the ball has stopped close to him. He can ask permission to pick it up and throw it to a fielder or the bowler to speed up the game.

9. Hitting the ball twice: The batter is given out if she deliberately hits a delivered ball with the bat twice. However, she is not given out if she tries to hit or defend the ball but it continues to roll towards the wickets and the second hit is to stop the ball from doing so. A second 'defending' block is allowed as long at the batter does not try to 'whack or strike' the ball away.

10. Timed out: This rule hardly ever occurs in a cricket match. A batter is timed out if it is his turn to bat (after a team-mate is out) but he does not get onto the field of play within 3 minutes of the previous team-mate getting out.

References

Australian Cricket Board. 2000. *Coaching Youth Cricket*. Champaign, IL: Human Kinetics.

American Sport Education Program. 2007. *Coaching Youth Softball*, 4th ed. Champaign, IL: Human Kinetics.

Beat the Runner
Ages 5 to 16

Key Skills and Fitness Components Developed

Skills

- Fielding skills (throwing and catching)
- Running between the wickets
- Wicketkeeping

Fitness Components

- Agility
- Balance
- Coordination
- Power
- Reaction time
- Speed

Equipment

- One cricket bat
- One wicket
- One tennis ball
- Five cones per eight participants
- Possibly chalk

Game

Arrange the participants into groups of eight, and then separate each group into two teams of four. One team starts as fielders; the other team starts as runners. For each group place a wicket and three cones on the ground to make an area of approximately 20 by 20 metres (22 by 22 yd). Place another two cones (called run cones) approximately 1 metre apart and approximately 5 metres (5.5 yd) away from the cone where fielder number 4 is standing (see figure on page 85 for the game set-up). If the surface of your playing area is suitable (e.g., in a sports hall or on concrete), use chalk to draw a line between the run cones. The chalk line is the equivalent of a batting, or popping, crease (see the introduction of this chapter).

One of the fielders starts with the ball and stands beside the wickets (call this fielder number 1). The remaining participants on her team each stand beside one of the cones. Number these fielders 2, 3 and 4, working in an anti-clockwise direction from number 1. One runner stands with the bat by the wickets. You can draw another batting crease on the floor (to the side of the wickets) using the chalk to indicate where the runner must start and finish her two runs. The runner does not use the bat to hit the ball, but carries it when running between the wickets. This will improve the batters ability to use and carry the bat when they are running to score runs during cricket match play. When running between the wickets, batters will touch the bat over the batting crease line when running two runs, or slide it along the floor to give themselves extra reach when they are close to being run out. The remaining runners line up approximately 5 metres (5.5 yd) away from the wickets.

When the participants are set up, shout 'go' to start the game. The fielding team tries to throw the ball to each other around the outside of the square. Fielder number 1 throws to

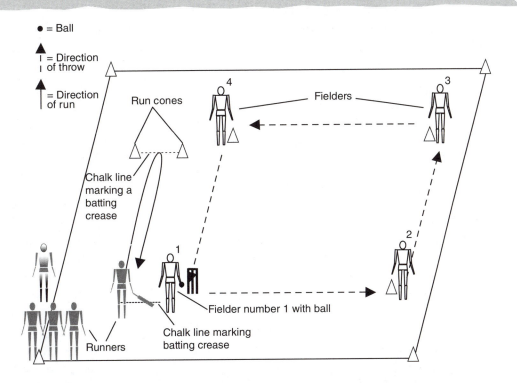

- • = Ball
- ▲ = Direction of throw
- ▲ = Direction of run

Run cones

Fielders

4

3

Chalk line marking a batting crease

1

2

Fielder number 1 with ball

Chalk line marking batting crease

Runners

number 2, number 2 to 3, number 3 to 4 and number 4 throws the ball at the wickets or into number 1's hands so she can break the wickets. The runner sprints to the run cones and back to the start as quickly as possible. When she gets to the run cones, the runner touches the end of her bat on the floor between the two run cones or over the line if you have drawn one. To score a point, the runner has to get to the run cones and back to her start position before the fielders can pass the ball around the square and break the wickets. If the fielders run out the runner, they prevent the runner from scoring a point. Runners take turns to compete against the fielders. Once they have all had three turns running, the teams swap roles. When both teams have taken a turn being the runners, the team who has the most points wins.

Safety Tips

- Runners who are not competing against the fielders should stand well out of the way and keep their eyes on the ball to avoid being hit by stray throws.

- The runner who is competing against the fielders should not run too close to where the fielders are likely to throw the ball. Draw the batting creases at least 5 metres (5.5 yd) from the wickets and the cone where fielder number 4 is standing.

Advice

- Set the distance from the start to the run cones so that the race is competitive. If the runners are scoring points too easily, move the run cones slightly farther away, but move them closer if the runners are struggling to score points.

(continued)

- Do not allow participants to run or throw the ball before you have started the game.

- Instruct the runner to slide her bat in when she is approximately 3 metres (3.3 yd) from the wickets when she is finishing the run. This gives her an extra reach and means she is less likely to be run out.

- Fielders should throw the ball to each other so it is easy to catch. Fielder number 4 should throw the ball at the wickets or to number 1 so it is just above the wickets. Throwing the ball so it lands just above the wickets makes it easier for number 1 to catch the ball and hit the wickets with it. If you are umpiring this game, stand to the side of the wickets (see figure on page 85) so you can judge whether the runner is run out when the fielders break the wickets.

Variations

- **Easier/harder:** To change the level of difficulty, change the distance the runner has to run. This can also be combined with having the fielders throw the ball over shorter or longer distances.

- **Game variation:** This game can be adapted for various throwing and fielding techniques using similar rules. For example, the ball could be rolled along the floor or thrown so it must bounce once.

- **Game variation:** The runner does not have to return from the run cones back to the start. She can decide to run only to the run cone and stop if she thinks she is going to be run out. Only 1 point is scored in this instance. She scores 2 points if she gets to the run cone and back. The runner should call 'stay' if they decide to only go for 1 run. They should then walk back to the end of the team's line.

- **Game variation:** Place run cones at three different distances (similar to Decision Run on page 92). The runner can decide which cone to run to. One point is scored for running to the first run cone and back. Two points are scored for running to the second cone and back, and three points are scored for running to the third cone and back.

- **Game variation:** Runners continue taking turns to run until the fielders have got a set number of runners out (e.g., 10).

- **Harder:** The fielders must catch the ball using only one hand.

- **Harder:** The runner must try to score 4 runs by running to the run cones and back twice. The fielders must pass the ball in sequence twice, reversing the direction on the second lap (e.g., fielder number 1 to 2 to 3 to 4 for the first lap then 4 to 3 to 2 to 1 for the second).

Caribbean Cricket

Ages 8 to 16

Key Skills and Fitness Components Developed

Skills

- Batting
- Catching
- Fielding
- Throwing
- Wicketkeeping

Fitness Components

- Agility
- Balance
- Coordination
- Power
- Reaction time
- Speed

Equipment

- Two cricket bats
- Two wickets
- Two tennis balls per 10 to 14 participants

Game

This is a really entertaining game that involves lots of switching roles, so everyone play-ing should get lots of involvement. Ideally, it is played indoors; however, groups should have approximately 10 to 14 participants in them, so it may not be possible to play inside in a sports hall or gymnasium if you have more than this recommended number. Each group should have two wickets, two bats and two balls. The wickets should be placed 20 metres (22 yd) apart (19 m [21 yd] for under-thirteens, 18 m [20 yd] for under-twelves). Two participants start as batters, two start as bowlers, one starts as the wicketkeeper and the remaining are fielders (see figure on page 88). All bowls are delivered from the same set of wickets, so the batter at the other wicket is the striking batter. The batters continue to bat until they are out. Batters can be out in the following ways: caught, bowled, run out, stumped, hit the ball twice and hit wicket. When a batter is out, he switches roles with the participant who got him out, as follows:

- If the bowler bowls him out, he becomes the batter.
- If a fielder catches or runs him out, he becomes the batter.
- If the wicketkeeper stumps or catches him out, he becomes the batter.

When the game begins, the bowlers take turns to bowl. If the striking batter misses the ball and the wicketkeeper fields the ball, the wicketkeeper becomes the bowler and moves to the bowling wicket. In this instance the bowler moves onto the off side (this is the left-hand side of the wickets, looking from the bowling wickets, if the batter is right-handed) to become a fielder. The fielders on the off side of the wicket all move one posi-tion around in a clockwise direction, and one of them becomes the new wicketkeeper. Participants change positions quickly; the new bowler needs to be ready to bowl the ball as soon as the next wicketkeeper is in position and everyone is watching the ball.

The batters try to score runs in the usual way, by running between the wickets. They may also score a 4 or 6 by hitting the ball so that it strikes the back wall of the hall. A

(continued)

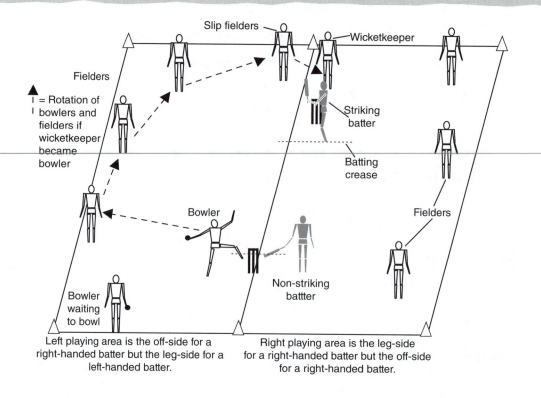

Slip fielders — Wicketkeeper

Fielders

▲
┃ = Rotation of
┃ bowlers and
  fielders if
  wicketkeeper
  became
  bowler

Striking batter

Batting crease

Bowler

Fielders

Non-striking battter

Bowler waiting to bowl

Left playing area is the off-side for a right-handed batter but the leg-side for a left-handed batter.

Right playing area is the leg-side for a right-handed batter but the off-side for a right-handed batter.

batter scores a 4 if the ball bounces before it hits the back wall, and a 6 if it hits without bouncing. Batters do not have to run if they hit a 4 or 6, but they must run any other time they hit the ball. This is sometimes referred to as the 'tip and run' rule by coaches. The tip and run rule states that batters must run if they hit the ball with the bat.

Because batters have to run if they hit the ball, there should be lots of run-outs, so fielders should be frequently changing with the batter. If a fielder picks up the ball after a batter has hit it or after another fielder has thrown the ball at the wickets during a run, then that fielder becomes the bowler. The bowler moves to the side where the new bowler was standing, and, if necessary, all of the players move around one position until the gap where the new bowler was standing is occupied. Participants keep their own scores throughout the game by continually adding up the runs they score when batting. Have them play for a set time (e.g., 15 to 20 minutes). The participant who has scored the most points is the winner.

Safety Tips

- Bowlers should deliver the ball when it is safe to do so. This means that when a bowler bowls other participants should not be standing between the wickets, and they should all be looking at the ball, especially the batter.

- All participants should keep their eyes on the ball when it is being bowled. This is particularly important for the wicketkeeper when she becomes a bowler (after fielding a ball) because she will be facing away from the striking batter when she is moving to the bowling wickets.

Advice

- To speed up the game, participants should get into their fielding positions quickly after a ball has been bowled.

Variations

- **Game variation:** Participants play in pairs and bat together. This means that if one of them is out, so is his partner. The participant who gets the batter out and his partner switch to become the two new batters.
- **Game variation:** To reward good bowling, if a bowler bowls a good delivery that beats the batter (and is not a wide), she continues to bowl. The wicketkeeper passes the ball back to the bowler, and she continues to bowl until the ball is hit by the batter and fielded by another participant or they bowl a wide.

Collide Catch
Ages 8 to 16

Key Skills and Fitness Components Developed

Skills
- Catching
- Throwing

Fitness Components
- Balance
- Coordination
- Reaction time

Equipment
One tennis ball per two participants

Game
Arrange the participants into groups of four, and give each group two tennis balls. For the set-up of this activity, see the figure on this page. Participants stand in a square formation. Although *all four participants in each group are competing against each other*, the participants work in pairs to throw the balls. The participants facing each other across the centre of the area constitute a pair. There should be approximately 5 to 7 metres (5.5 to 7.7 yd) between the participants in each pair.

Each participant in one of the pairs (facing each other) starts with a ball and adopts the low stance of a wicketkeeper or slip fielder. Each participant in the throwing pair throws his ball to his partner repeatedly, using an underarm action. The partners should try to release the balls at the same time so they collide mid-flight. They should also try to throw the balls so that if the balls do not collide in the middle, they can easily be caught by their partner. All of the participants should be ready to catch one of the balls if they collide. If a participant catches a ball after a collision and before the ball bounces, he scores a point. If the balls do collide in the centre of the group, they are given to the other pair of participants, who take their turn to throw the balls to each other. This happens regardless of whether either ball is caught after the collision. Participants continue for a set time (e.g., 3 minutes) or until one participant has scored a set number of points (e.g., 10). Change the groups; then start the fun again.

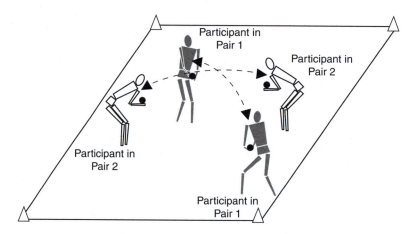

Participant in Pair 1

Participant in Pair 2

Participant in Pair 2

Participant in Pair 1

Safety Tips

- Use soft balls only.
- Participants should not stand too close to each other.
- Participants should not throw the ball too hard.
- Set groups far enough apart to avoid participants being struck by stray balls from other groups.

Advice

- To facilitate partners catching each other's balls when they do not collide, suggest that they toss them so they are at about shoulder height in the centre. Then they will drop so that the partners can catch them between knee and hip height.
- Allow participants to practise the throw by giving a ball to each of the pairs. They should develop throwing the ball, so the throw has the correct pace and reaches their partner at the correct height, so it is easy to catch. When they have developed this skill, play the game.
- If two participants are having difficulty throwing at the same time, ask them to count down from 3 to zero so they are more accurate at releasing at the same time.
- Participants should keep their own scores throughout the game.
- Advanced participants should try to catch and throw quickly so there are lots of collisions. However, they must still try to throw at the same time as their partner.

Variations

- **Game variation:** Within each group compete in pairs. A participant scores a point for the team if she catches a ball after a collision. Pairs gain 2 points if they each catch a ball after a collision. Play for a set time (e.g., 3 minutes) or to score a set number of points (e.g., 10).
- **Game variation:** Participants in each group work together against the other groups to score as many points as possible in a set time (e.g., 3 minutes) or to be the first group to score a set number of points (e.g., 10).
- **Small groups:** Have participants play in groups of three. Participants should take turns to work in a pair, with the other participant standing to the side. All participants try to catch a ball after a collision to score a point. After there has been a ball collision, the participant standing at the side switches with one of the pair.
- **Sport-specific:** This game can be adapted for use in other sports that require throwing and catching skills (e.g., rounders, softball, baseball). Use a tennis ball with younger children but relevant balls can be used with older or more advanced participants. It can also be adapted for use in soccer sessions when coaching or teaching goalkeepers. Use relevant balls for the activity that the participants are playing.

Key Skills and Fitness Components Developed

Skills

- Batting (including running between the wickets)
- Catching
- Fielding
- Throwing
- Wicketkeeping

Fitness Components

- Agility
- Balance
- Coordination
- Power
- Reaction time
- Speed

Equipment

- Two cricket bats, one tennis ball and one wicket per 10 to 14 participants
- Cones
- Possibly chalk

Game

Arrange the participants into groups of 10 to 14; then separate each group into two equal teams. Set up the wicket and cones as shown in figure on page 93. Place the wicket on the ground and use the cones to mark out three run lines approximately 15, 20 and 25 metres (16, 22, and 27 yd) away from the wicket. If the surface of your playing area is suitable (e.g., in a sports hall or on concrete), use chalk to draw a line between the two cones marking each run line. The run lines are equivalents of a batting, or popping, crease (see the introduction of this chapter).

One team starts batting, and the other starts fielding. The fielding team nominates one participant to be the wicketkeeper and stand behind the wicket. The rest of the team spreads out, trying to cover as much of the outfield as possible. One batter starts as the striking batter, and the rest of the team members stand or sit behind the wicket well out of the way of the fielders. The striking batter steps up to the wicket to bat. With younger or less able groups it may be beneficial for you to bowl. You should do this from a distance of approximately 12 metres (13 yd) from the wicket.

When bowling to younger participants, deliver the ball at the wicket with an underarm action. The batter tries to hit the ball away, or defend, by stopping the ball from hitting the wicket. *The batter has to run regardless of whether she hits the ball.* The fielding team tries to retrieve the ball as quickly as possible and throw it to the wicketkeeper to run the batter out or prevent her from scoring runs. The batter tries to score runs in the following ways:

- If she runs to any of the lines and decides not to return straightaway to the wickets, she scores 1 run.
- If she runs to the first line and then straight back to the wickets, she scores 2 runs.

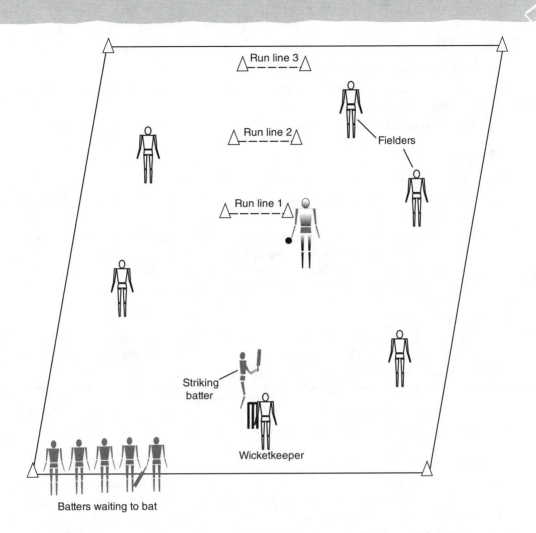

Run line 3

Run line 2

Fielders

Run line 1

Striking
batter

Wicketkeeper

Batters waiting to bat

- If she runs to the second line and then straight back to the wickets, she scores 4 runs.
- If she runs to the third line and then straight back to the wickets, she scores 6 runs.

If the batter decides not to run straight back, she should wait at the line nearest the wickets ready to run back as soon as the ball has been bowled to the next batter. The fielding team can run the first batter out when she tries to return to the wickets. This batter must run when the next batter takes her turn to receive the next ball. No other points are scored for a batter who returned to the wickets after waiting for the next team-mate to hit, but the team-mate (next hitter) can still score 2, 4 or 6 runs if she hits the ball and gets to one of the lines and back without stopping. If any of the batters are out (bowled, run out or caught), then the batting team loses 5 runs from its score.

After taking their turn to bat and completing their runs, participants join the back of their team's line ready to bat again when it is their turn. The batting team continues for a set time (e.g., 7 to 10 minutes), or until each batter has received a set number of bowls (e.g., four each). The teams then swap roles, and when both teams have taken their turn to bat, the team with the most runs win.

(continued)

Safety Tips

- Fielders should stand at least 10 metres (11 yd) from the batter.
- Fielders should not stand between the wicket and the run lines because the batter may run into them.
- Warn the fielders to be careful of collisions when chasing the ball.

Advice

- Remind batters that they must run even if they miss the ball.
- Fielders can rotate positions every six deliveries so that they all get a chance to be the wicketkeeper.
- With older or more experienced participants, this game is best played in a sports hall because the batters will hit the ball farther outdoors. This can make the game too easy for more skilled batters. Alternatively, having them bowl to each other (see variation in next section) makes it harder for the batters to hit the ball.

Variations

- **Game variation:** Allow the fielders to bowl themselves. With older or more experienced participants, make the bowlers deliver using an overarm action from an appropriate distance (see chapter introduction for more information).
- **Game variation:** If a batter is caught out, the teams switch roles.
- **Harder:** Batters have to run to one of the lines and back without stopping. If the batter misses the ball, the wicketkeeper must throw the ball to one of her team-mates, who must pass to a different team-mate before the ball is thrown at the wickets or back to the wicketkeeper.
- **Harder:** Change the rules so that in any one inning, batters are not allowed to bat again if they are out. In this instance an inning should be timed or the team should be given a set number of deliveries (e.g., four each). If all of the batters are out before the end of this time or a set number of deliveries, then the teams switch roles.

Four, Two or Out

Ages 8 to 16

Key Skills and Fitness Components Developed

Skills

· Catching

· Fielding

· Throwing

Fitness Components

· Agility

· Balance

· Coordination

· Power

· Reaction time

Equipment

• One tennis ball per 12 participants

• Cones

Game

Arrange the participants into groups of 12; then separate each group into two teams of six. Number the teams 1 and 2. For the set-up of this activity, see figure on page 96. Cone out a playing area approximately 20 by 30 metres (22 by 33 yd) for each group. It should be a rectangular area divided into three sections. The middle section is called the defensive area and should be approximately 20 by 20 metres (22 by 22 yd). The outer areas are throwing area 1 and throwing area 2. The lines separating the defensive area and the throwing areas are the goal lines; goal line 1 separates the defensive area from throwing area 1, and goal line 2 separates the defensive area from throwing area 2. Team 1 begins as the fielding team and stands in the defensive area. Team 2 begins as the throwing team; three of them stand in throwing area 1, with the remaining three standing in throwing area 2.

One of the participants from Team 2 in throwing area 1 starts with the ball. He tries to throw the ball through the defensive area to his team-mates in throwing area 2 (over goal line 2). He must not step over or past goal line 1 when he releases the ball. The ball must be thrown through the defensive area below a specific height (e.g., 183 cm [6 ft] or the tallest of the participants), so the thrower cannot throw the ball over the top of the fielders' heads. He is awarded 2 points if he throws the ball through the defensive area and a team-mate catches it before a bounce or after it has bounced once. One point is awarded if the ball travels over goal line 2 but is not caught by a team-mate in the other throwing area before it bounces. If the fielding team stops the ball going through the defensive area, the thrower's team loses 1 wicket or has 1 out (see the introduction to this chapter). If a fielder manages to catch a ball before it bounces, the fielding team lose 2 wickets (have 2 outs).

If the fielders stop the ball, they pass it to one of the participants in throwing area 2 because throwing alternates between the participants standing in the two throwing areas. Team 2 continues throwing until it has lost 10 wickets (10 outs) or for a set time (e.g., 3 to 5 minutes); then the teams swap roles. If they are playing the timed version, at the end of the set time, 2 points are removed from the throwers' score for each wicket (out). For example, if a team scores 35 points but have lost 5 wickets then their final score

(continued)

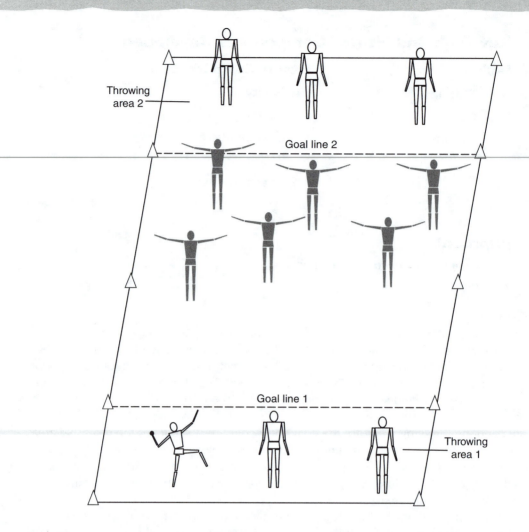

Throwing area 2

Goal line 2

Goal line 1

Throwing area 1

would be 25. After both teams have taken their turn as the throwers, the team with the most points wins.

Safety Tips

- Participants should be suitably warmed up before playing the game because it involves ballistic movements.
- Fielders in the defensive section should not stand too close to the participant who is throwing the tennis ball.
- The size of the area depends on the age and experience of the participants. It should be challenging yet safe. Because beginners or younger participants will struggle to throw the ball through a large area, they will be frequently unsuccessful if the area is too big. A small area, on the other hand, is not advisable for more advanced or older participants because it becomes dangerous for the fielders.

- Fielders should not stand in a line (parallel to the goal lines) across their area. They should stand so that, if they dive to their side, they do not collide with a team-mate. Inform participants to call their own names when they are diving to field a ball so that their team-mates can move out of their way.

Advice

- Instruct participants in correct throwing, catching and fielding techniques.
- Have participants keep their team's score throughout the game.

Variations

- **Easier/harder:** Change the size of the area depending on the age or ability of the participants. A longer defensive area or narrower playing area makes the game more challenging for the throwers (but easier for the fielders).
- **Game variation:** Place two wickets approximately 5 metres apart (not too close to the edge of the playing area) on each of the goal lines. The fielders can try to hit the wickets on the goal line that they are trying to score past when throwing and score 6 points if they manage to do this. Other than that variation, the scoring system is the same as the original version of the game.
- **Game variation:** Participants play individually against the other members of the group. If a participant is a thrower and a ball that he throws is caught or stopped by a fielder, the two participants swap roles. If the ball is thrown over the goal line and is caught (before it bounces or before it has bounced twice), award the thrower and the catcher two points. Award one point to the thrower for throwing over the required goal line when it is not caught before the bounce or having bounced more than once. Four points are awarded for a fielder catching the ball before it bounces. Have them play for a set time, after which the participant with the most points is the winner.
- **Harder:** Instead of throwing the ball, the throwers can hit the ball using a bat. The game can be adapted for hitting a variety of shots. This is similar to Drop, Bounce, Hit (see *Fun and Games*, page 70). If using this variation, make the defensive area bigger and do not allow fielders to stand within 10 metres (11 yd) of the batter.
- **Sport-specific:** This game can be adapted for use in rounders, softball and baseball using the same rules.

<table>

Key Skills and Fitness Components Developed

Skills	Fitness Components
· Catching	· Agility
· Fielding	· Balance
· Throwing	· Coordination
	· Power
	· Reaction time

</table>

Equipment

- One tennis ball and one wicket per six to eight participants
- Cones

Game

Arrange the participants into groups of six to eight, and then separate each group into two equal teams. Use cones to mark out the playing area for each group. Create a rectangular area divided into three sections. The lines separating the middle section are the throw lines. The middle section is a no-throw area. Place the wicket in the centre of the no-throw area. Participants from Team 1 stand in one of the end sections, and participants from Team 2 stand in the other (see the figure on this page). The end lines (the shorter sides of the playing area) behind the teams are goal lines that the teams are trying to defend. Number the teams 1 and 2.

A participant from Team 1 begins with the ball, and when the game starts, she throws it at the wicket. Throws must be taken from behind her team's throw line, so not in the no-throw area. If the ball hits the wickets, 3 points are scored for that team. Participants try to throw the ball so that if it misses the wickets it passes through to the opponents'

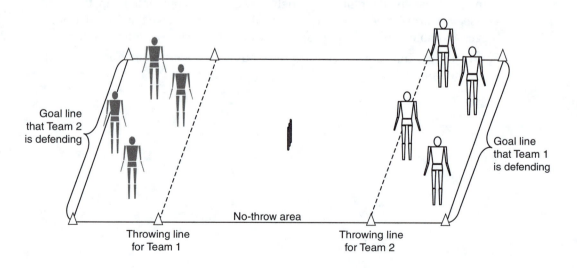

Goal line that Team 2 is defending

Goal line that Team 1 is defending

No-throw area

Throwing line for Team 1

Throwing line for Team 2

goal because 1 point is scored if the ball passes through the opponents' goal. For a goal to be scored, the ball must pass below a certain height (e.g., waist or head height), although the ball can bounce or travel directly across the goal line. If the ball hits the wickets and travels over the opponents' goal line, 4 points are awarded to the thrower's team. The opposing team tries to stop the ball from going through the goal using fielding techniques. A participant can also score a point if she catches a ball that has been thrown by an opponent before it bounces. A participant from Team 2 now attempts to throw the ball at the wickets and through the opponents' goal. Participants take turns throwing, alternating between teams. The game continues for a set time (e.g., 3 to 4 minutes) or until one team scores a set number of points (e.g., 15 to 20).

Safety Tips

- Ensure participants are suitably warmed up before playing the game because it involves ballistic movements.
- Do not allow participants to throw in the no-throw area.
- Choose the size of the no-throw area based on the age and experience of the participants. It should be challenging yet safe.

Advice

- When defending, team-mates should not stand in a line with each other parallel to the goal or throwing line. Participants should stand so that if two of them dive for the same ball, they will not collide into each other.
- Instruct participants in the correct throwing, catching and fielding techniques.

Variations

- **Easier**: Place two sets of wickets next to each other in the centre of the area to make it easier for the participants to hit.
- **Easier/harder**: This game can be played with different numbers on a team.
- **Easier/harder**: Make the no-throw area smaller or bigger depending on the age or ability of the participants. A longer or narrower no-throw area makes the game more challenging.
- **Harder:** Have only one stump (a wicket is three stumps) for the participants to hit.
- **Game variation:** Place three or five sets of wickets between the two teams. The wickets should be spaced out with a distance of approximately 5 metres (5.5 yd) between them. Participants throw at any of the wickets and score when they hit one. The participants cannot score by hitting a wicket that has already been hit. Continue until all of the wickets have been hit; the team that hits the most wickets wins.
- **Game variation:** Add a second ball, but insist that participants from the same team cannot throw the ball at the same time. Do not play this variation with a cricket ball for safety reasons.
- **Sport-specific:** The game can be adapted for use in rounders, softball and baseball using the same rules. If you do not have wickets, use an alternative object.

Knock-Down

Ages 8 to 16

Equipment

- Five bibs (pinnies)
- Two wickets and one tennis ball per 10 participants
- Cones

Game

Arrange the participants into groups of 10; then separate each group into two teams of five. Have one team put bibs on. For the set-up of this activity, see figure on page 101. Use cones to mark out a playing area for each group. Place the wickets in the middle of the area as in figure on page 101, and mark out a circle using cones around each of the wickets. The wickets should be in the centre of the circles, which should be approximately 10 metres (11 yd) in diameter.

A participant from one of the teams starts with the tennis ball. The team in possession of the ball tries to make a set number of passes (e.g., 5). Team members must throw the ball to each other to make the passes. They can move when they do not have the ball, but when they are in possession of the ball, they are not allowed to move. Once they have made the set number of passes, they are allowed to throw the ball at either of the wickets. A point is scored for hitting either of the wickets after making the set number of passes. If a participant drops the ball or a throw doesn't reach a team-mate and that team retains possession of the ball, the players start counting the passes from zero again. Participants have only 5 seconds to pass the ball when they have it, and possession is passed to the opponents if one of them holds on to the ball for longer than 5 seconds.

The opposing team tries to prevent the team in possession of the ball from making the set number of passes. If they manage to intercept the ball and gain possession, they try to make the set number of passes and then throw the ball at the wickets. If a team hits the wickets, the game may have to stop for the wickets to be set up again. After scoring a point, the team that hit the wickets regains possession. If a participant misses the wickets when aiming a shot at them, any of the participants on either team can pick up the ball. When a ball is picked up after a missed throw at the wickets, the team that gains possession of the ball must make the set number of passes before taking the next throw at the wickets.

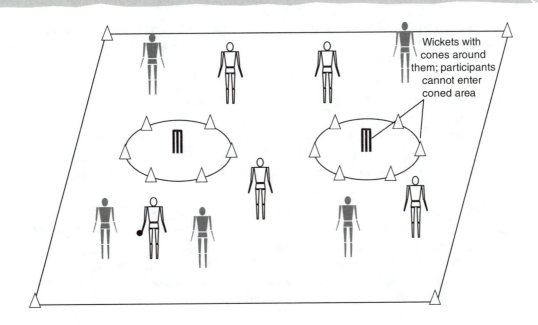

Wickets with cones around them; participants cannot enter coned area

Participants are not allowed to enter into either of the circles around the wickets, unless it is to set up a wicket that has been knocked over. If a participant throws or drops the ball so that it rolls out of the area or rolls and stops in a circle, then possession is given to the opposing team. Have teams play for a set time (e.g., 5 minutes) or until one team has scored a set number of points (e.g., 10).

Safety Tips
- Ensure the participants are suitably warmed up before playing the game because the game requires ballistic actions.
- Warn the participants to be careful of collisions.
- Make sure groups are not set up too close together to avoid participants being struck by stray balls from other groups.

Advice
- Participants may not move when they have possession of the ball.
- Encourage participants to run into a space to receive a pass from a team-mate.
- When a team is defending, instruct the players to each mark, or guard, an opponent.

Variations
- **Easier:** Reduce the set number of passes the team has to make before players are allowed to throw the ball at the wickets.
- **Easier:** Place two sets of wickets next to each other as the targets, or make the circles smaller.

(continued)

- **Game variation:** One team must hit one of the wickets to score, and the opponents must hit the other. Teams are allowed one participant inside the opposing team's circle. This participant can try to stop the ball from hitting the wicket that team is defending.

- **Harder:** If a participant drops the ball when trying to catch it, the opposing team gains possession of the ball.

- **Harder:** Participants can use only one hand to catch and throw the ball.

- **Sport-specific:** This game could be adapted for use in other striking and fielding games (e.g., baseball, rounders or softball). If you do not have wickets, use an equivalent (e.g., large cones).

- **Sport-specific:** This game could be adapted for use in basketball, netball or rugby sessions. Use relevant sports balls with a large cone (or equivalent) for the targets.

- **Sport-specific:** This game could be adapted for use in soccer sessions. Use a soccer ball and a large cone for the targets. Participants kick the ball to pass to each other and to hit the target. Alternatively, if coaching or teaching goalkeepers, then the participants should throw or roll the ball.

Leg as Wicket

Ages 5 to 13

Key Skills and Fitness Components Developed

Skills
- Batting
- Catching
- Fielding
- Throwing

Fitness Components
- Agility
- Balance
- Coordination
- Power
- Reaction time

Equipment

- One small sponge ball (or tennis ball, but not harder than this) and one bat per 10 to 12 participants
- Cones

Game

Arrange the participants into groups of 10 to 12. Use cones to mark out a circle approximately 15 metres (16 yd) in diameter. One participant stands in the centre of the circle with the bat, while the remaining participants stand on the outside of the circle as fielders (see the figure on this page). One of the fielders starts with the ball. The ball should not be too hard (a sponge-type ball is preferable).

The participant with the ball throws it at the batter to try to hit him on the legs. To count as a hit the ball must have bounced once on the floor, or hit the batter below the knee if it does not bounce first. The batter uses the bat to stop the ball hitting him on the legs by playing defensive cricket shots. If a ball misses the batter and travels to a fielder,

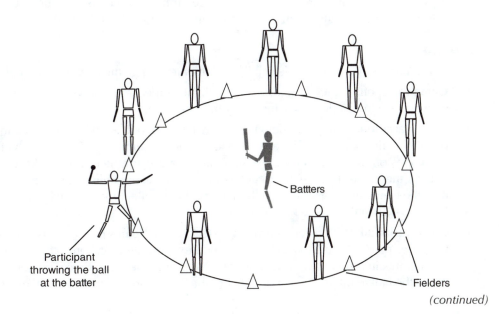

Participant throwing the ball at the batter

Battters

Fielders

(continued)

or the batter hits the ball to one of them, the fielder should pick up the ball and throw it at the batter, again trying to hit him on the legs. The batter continues until the ball hits him on the legs. When the batter has been hit on the legs, he switches roles with the fielder who threw the ball that hit him. A batter can also be out if he plays the ball into the air and a fielder catches it. In this instance the fielder who catches the ball becomes the batter. The batter cannot simply jump or dodge out of the way; he must attempt to play defensive shots. You can make a rule that if a batter does not hit the ball on five consecutive throws, he is out. However, this is only if the throws have been close to the batter because the batter should not try to play balls that are thrown out of his reach.

Safety Tips

- Use soft balls only.
- Make the circle big enough so that fielders are not too close to the batter.
- Participants should not throw the ball too hard.
- Fielders must throw the ball low so they do not hit the batter above the legs.
- Do not allow fielders to throw the ball from inside the circle.
- Make sure groups are not set up too close together to avoid participants being struck by stray balls from other groups.
- Make sure the batter uses defensive shots only.

Advice

- If a batter continues for a long time (e.g., 20 throws), allow the fielders to take a step towards the batter or add another ball.
- To speed up the game, encourage fielders to throw the ball as soon as they have it.
- If using a large, open area, place some spare balls behind one of the fielders in case a ball travels well past the fielders. Participants use a spare ball if the ball travels a long distance from the circle. Once all the spare balls have been used up or whenever a batter switches, participants should collect the balls.

Variations

- **Easier/harder:** Make the circle smaller or larger to change the degree of difficulty.
- **Game variation:** Rather than throw the ball, the fielders must bowl the ball at the batter. Make the circle bigger if playing this variation.
- **Game variation:** Arrange participants into two teams; one team bats first, and the other team fields. Batters will take turns to bat for a set time (e.g., 5 minutes), with each one continuing until they are hit. Batters waiting for their turn should stand outside the circle. Fielders try to get as many outs as possible in the 5 minutes then the teams switch roles. Once both teams have batted, the team who had the least outs when they were batting wins.
- **Game variation:** Within each group of 10 to 12, participants play in pairs against the other pairs. Place a wicket in the middle of the area. When batting, both participants in a pair have a bat and they will bat at the same time. The fielders throw the ball to hit the wicket or either of the batters' legs with the ball. If one of

the batters is out, so is her partner. If a fielder gets a batter out, the fielder and his partner switch roles with the batters. Batters should stand on opposite sides of the wickets. One batter should try to stop throws from the fielders standing around half of the circle from hitting the wickets and her partner should try to stop throws from the other fielders around the other half of the circle.

- **Small groups:** With smaller groups make a semi-circle near a wall or other suitable obstacle. The batter stands by the wall in the centre, and the fielders stand around the outside of the semi-circle. Balls that are thrown and miss the batter should rebound back to the fielders.
- **Sport-specific:** This can be adapted to other passing or throwing games (e.g., netball or basketball). The participant in the centre of the circle does not have a bat. The fielders use relevant throwing techniques to throw the ball so it strikes the centre participant below the knees.

One Hand, One Bounce

Ages 8 to 16

Key Skills and Fitness Components Developed

Skills
- Batting
- Bowling
- Catching
- Fielding
- Throwing

Fitness Components
- Agility
- Balance
- Coordination
- Power
- Reaction time
- Speed

Equipment
- One cricket bat, tennis ball and wicket per five to seven participants
- Cones

Game

This is an activity that develops good defensive techniques while batting, as well as close catching and fielding techniques. Arrange the participants into groups of five to seven, and give each group a set of wickets, a ball, a bat and a cone. Set up the activity as shown in the figure on this page. There should be one participant serving, or bowling, one batter and one wicketkeeper; the rest of the participants are fielding.

The participant who is serving throws the ball at the wicket from a cone placed approximately 15 metres (16 yd) away. The ball should be thrown so it bounces once before it hits the wickets. More advanced participants can bowl the ball instead of throwing it. The distance between the cone and wicket should be 20 metres (22 yd), (19 m [21 yd] for under-thirteens, 18 m [20 yd] for under-twelves) The batter tries to defend the ball using her bat to stop it from hitting the wickets. The batter should *play only defensive strokes or shots* and *should not hit the ball too hard*. If the ball is going to miss the wicket, the

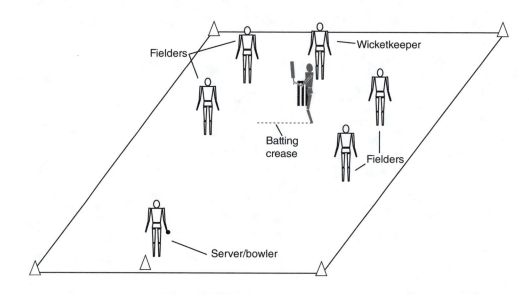

batter may decide to leave the ball. The fielders should surround the batter, but should not stand too close to her.

If the batter hits the ball, the fielders try to catch it. Fielders score 3 points if they catch someone out. The fielders can catch the ball with one or both hands before it bounces on the floor or after *one* bounce if they catch it using one hand. The batter faces 12 bowls and scores a point for each ball that is left that does not hit the wicket or for each ball hit that is not caught by a fielder. Each time the batter is out (bowled or caught), she loses 1 point. The server, or bowler, gains 1 point if she bowls someone out.

Once the batter has had her 12 bowls, rotate positions. The participants all rotate in a clockwise direction; the wicketkeeper becomes the batter, the batter moves to field, the fielders rotate positions so that one of them will be the server and another will be the wicketkeeper. Repeat this process until all of the participants have taken a turn at bat. Participants should add up their points throughout the game. Once they have all taken a turn at bat, the one with the most points wins. If you are playing the game again, participants should change their starting positions so that each batter will receive serves or bowls from a different opponent.

Safety Tips

- Ensure that the batters use only defensive shots to play the ball, and that they do not hit the ball too hard.
- In this game the fielders can stand approximately 5 metres (5.5 yd) from the batter, because the batter can play only defensive shots. However, in other games fielders should stand at least 10 metres (11 yd) from the striking batter.
- Fielders should not stand between the server and the batter.
- If the server, or bowler, is throwing overarm, ensure that she does not throw the ball too hard.

Advice

- Have participants keep their own scores throughout the game.
- Have participants rotate positions correctly so that each one has a turn to bat, bowl, wicketkeep and field.

Variations

- **Easier/harder:** With younger or less able participants the serve should be a fairly gentle, looping underarm throw, but a harder overarm throw is preferable with older or more able participants.
- **Game variation:** Batters continue batting until they are out. If a fielder catches a batter out or the server bowls her out, they swap roles.
- **Game variation:** Play in teams; one starting as batters and the other as fielders. Teams have a set number of serves (e.g., 30 to 50). One batter is the striking batter and her team-mates line up 10 metres (11 yd) behind and to the side of the wickets. A batter continues facing until she is out. If she is out, she loses 3 points from the team's total, and then joins the back of the line to bat again. The participant who was at the front of the batting line becomes the striking batter. Teams swap roles once the batters have had their set number of serves.

Key Skills and Fitness Components Developed

Skills

- Catching
- Fielding
- Running between the wickets
- Throwing

Fitness Components

- Agility
- Balance
- Coordination
- Power
- Reaction time
- Speed

Equipment

- Three cricket bats, two wickets and one tennis ball per 10 to 14 participants
- Cones
- Chalk

Game

For the set-up of this activity, see figure on page 109. The wickets should be placed 20 metres (22 yd) apart (19 m [21 yd] for under-thirteens and 18 m [20 yd] for under-twelves). If the surface of your playing area is suitable (e.g., in a sports hall or on concrete), use chalk to draw batting creases (see the introduction of this chapter for further information). Place two cones on the floor, one on each side of the wicket, approximately 5 to 7 metres (5.5 to 7.7 yd) from it. Separate each group into two equal teams. One team starts as the fielding team, and the other starts as the running team. One of the runners starts with a bat and he should stand by the wickets between the two cones. The remaining runners line up behind one of the cones and the two participants at the front of the line are given a bat. One participant from the fielding team starts as a wicketkeeper. The wicketkeeper should stand by the wickets that are between the two teams (see figure on page 109). The remaining participants in the fielding team line up behind the other cone.

When the teams are set up, roll a ball out in front of the fielding team. As soon as you have rolled the ball out, the runner by the wickets tries to run to the other wickets and back to score 2. At the same time the fielder at the front of the line chases after the ball to retrieve it. When he gets to the ball, he picks it up and throws it at the wickets or to the wicketkeeper. The batter should touch their bat on or over the batting crease at the first wicket, and slide their bat over the batting crease when they return back to the wickets where they started. If the runner gets back before the fielder or wicketkeeper hits the wicket with the ball, then he scores 2 points. If the fielder or the wicketkeeper hits the wicket with the ball before the runner gets back, the batting team loses a point.

The fielder who chased after the ball now becomes the wicketkeeper, and the wicketkeeper joins the back of his team's line. The runner joins the back of his team's line after handing the bat to the participant who is nearest to the front of the line who does not have one. The runner who is at the front of the line moves to the wickets and gets ready to run. As soon as the next participants are ready, roll the ball out to repeat the

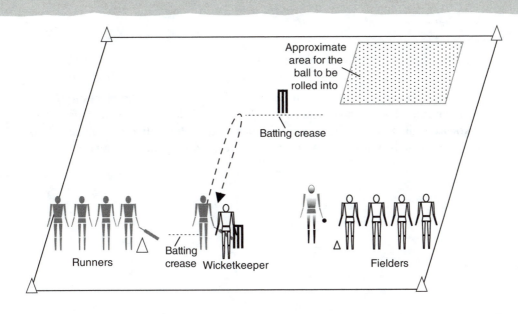

Approximate area for the ball to be rolled into

Batting crease

Batting crease

Runners

Wicketkeeper

Fielders

process. When all of the fielders have chased the ball three times, the teams swap roles so the runners become fielders and the fielders become runners. When both teams have fielded the ball, the team with the most points wins the game.

Safety Tips

- Ensure the participants are suitably warmed up before playing because the game requires ballistic actions.
- Participants in the lines should not stand too close to the wickets, and all participants should keep their eyes on the ball in case the fielder is not accurate with the throw.
- Runners should hand the bat to their team-mates when passing it; they should not throw the bat.

Advice

- If the ball is rolled too far, the batter will score 2 runs easily; but if it is not rolled far enough, the fielder should easily run out the runner. The ball should be rolled so it is competitive for the runner and the fielder.
- Do not allow participants to run before you have rolled the ball.
- Instruct runners to slide their bats along the floor when they are finishing the second run. They should start sliding the bat approximately 3 metres (3.3 yd) from the batting crease until the bat has passed it. This gives them an extra reach, meaning that they are less likely to be run out.
- If the fielder is picking the ball up with his right hand, the ball should be beside the outside of his right foot when he picks it up (the opposite is true for left-handed throwers).
- Ideally, fielders' throws should be just above the wickets to the hands of the wicketkeeper.

(continued)

Variations

- **Game variation:** The runner does not have to run 2. He can decide to run only 1 if he thinks he is going to be run out. Only 1 point is scored in this instance.

- **Game variation:** This game can be adapted for various fielding techniques using similar rules. For example, you can start with the wicketkeeper at the other wickets. Roll the ball in front of the fielder, who has to run to the ball, pick it up and throw it underarm at the wickets. The runner only has to score 1 run without being run out.

Three-Ball Throw

Ages 5 to 13

Key Skills and Fitness Components Developed

Skills

· Catching

· Fielding

· Running

· Throwing

Fitness Components

· Agility

· Balance

· Coordination

· Power

· Reaction time

· Speed

Equipment

One hoop, three tennis balls, and two cones per eight participants

Game

Arrange the participants into groups of eight; then separate each group into teams of four. Number the teams 1 and 2. Team 1 starts as the running team, and Team 2 starts as the fielding team. For the set-up of this activity, see figure on page 112. For each group place a hoop on the floor. The fielders stand beside the hoop. Place two cones on the floor. The first one is approximately 10 metres (11 yd) from the hoop, and the other is 5 to 7 metres (5.5 to 7.7 yd) from the first cone. One of the runners becomes a thrower and is given the balls. The thrower stands next to the hoop. The other runners line up next to the cone that is nearer to the hoop.

When the participants are ready, the thrower with the balls tosses them away from the hoop. She should throw the balls one at a time and aim to get as much distance as possible each time. After throwing, the participant should join the back of her team's line. As soon as the thrower has thrown the last ball, the fielders run to retrieve them, while the runners try to score as many points as possible by running to the other cone and back. The runners take turns to run and score a point each time one of them completes a run. The fielders must get all of the balls inside the hoop and should work as a team to retrieve them. The runners each have a turn to be the thrower to toss the tennis balls. When they have all taken their turn, the teams switch roles. The team scoring the most points once both teams have thrown wins.

Safety Tips

• Ensure participants are suitably warmed up before playing the game because it involves ballistic movements and sprinting.

• Runners should try to keep their eyes on the fielders when they are throwing to ensure that they do not get hit by balls that are thrown towards the hoop.

• Fielders should be careful when they are throwing a retrieved ball. If two of them throw the ball at the same time, the team-mate who is catching them may get hit. They should wait until they have eye contact with the catcher and call her name to get her attention before throwing the ball.

(continued)

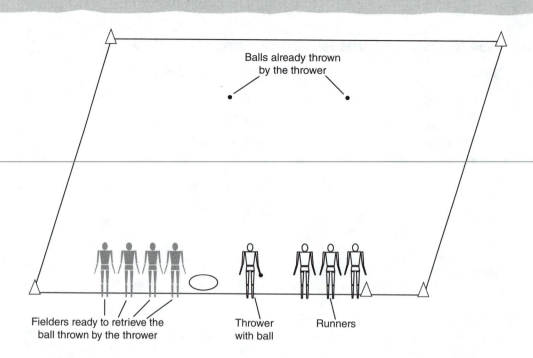

Balls already thrown by the thrower

Fielders ready to retrieve the ball thrown by the thrower

Thrower with ball

Runners

Advice

- Participants should not move until the last ball has been thrown.
- Runners must not run until the previous runner is past the cone on their return sprint.
- This game cannot be played on fast-rolling surfaces (e.g., on concrete playing areas or an Astroturf).
- If more than one group is playing this game, the groups should be lined up beside each other with a suitable space between them. Alternatively, groups could be set up so that they throw from a central point. Groups should not be allowed to throw their balls into another group's area. This is to ensure safety as well as preventing fielders from getting confused as to which balls they should collect after they have been thrown.
- Fielders should work together to retrieve all of the balls. Fielding teams may want to send three participants after the tennis balls. The remaining fielders stay by the hoop to catch the balls that are thrown back in.
- Fielders who are fast runners or powerful throwers should retrieve the balls that are farthest from the hoop.

Variations

- **Game variation:** Participants play in teams of four. The thrower hurls four balls. The fielders each need to retrieve a ball and need to work in pairs to retrieve them. After the balls have been thrown, one participant from each pair runs to collect a ball and throws it to her partner, who stays by the hoop. Once the ball is placed in the hoop, they switch roles; the participants who were waiting by the hoop run to collect one of the other balls, and the participant who collected the first one runs to the hoop to catch the ball when it is thrown back in.

- **Game variation:** The throwers are each given one of the balls, and they all throw them at the same time before starting to run.
- **Game variation:** Instead of throwing the ball, the participants hit the ball away with a cricket bat (or similar).
- **Sport-specific:** The game can be adapted for use in rounders, softball or baseball sessions using the same rules.

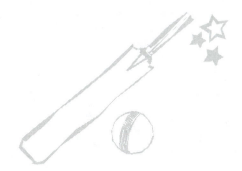

four

Hockey Games

The activities in this chapter relate to hockey. Collectively, the activities develop shooting, dribbling, passing and receiving skills. Most activities require minimal equipment apart from hockey sticks and balls.

It is possible to use most of the activities with indoor equipment in a gym or sports hall. Outdoors, the ideal surface for these activities is an AstroTurf or artificial surface. Most activities can be carried out on grass.

For safety reasons, when instructing younger participants, use mini hockey balls and smaller sticks. All participants should wear shin guards for protection. Some activities require a goalkeeper. If you do use a goalkeeper, that player must wear full safety equipment. This equipment is expensive and time-consuming to put on, so unless you have a longer session, it is not always practical to have goalkeepers. Where an activity suggests that you use a goalkeeper, alternative options are provided so everyone can take part. This information is found in the Variations section of each activity. Many of the hockey activities can be adapted for use with other invasion games, particularly soccer.

Ball Swap
Ages 5 to 16

Key Skill and Fitness Components Developed

Skill

Dribbling

Fitness Components

- Agility
- Balance
- Coordination
- Reaction time
- Speed

Equipment

- One hockey ball and hockey stick per participant
- Cones

Game

This is a good activity for use as part of a progressive warm-up. Cone out your playing area. Each participant has a hockey stick and a ball. Moving in various directions, the participants should dribble their ball around the inside of the area, slowly building up the speed of their movements. As the group is moving around the area, have the participants practise a variety of dribbling skills.

As one of the participants dribbles past you, call 'ball swap'. The participants must leave their balls and quickly find one that was being dribbled by someone else. At this point try to pick up one of the balls. Ideally, a participant dribbling past you will leave her ball to get another one, so the ball will be right in front of you to pick up before another participant can get it. The participant who does not get a ball performs a fun challenge, such as saying something funny or performing an animal impression. Give the participant who performed the fun challenge the ball you picked up; then start the fun again.

Safety Tips

- Make the area big enough for all participants to move around in easily.
- Warn participants to be careful of collisions. They can do this by looking around and ahead of them between touches of the ball.
- Warn participants to be cautious if they are competing to get the same ball once you call 'ball swap'. They should be careful not to run into each other and not to hit anyone else with their stick.
- If using this activity as a warm-up, have participants dribble around for a few minutes before calling 'ball swap' so their muscles are warm and prepared for sprinting to get another ball. Some stretches can be interspersed into the first few minutes of dribbling.

Advice

- Try to vary the skills and movements the participants have to perform when they are dribbling their balls around the area.

- Participants must not dribble around next to another participant. They must move in different directions.

- Once you call out 'ball swap', if you are unable to quickly pick up one of the balls before all of the participants get one, the participant who is last to get a new ball has to perform the fun challenge.

- Here are some key coaching points for dribbling:
  - Keep close control of the ball.
  - Keep looking around for spaces between touches.
  - Maintain the correct grip when changing direction. (When changing direction, rotate the stick in the bottom hand before gripping the stick again. The grip with the top hand does not change, but the stick is rotated by turning the forearm and wrist.)

Variations

- **Game variation:** Once all the participants except one have balls, count down from 10 to zero. The participant who does not have a ball has 10 seconds to try to knock another participant's ball out of the area. If she manages to do this, the participant who had her ball knocked out of the area performs the fun challenge. Alternatively, the participant who does not have a ball must take one from one of the other participants. Whichever participant doesn't have a ball has to perform the fun challenge.

- **Game variation:** Use cones to separate the area into two halves. Half of the participants dribble around inside one of the areas, and the other half dribble around inside the other. When you call 'ball swap', participants must switch areas and get a ball from the other area. When the game starts again, participants dribble around the area they have just moved into. The last participant to get a ball performs the fun challenge.

- **Harder:** When you have called 'ball swap', participants must run around one of the cones on the side of the area before getting a new ball.

- **Small groups:** Use this variation when you have fewer than 8 participants in your group. Participants who do not get a ball are out. After each call of 'ball swap', take one ball away. The two participants who are left with a ball at the end are the winners. Once a participant is out, she is given a ball, which she must dribble around the outside of the area working on the skills until the winners are decided and a new game is started.

- **Sport-specific:** This game can be adapted for use in other sports that involve dribbling, such as soccer and basketball.

Collect a Cone

Ages 5 to 16

Key Skills and Fitness Components Developed

Skills

- Hitting
- Passing

Fitness Components

- Balance
- Coordination

Equipment

- One hockey ball and hockey stick per participant
- Cones

Game

Arrange the participants into groups of two to five. For each group use cones to set up a hitting line, and have the participants stand on this line. Each participant should have a hockey stick and a ball. Scatter cones on the floor in front of the participants. There should be three to six cones per participant (see the figure on this page).

When the game begins, each participant tries to hit his ball at a cone. After each shot participants collect their balls and dribble them back to the hitting line to take another shot. If they hit a cone, they pick the cone up, carry it back to the hitting line and place it on the floor behind them. If a participant's ball hits more than one cone, he should collect any that are hit. Have them play for a set time (e.g., 3 minutes) or until all of the cones have been collected. Count the number of cones collected by each participant; whoever collects the most is the winner. Place the cones back out and start the fun again.

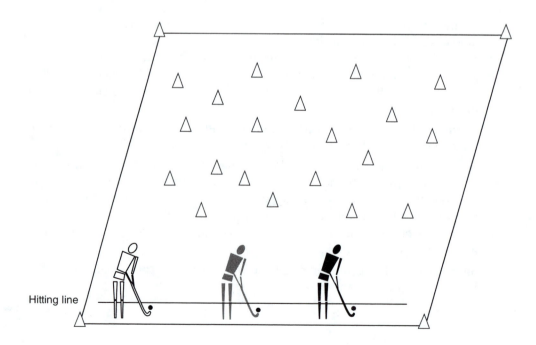

Hitting line

Safety Tips

- If the participants are using hard balls, warn them not to hit the ball too hard and to be careful of the other participants when hitting at the cones.
- Participants should wait until there is no one in front of them before they take a shot.
- Participants should watch the other players' balls when they are collecting their own. They should dodge any stray passes hit by opponents.
- Warn participants to be careful of collisions.

Advice

- If playing this game on a fast-rolling surface (e.g., in a sports hall or on AstroTurf), you will need a wall, fence or other suitable barrier behind the target cones to stop participants' balls from travelling too far after they have been hit.
- Encourage fair play; participants should only collect cones that they have actually hit.

Variations

- **Easier/harder:** Change the difficulty level by changing the distance of the cones from the hitting line.
- **Game variation:** The game can be played in teams (e.g., participants work in pairs to collect cones for their team).
- **Sport-specific:** This game can be adapted to other sports that involve passing. For example, soccer players can kick their balls at bigger targets (e.g., larger cones).

Get There First
Ages 5 to 13

Equipment

- One hockey stick and ball per participant
- Cones

Game

This activity can be used as part of a progressive warm-up. Cone out a large square playing area that is big enough for all of the participants to move around in. The sides of the area should each be given a name from a specific category. Use a category that the participants are familiar with. For example, with younger participants you may choose 'favourite fruits'. Ask some of the participants what their favourite fruits are and choose four of these to name the four sides of the area (e.g., orange, apple, banana and pear). Participants should each have a hockey stick and a ball. They dribble their balls around the area in various directions, slowly building speed. If you call out one of the names of the lines, the participants have to dribble their ball to that line, stop their ball on it and have their stick next to the ball. The first participant to do this gains a point. The last participant to do this has to perform a fun challenge, such as saying something funny or performing an animal impression.

Participants then dribble their balls around the area again, ready for you to call out the name of another line. Have them play for a set time (e.g., 5 minutes); the participant who scores the most points at the end is the winner. Alternatively, have them play until one participant has scored a set number of points (e.g., 5).

Safety Tips

- Make the area big enough for all of the participants to move around in.
- Warn participants to be careful of collisions. They can do this by looking around them between touches of the ball.
- Encourage participants to dribble towards a part of the line that does not have too many other participants dribbling towards it, or standing on it.
- If using this game as a warm-up, have participants dribble around for a few minutes before calling out the name of one of the lines.

Advice

- Try to vary the skills and movements the participants have to perform when they are dribbling their balls around the area.

- Add the name of one line at a time, because the participants may not remember all of the names if you say them all at the start.

- With younger participants it may be useful to play the game for a few minutes jogging and running around the area without the hockey balls so they learn the names of the sides first. Add the balls once they know how to play and can remember the names of the lines.

- Make sure younger participants move, stop or dribble the ball using their hockey sticks only. They should not use their hands or feet to control the ball.

- Other categories you could use with younger participants could include their favourite cartoon character, drink or sport.

- With older participants the categories could be their favourite hockey team, school subject, sporting activity or car.

Variations

- **Game variation:** Participants do not dribble their ball inside the area waiting for you to call a name. Instead, they start on one of the lines and dribble to a new line once you called it. If you call out the name of the line that the participants are already standing on and they move off this line, they have to perform a fun challenge.

- **Game variation:** This is a progression to the previous variation. Choose a few of the participants to be defenders. Once you call the name of a line, the defenders try to stop the other participants from dribbling their balls to the line. If they manage to take the ball off the dribbler, then they switch roles. A point is scored each time a participant gets to a line with a ball.

- **Sport-specific:** This activity can be adapted for use in other sports that involve dribbling, such as soccer and basketball.

Mines

Ages 5 to 16

Key Skills and Fitness Components Developed

Skills

· Hitting

· Passing

· Receiving

Fitness Components

· Balance

· Coordination

Equipment

• Cones

• One ball per two participants

• One hockey stick per participant

Game

For the set-up of this activity, see the figure on this page. Participants work in pairs against the other pairs. Use cones to mark out two hitting lines approximately 20 metres (22 yd) apart. In front of the participants scatter cones on the floor; these are the mines. There should be 6 to 10 mines per pair. Each participant has a hockey stick, and each pair has a ball. One participant from each pair stands behind one of the hitting lines with the ball, and their partners stand opposite them behind the other hitting line.

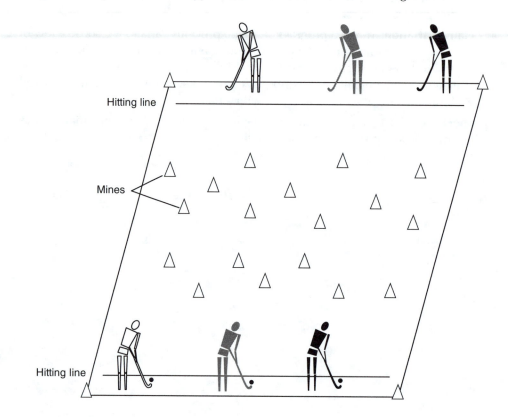

When the game begins, participants try to hit their balls to their partners. They must pass the ball from behind their hitting line, so it travels along the floor and misses the mines. A point is scored each time the participants pass the ball through the mines without hitting one. Every 20 to 30 seconds participants behind one of the hitting lines should switch positions. Their partner should move, too, so they are opposite them. This ensures that the participants hit from different areas. Play for a set time (e.g., 2 minutes); the pair that scores the most points wins. Rearrange the positions of the cones; then start the game again.

Safety Tips

- Participants should not hit the ball too hard.
- Pairs should face each other to hit the ball across; they should not hit across other pairs.
- If a pair's ball stops inside the area where the mines are, one of them should go in to collect it. Other participants must not take their shot if the player collecting the ball moves into their hitting line. They must wait to resume playing after the participant has moved out of the mine area.
- If participants are collecting a ball that has stopped in the mines, then they should watch the other pairs' balls, so they can dodge any stray passes.

Advice

- When setting up the cones, do not leave large gaps where participants can easily pass the ball through.
- Encourage fair play; participants should give themselves a point only when the ball travels through the mines without touching them.

Variations

- **Easier/harder:** Change the level of difficulty by removing or adding mines.
- **Sport-specific:** This game can be adapted for use in soccer sessions using the same rules except that participants kick or pass the ball through the mines. Use larger cones for the mines.

Pass Through the Target
Ages 5 to 16

Key Skills and Fitness Components Developed

Skills
- Hitting
- Passing
- Receiving

Fitness Components
- Balance
- Coordination

Equipment
- Cones
- One hockey ball per three to six participants
- One hockey stick per participant

Game

Use this activity as part of a progressive warm-up, as a skills practice or as a competitive race. This activity can be used to develop passing and controlling skills. Arrange the participants into teams of three to six. Use cones to set up a playing area for each team (see figure on page 125). Each participant has a hockey stick, and each team has a ball. Create a lane approximately 20 metres (22 yd) long and 10 metres (11 yd) wide. At the end of each lane use cones to mark out a target and have one participant from each team stand behind the target. At the opposite end of the lane, use cones to mark a hitting line, and have the remaining participants line up behind this line.

When the game starts, the participant at the front of the line hits or passes a ball at the target. A point is scored each time a participant hits the ball through the target. The other participants who are lined up need to stand a safe distance behind the striking hitter, so they are not hit by the hitter's stick as they take their shot. After taking a shot, the striking hitter moves to the back of the line so that the next participant can take her turn to pass the ball at the target. Make sure participants hit from behind the hitting line. The participant behind the target hits the ball back to her team after each shot. When a participant manages to hit the ball through the target, she swaps places with the participant who is standing behind the target hitting the ball back. Have them play for a set time (e.g., 2 minutes), after which the team with the most points is the winner. Alternatively, you can determine the winning team by having them play until one team has scored a set number of points (e.g., 10).

Safety Tips
- Space the lanes so that participants standing behind the target are not hit by stray shots from the other groups.
- Participants who are waiting for their shots should stand well back from their team-mate who is striking the ball.
- Participants should not strike the ball if any participants are running in their lane (e.g., when two participants are switching after one of them has scored a point, or if one participant is collecting a stray ball).

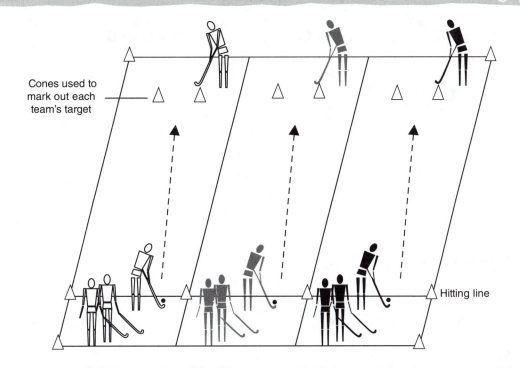

Cones used to mark out each team's target

Hitting line

- Participants who are in the lines should be watchful of balls being hit back to the hitting line, even when it is not their turn to strike the ball.

Advice

- Ask participants to count out their team's score after each point is scored so that all participants know how many points each team has scored.
- With younger participants or beginners set the target up in front of an obstacle (such as a fence or wall) so that the ball does not travel too far if the participant stopping and returning the ball misses it.

Variations

- **Easier/harder:** Change the distance between the hitting line and the target or the size of the target depending on the age or ability of the participants.
- **Game variation:** Each participant must score 1 point for the team to win the game. Once a participant has scored, she helps to pass the ball back from behind the target. After the first participant has scored, the participant who started behind the target joins the other hitting players so she gets a chance to hit at the goal.
- **Sport-specific:** This game can be adapted to other sports that involve passing (e.g., soccer).
- **Sport-specific:** This game can be adapted for use in cricket sessions. Change the goal for a set of wickets, and have participants either bowl or throw the ball to hit the stumps.

Agility Score

Ages 5 to 16

> ## Key Skills and Fitness Components Developed
>
> ### Skills
> All attacking and
> defending skills
>
> ### Fitness Components
> · Agility
> · Balance
> · Coordination
> · Power
> · Reaction time
> · Speed

Equipment

- One hockey ball and hockey stick per participant
- Cones
- One hockey goal and one set of goalkeeper equipment per 8 to 12 participants

Game

For the set-up of this activity, see figure on page 127. Arrange the participants into groups of 8 to 12; then separate each group into two equal teams. Use cones to mark out a start line for each team. The start lines for each team should be 3 to 5 metres (3.3 to 5.5 yd) long and be positioned approximately 20 metres (22 yd) from the goal, with a distance of 5 metres (5.5 yd) between them.

Moving away from one of the start lines, place three run cones. Place the first run cone (cone 1) approximately 5 to 8 metres (5.5 to 8.7 yd) from the team's start line, the second cone (cone 2) 5 metres (5.5 yd) from cone 1 and the third cone 5 metres (5.5 yd) from cone 2 (see figure on page 127). Repeat this process for team 2. A participant from each team stands behind the team's start line. The rest of the participants line up to the side of their team's start line. Place a ball on the floor between the participants and the goal. This should be a few metres outside the shooting circle. The shooting circle is the area the attackers must try to get the ball into so they can score goals. Goals can only be scored from shots taken from inside the shooting circle.

Call out the number of a cone (e.g., 'cone 2'). Participants must run to the cone you call out, run around it and run back to their start line. They must pass the start line and try to get to the hockey ball first. The participant who gets to the ball first becomes the attacker and his opponent becomes the defender. The attacker tries to score past the goalkeeper while the opponent defends, trying to stop him scoring. If the defender gains possession of the ball, he tries to score past the goalkeeper while the opponent defends. The attacker cannot shoot from outside the shooting circle, so he must dribble the ball into it before attempting to score. The pair continues to play until a goal is scored or the ball goes out of play.

After the attack, participants collect the ball they have been playing with, return it to you and then join the back of their team's line. Place another ball on the floor for the

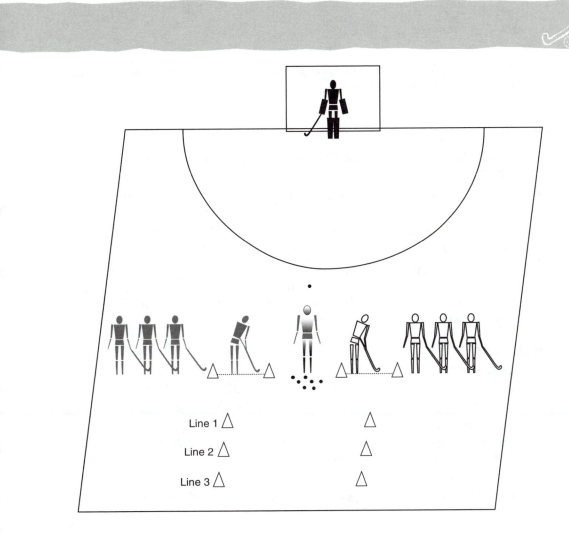

Line 1 △   △

Line 2 △   △

Line 3 △   △

next participants, who should move to the start line ready for you to call the next number. Each time a participant scores a goal, he gains 1 point for his team. Have them play for a set time (e.g., 5 minutes), and then switch the teams so that they are running from the other start line (this makes the game fair because there is a slight advantage to being on the right-hand side of the goalkeeper). After they have played again for the set time (5 minutes), the team with the most points wins. When switching the teams to the other side, rotate the positions in the lines so participants are competing against different opponents.

Safety Tips

- Set groups up side by side with a gap between their playing areas. This should minimise the risk of participants being hit by stray shots from the other groups. You can still call out the lines for the participants to run to, or a participant within each group can be in charge of that group's game.

- Goalkeepers must wear safety equipment.

- Participants should be careful when they compete for the ball after the sprint. The participant who gets there second must slow down or change the angle of his run so he does not trip his opponent or run into him.

(continued)

- If participants are collecting balls behind the goal when another pair is attacking and defending, warn them to keep their eyes on the ball so they do not get hit by stray shots.

Advice

- Give participants enough rest between turns because this is quite an intense activity.
- Carry out this activity with a fence close behind the goal so that missed shots do not travel far.
- After taking their turn to run, participants should quickly move to the side of the area and return to the back of their line so the next pair can be started.
- Unless you have participants who specialise in the goalkeeper position, change the keeper regularly. It takes quite a while to change into and out of the equipment, so bear this in mind when choosing whether this game is applicable in a shorter teaching or coaching session.

Variations

- **Game variation:** Call out two numbers. The participants must run to the cone of the first number called, return to the start and then run to the next line called before running past the start line to the ball, (e.g., 'Cone 1 and 3').
- **Game variation:** If you do not have goalkeeper equipment, allow the shooter to score by using a push-pass only. The shot must also be pushed, so it rolls along the floor and does not travel in the air.
- **Sport-specific:** This game can be adapted for use in other games that involve dribbling and shooting using similar rules (e.g., basketball and soccer).

Four Goals

Ages 8 to 16

Key Skills and Fitness Components Developed

Skills

· Attacking and defending skills

· Passing

· Receiving

· Support play

Fitness Components

· Agility

· Balance

· Coordination

· Endurance

· Power

· Reaction time

· Speed

Equipment

- One bib (pinnie) per two participants
- One hockey stick per participant
- One hockey ball per 12 participants
- Cones

Game

This game is played using similar rules to a normal hockey match, but instead of scoring into goals, participants must pass the ball through mini-goals to score. For the set-up of this activity, see figure on page 130. Arrange the participants into groups of 12; then separate each group into two teams of six. One team in each group puts bibs (pinnies) on. For each group, cone out a large playing area and use the remaining cones to mark out four mini-goals. The mini-goals should be approximately 5 metres (5.5 yd) in length, and they should not be too close to each other or the boundary of the area.

One of the teams starts with the ball, and when the game begins, members of this team try to score points by passing the ball through the mini-goals. *If a participant plays the ball through one of the mini-goals, a team-mate must control it on the other side for the point to be allowed.* The ball can be passed though the mini-goal from either side to score a point. Teams cannot score through the same mini-goal twice in a row. This means that if they score through one of the mini-goals, they must score through a different one for the next point. The opposing team works to stop the ball being passed through the mini-goals. If the opposing team gains possession of the ball (by an interception or by tackling [using the stick to hit the ball or steal the ball from them]), then that team works to score points by passing the ball through the mini-goals.

Safety Tips

- Warn participants to be careful of collisions.
- Leave enough space between playing areas so that participants do not run onto other playing areas while moving down the sides of their own.

(continued)

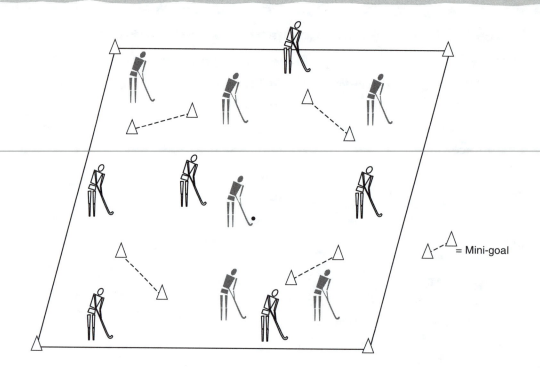

= Mini-goal

Advice

- Ideally, the cones marking out the mini-goals should be different (e.g., a different colour or size) to the ones marking out the boundary for the area.

- Remind participants that they cannot score through the same mini-goal twice in a row and that a point is not scored if a participant dribbles the ball through one of the mini-goals. Also remind them that the ball must be controlled on the other side of the mini-goal when it has been passed through.

- Participants should not crowd the ball and should use all of the space. Encourage the participants to keep looking around for the best team-mate to pass to when they have possession of the ball.

- If focusing on defending, encourage the participants to mark specific opponents.

Variations

- **Easier:** Add one or two floating players. These players help whichever team is in possession of the ball.

- **Easier/harder:** Change the numbers of participants on each team.

- **Easier/harder:** Change the size of the area or the size of the mini-goals, or both, to increase or decrease the level of difficulty.

- **Game variation:** To change the emphasis of the game to dribbling, participants can only score by dribbling the ball through a mini-goal. A participant can score only a maximum of 2 points before a team-mate must score the next point.

- **Harder:** Limit the number of touches the participants can have (e.g., three) when they are in possession of the ball. Once participants have taken two touches, the final touch must be a pass or shot through a goal.

- **Harder:** One team can score only through two of the goals, and the opponents must score through the other two.

- **Sport-specific:** This game can be adapted to other sports that involve passing, such as soccer.

Make the Pass

Key Skills and Fitness Components Developed

Skills
- Attacking and defending skills
- Passing
- Receiving

Fitness Components
- Agility
- Balance
- Coordination
- Endurance
- Power
- Reaction time
- Speed

Equipment
- One bib (pinnie) per two participants
- One hockey stick per participant
- One ball per 10 to 12 participants
- Cones

Game

This game becomes progressively more difficult as the participants' skill level and understanding improve, which means that the challenge should get increasingly more demanding in relation to their learning and ability.

For the set-up of this activity, see figure on page 133. Arrange the participants into groups of 10 to 12; then separate each group into two teams with equal numbers in each. Number the teams 1 and 2, and have one team put bibs (pinnies) on. All of the participants should have hockey sticks. For each group, cone out a large playing area and use other cones to separate the area into two halves. Teams should stand in opposite halves of the area.

Once you have set up the area and explained the rules, pass the ball to one of the teams. The participants from this team are attackers, and they must make six passes to each other to score a point. One member of the opposing team becomes a defender and runs across the halfway line trying to stop the team in possession from making six passes.

If the defender gains possession of the ball, he passes it across the halfway line to his own team. He then runs back to his own half of the area to help his team-mates make six passes. The teams switch roles so the defenders are now attackers. Again, a participant from the opposing team crosses the halfway line to try to stop the other team from making six passes.

If a team scores a point, it retains possession and tries to score another point by making another six passes. If the ball goes out of play, it has to be hit back into play from the place where it left the area. The team that did not touch the ball last before it left the area has possession of the hit-in.

Once a team has scored 5 points, the opposing team can send another defender into the opposing team's area. This means that after a team has scored 5 points, two opponents

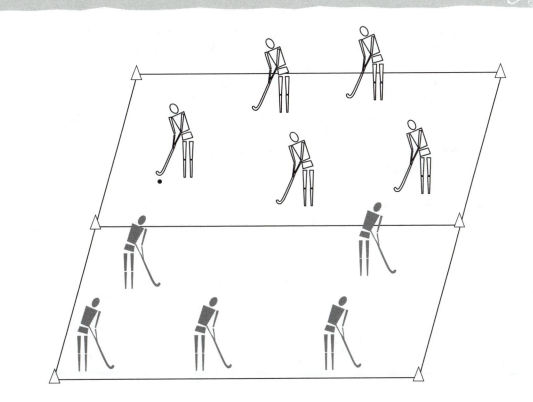

go in to defend; when 10 points have been scored, three opponents go in to defend. This continues until five participants go across to be defenders. Have them play for a set time (e.g., 5 to 10 minutes) or until one team has scored a set number of points, such as 20.

Safety Tips

- Warn participants to be careful of collisions.
- If a few groups are playing, leave enough space left between playing areas so that participants do not run onto other groups areas while moving down the sides of their own.

Advice

- Participants should not stand too close to other team-mates and should use all of the space available in their half of the area.
- Encourage attackers to use short passes when the defenders are not close to them, but to send the ball over longer distances when the defenders have closed them down.

Variations

- **Game variation:** Teams send three defenders into the opposing team's area. The team in possession must make five passes to score a point. Once they have scored 1 point, they must make six passes to score a further point. This continues so they must make one extra pass every time they score a point. Participants from each team take turns to be the defenders.

(continued)

- **Game variation:** If Team 1 has possession of the ball in their half of the area, then one participant from Team 2 becomes a defender and moves into Team 1's area. If Team 1 completes the set number of passes, then Team 2 can send in another defender to stop Team 1 scoring a further point. Team 2 continue to send in a defender each time Team 1 makes the set number of passes. Each time a team gains possession, the defenders start with one defender moving into the opposing team's area.

- **Harder:** Participants are limited to the amount of touches they make when they are in possession of the ball. For example, they can touch the ball only twice before they have to make a pass.

- **Sport-specific:** This game can be adapted for use in other sports that involve passing and receiving, such as basketball, netball, rugby and soccer.

Key Skills and Fitness Components Developed

Skills
- Attaching
- Defending
- Goalkeeping
- Passing
- Shooting

Fitness Components
- Agility
- Balance
- Power
- Reaction time
- Speed

Equipment

- One bib (pinnie) per two participants
- One hockey stick per participant
- One ball, two goals and two sets of goalkeeper equipment per 12 participants
- Cones

Game

Arrange the participants into groups of 12; then separate them into two teams of six. Number the teams 1 and 2, and have participants from one team put bibs (pinnies) on. For the set-up of this activity, see figure on page 136. Using cones, mark out a playing area of approximately 20 by 20 metres (22 by 22 yd) for each group. Set up the goals on opposite sides of the area, and use other cones to separate it into two halves. Each team defends one of the goals and is set up as follows:

- A goalkeeper (wearing correct equipment) in the team's goal
- Four participants playing as shooters standing in the same half as the goalkeeper
- One participant playing as a goal poacher standing in the other half

When the game starts, the participants can move around inside their half of the playing area, but they cannot move into the other half. Participants try to score into the opposing team's goal. The shooters must try to shoot from longer distances, but the goal poacher can score from close range. Team-mates, who are shooters, should pass to each other if a defender is blocking their shot to the goal, or if a defender is attempting to steal or tackle the ball from them. Using defending skills, the team not in possession of the ball tries to stop their opponents from scoring. If a defender gains possession of the ball, they should look to score past the opponent's goalkeeper. After a few minutes, have each team switch one of the shooters with the goal poacher. Have them play for a set time (e.g., 10 minutes) or until one team has scored a set number of goals (e.g., 10).

Safety Tips

- Warn participants to be careful of collisions.
- Groups should not work close to other groups, to avoid participants being hit by stray shots from other groups. Always set up the groups side by side so that balls that are shot from one group do not go into another group's area.

(continued)

135

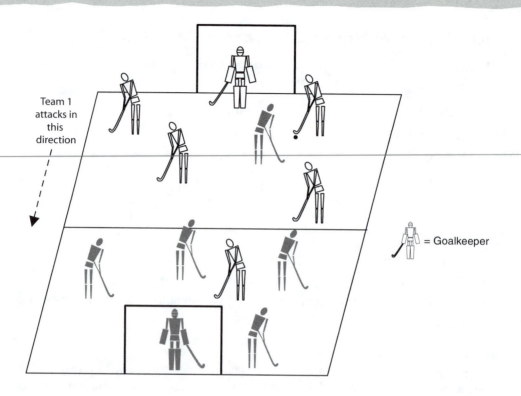

Team 1 attacks in this direction

= Goalkeeper

- If participants are older or more experienced, they should shoot from a greater distance (e.g., 10 to 12 m [11 to 13 yd]).

- Participants need to be careful not to hit others with their hockey sticks when they are shooting the ball.

- This game can only be played with goalkeepers if they have full protective equipment on. If there is no equipment available then shots must be taken so that the ball travels along the floor.

Advice

- The goal poacher should follow in shots in case they rebound off the goalkeeper.

- Remember to regularly swap the goal poacher so all team members get lots of practice shooting from distance.

- If possible, have some spare balls around the area so that one of these can be used if the ball is hit out of the area. This should keep the game going and the participants will get more practise.

- Here are some key coaching points about shooting:
    - Take a big step forwards when striking the ball.
    - Keep your eyes on the ball.
    - Participants should keep their head over the ball when striking it.
    - Shots should be steady, not rushed. Encourage *accuracy before power*.

- Take a big backswing with the hockey stick and follow through after hitting the ball.
- Hit the ball when it is in line with your body and not too close to your feet.

Variations

- **Easier/harder:** Change the number of goal poachers, shooters, or both, to change the level of difficulty for the shooters.
- **Sport-specific:** This game can be adapted to soccer using similar rules.

Ten Passes
Ages 8 to 16

Key Skills and Fitness Components Developed

Skills	Fitness Components
· Defending skills	· Agility
· Passing	· Balance
· Receiving	· Coordination
	· Endurance
	· Power
	· Reaction time
	· Speed

Equipment

- One hockey stick per participant
- Two balls per 20 to 24 participants

Game

Arrange the participants into groups of 20 to 24; then separate them into two equal teams. Two participants from each team start as defenders. The remaining participants are passers, and they form a circle in their team. The size of the circles depends on the age or the ability of the participants, but they should be approximately 15 metres (16 yd) in diameter. The defenders stand in the centre of the *opposing* team's circle. Give one of the passers from each team a ball.

When the game starts, the passers have a set time to score as many points as possible. To score a point, the passers must complete 10 passes to each other. The passers are allowed to move a metre to either side, but they cannot move forwards or backwards to receive or pass the ball. The defenders try to intercept the ball to prevent the passers from making eight passes. If the defenders gain possession of the ball, they pass it back to the passers so they can start again, but the passers must start counting the passes from zero again. This also happens if the passers hit the ball so it goes outside of the circle. If a ball being passed is deflected by the defender's hockey stick but the ball is still received by a passer, the number of passes continues and the team does not have to start from zero again.

After the set time, each of the defenders switches roles with a team-mate. Teams keep score of how many points they score throughout the game. Once every participant has taken a turn to defend, the team that has scored the most points win.

Safety Tips

- Warn participants to be careful of collisions.
- Leave a suitable distance between the groups' circles so that stray balls that leave a group's circle do not enter another group's circle.
- Have some spare hockey balls around the outside of the circles. If a ball is hit out of a circle, the participants should use another one. Participants should collect

the balls at the end of each round when the defenders are switching roles with team-mates.

Advice

- The size of the circle should be challenging for the passers. A circle that is too big can make it too easy for the passers, but having the circle too small can make the game too hard for passers.

- Instruct passers to throw short passes to participants who are close to them in the circle. Once they draw the defenders to them, they should throw a longer pass across to one of the participants from opposite them in the circle.

- Try to group the participants by ability.

Variations

- **Easier/harder:** Change the number of passes the passers must make to score a point or the size of the area (or both) to make the game more or less difficult. Modify the size of the circle depending on the age or ability of the participants.

- **Game variation:** Start with a fairly big circle. Every time the passers make the set number of passes, they take one big step inwards to make the game more challenging.

- **Game variation:** The passers have to make an increasing number of passes to score a point. They start by having to make five passes to score a point, and this increases to six and more as the passers score more points. However, being a defender for a long period of time can be tiring, so make sure defenders are only in for short periods (e.g., no more than 60 seconds). If the defender gets too tired, the game becomes too easy for the passers, so there is little or no challenge for them.

- **Game variation:** A point is scored for every successful pass. Passers keep counting up when they make successful passes. If the defenders gain possession of the ball or the ball is hit out of the area, then the passers start counting from zero again when they next start passing. Teams compete to score the highest number of passes in one sequence. Similar to the original version, defenders are changed after 2 minutes. Once all the participants have taken a turn to defend, the group with the best record wins. For example, a team would win if their best number of passes was 12 when their opponent could only manage 10 passes in a row.

- **Game variation:** This variation is frequently played by adults and may not be appropriate for children. Passers keep going until the defenders gets the ball or the ball leaves the circle. The participant who messes up switches with the defender (and the participant standing to his right if two defenders are required). This game is not advisable when instructing younger children because quite often the participant with the lowest ability remains the defender for long periods of time. This can be a negative experience and detrimental to his confidence and learning, and so should be avoided.

- **Small groups:** If you have between 10 and 16 participants in the group, have them play the game in pairs. Two participants are defenders while the rest are passers. The passers stand in a circle and try to score points by making the set number of

(continued)

passes for the set time. After all the pairs have defended, the pair with the fewest points scored against them wins.

- **Small groups:** If you have fewer than 10 participants in the group, have them play the game individually, using the same rules as the version outlined previously. Participants defend on their own. Once again the participant who had the fewest passes made against them, after all the participants defend, wins.

five

Rugby Games

The activities in this chapter relate to rugby and include a mix of warm-up ideas, technical practices and conditioned games. A number of them involve support play and passing because these are two of the most important skills a rugby player needs. The conditioned games involve attacking and defending tactics, and participants will improve their knowledge of how to outwit opponents with regular practice. The activities are suitable for playing in rugby union or rugby league sessions. However, if you are coaching older participants and want to use full-contact tackling be sure to use the correct tackling laws for your specific code (see safety information regarding tackling later in this introduction).

Rugby uses revised rules to make the game more enjoyable for younger children. Touch and tag rugby are modified, non-contact versions of the game. In both versions tackling does not involve holding an opponent or trying to get him onto the ground, which reduces the risk of injury.

The Rugby Football Union (RFU) recommends that participants under eight years old play mini-tag rugby, which requires that participants wear belts with two tags, one on each side, attached by Velcro. An opponent tackles a player running with the rugby ball by removing a tag from his belt. In touch rugby a defender tackles the ball carrier by touching or tapping with a hand on each of his hips. The touch should be on the side of the ball carrier's body. In both mini-tag rugby and touch rugby, once the ball carrier is tackled, he must stop and pass the ball to a team-mate. After a specified number of tackles (e.g., 5 tackles), the attacking team loses possession to the opponents. Throughout this chapter, tackling is referred to as touch or tag tackling.

If you have enough tag belts, use them whenever possible. If you do not have enough tag belts for each of the participants to have one, then use touch tackles. It is possible to use all the activities with full-contact tackling, but only after you have taught participants the correct techniques for tackling and falling safely. If you are unsure how to teach tackling progressions, gain relevant rugby coaching qualifications before allowing participants to use full-contact tackling when playing the games in this chapter.

No kicking games were included in *Fun and Games*; instead, activities focused on improving participants' passing techniques and support play. In this book there is a greater emphasis on kicking; the games that involve kicking are specifically aimed at older or more able participants.

It is important to understand the key rugby terms used in this chapter. If required, you can find more information on the International Rugby Board website (www.irb.com) in the Laws and Regulations section.

- **Dummy pass:** A fake pass to a team-mate. The player pretends to pass the rugby ball, but keeps hold of it at the usual point of release.

- **Forward pass**: A pass made in the direction of the opponents' goal line. When in possession of the rugby ball, a player cannot pass to a team-mate who is standing nearer the opponents' goal line. Participants new to rugby frequently make this mistake. Some of the games included here allow players to pass in any direction because the games are intended to be used as part of a warm-up or to develop passing techniques. The games that involve passing skills and players attacking a goal line require the players to pass the rugby ball backwards as stipulated by the laws of the game.

- **Goal line, try and in-goal area:** On a rugby pitch there is an in-goal area at either end (these are similar to end zones in American football). The lines that separate the field of play and the in-goal areas are called the goal lines. Teams defend one in-goal area and attack the other one when in possession of the rugby ball. Teams score a try by grounding the rugby ball on the ground in the opponents' in-goal area. The scorers must hold the rugby ball in the hands or arms when bringing it into contact with the ground. Alternatively, a team can score a try if the rugby ball is already on the ground in the in-goal area. In this instance the try scorer needs to put downward pressure on the rugby ball with her arms, hands or upper body. You can create goal areas in the activities if needed. The term *goal line* is used throughout the chapter. Attackers score tries by grounding the rugby ball on or over this line.

- **Knock-on:** If the rugby ball is dropped and travels towards the opponents' goal line, it is said to be knocked on. This often occurs when a player attempts to receive a pass from a team-mate. The rugby ball must touch an opponent or the ground as a player loses possession to be classified as a knock-on. If a participant drops the ball but it travels backwards, this is not a knock-on and the game continues.

- **Maul:** A maul is a phase of play that consists of at least three players. It occurs when a player carrying the rugby ball is held by one or more opponents and one or more of the ball carrier's team-mates bind to the ball carrier. All players in a maul must remain on their feet and be moving towards a goal line. An example of this is when a player is held up in the tackle. One or two team-mates may assist by grabbing the ball carrier's shirt and pushing him towards the goal line. The maul starts when the team-mates have bound to the ball carrier. Participants will only need to know about mauls once you have introduced full-contact tackling because mauls do not occur in touch or tag versions. This is also the case with rucks and rucking (discussed next).

- **Ruck:** A ruck is a phase of play in which one or more players from opposing teams are contesting a rugby ball on the ground. This often occurs when a player is tackled and put onto the ground. This player must then promptly release the rugby ball. A player who is on her feet and close to the action usually picks the ball up and the game continues. However, if a player from each of the teams arrives at the tackle and they compete for the rugby ball, they usually grab hold of each other, trying to push each other out of the way. When this happens, it is called a ruck. More players can join the ruck and try to help their team-mate by pushing the opponent out of the way, leaving the ball available for a different team-mate to pick up.

- **Rucking:** Players contesting the rugby ball in a ruck are said to be rucking. These players must stay on their feet and cannot go down on their knees, otherwise a penalty will be given to the opponents.

- **Tackle:** Throughout this chapter, tackling is referred to as touch or tag tackling. You can incorporate full-contact tackling in activities that include touch or tag tackles. You must be suitably qualified to teach full-contact tackling, and you must take participants successfully through the teaching progressions for tackling before including them in your sessions.

Pass in Sequence
Ages 5 to 16

Key Skills and Fitness Components Developed

Skills
- Catching
- Passing

Fitness Components
- Balance
- Coordination
- Reaction time

Equipment

Three rugby balls per six to eight participants

Game

Arrange the participants into teams of six to eight, and give each team one rugby ball. The participants in each team stand in a circle approximately 6 metres (6.6 yd) in diameter and decide on a passing order. Teams must pass the ball to each other so that each team member has received and then passed the ball. Participants cannot pass the ball to the team-mates standing on either side of them within the circle. If they pass in the correct sequence, the participant who started with the rugby ball will be the last to receive a pass. Once this is done, they have completed one lap.

The figure on page 145 illustrates how the passes could be made in groups of six, seven and eight participants. Allow the participants to practise passing in their sequence for a few minutes. Once they are accomplished at passing in the correct order, start the game. When the game begins, each team must pass the ball in sequence until three laps are completed. The first team to complete the three laps wins and gains a point. To ensure that all participants receive a pass in the sequence, ask them to call their numbers out as they receive the ball. Repeat the game a few times; then have them modify their passing using various passing sequence challenges, such as the following :

- Reverse the passing sequence so the ball is passed in the opposite direction.
- Each team has two rugby balls, and they must pass both of these around the group to complete the three laps.
- Each team has two rugby balls, which they must pass in the opposite direction (reversing the sequence).
- Each team has three rugby balls, which they must pass in sequence. This version works better with larger team sizes (e.g., 8 participants per team).

Have them play for a set time (e.g., 10 minutes) or for a set number of rounds (e.g., 15); the team with the most points is the winner. Alternatively, have them play until one team has scored a set number of points (e.g., 5 to 10).

Safety Tips

- Participants should pass slowly until they are familiar with the passing sequence.
- All passes should be aimed at the centre of the body. This should reduce the risk of receivers being hit in the face by balls passed to them.

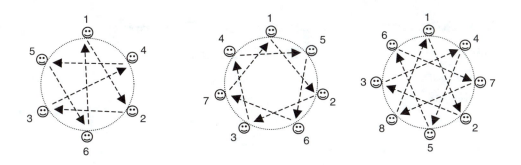

- Warn participants to keep their eyes on their own rugby balls and not to watch other groups because they are likely to be hit by the ball being passed to them by a team-mate.

Advice

- Participants should give a target with their hands to indicate where they want the pass to be given.
- Make teams' circles of the same diameter.
- If the teams do not have equal numbers in them, ask the participants to pass in sequence but to complete a set number of passes to win a point (e.g., 20).

Variations

- **Game variation:** Two teams compete against each other using the Tadpole Pass rules (see page 150).
- **Game variation:** Teams compete to see how many laps they can complete in a set time (e.g., 2 minutes). If they drop their rugby ball, they start counting from zero again.
- **Sport-specific:** This game can be adapted for use in other passing and receiving and throwing and catching activities using similar rules, such as cricket, basketball, netball and soccer. Balls should be kicked to pass them if using this game in soccer sessions.

Reactor Bounce

Ages 8 to 16

Key Skills and Fitness Components Developed

Skills
- Catching
- Kicking
- Receiving

Fitness Components
- Agility
- Balance
- Coordination
- Power
- Reaction time
- Speed

Equipment
- One rugby ball per four participants
- Cones

Game

Use this activity to develop the ability to use a rugby drop-kick technique. Arrange the participants into groups of four; then separate each group into teams of two and cone out a playing area for each one (see the figure on this page). There should be two 10-by-10-metre (11-by-11-yd) areas, one for each team. The distance between the two areas depends on the age or ability of the participants; a shorter distance is preferable for younger or less able participants.

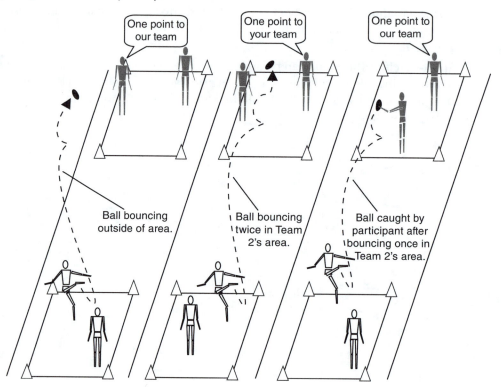

One point to our team

One point to your team

One point to our team

Ball bouncing outside of area.

Ball bouncing twice in Team 2's area.

Ball caught by participant after bouncing once in Team 2's area.

One participant begins with the rugby ball and is the kicker. She drop-kicks the ball so it travels across the area between the teams to bounce inside the opposing team's area. The participants receiving the ball must let the ball bounce. If the ball does not bounce inside the area, the participants receiving the kick are awarded a point. If the ball bounces inside the area, the participants receiving the kick try to catch the ball before it bounces again. If they succeed, they are awarded a point. If the ball bounces more than once, the team kicking is awarded a point.

Safety Tips

- Warn participants to be careful of collisions.
- Lead participants in a thorough warm-up before they play this activity because it involves ballistic kicking actions.
- Space groups so participants aren't hit by stray rugby balls that other teams have kicked.

Advice

- Ensure that the rugby balls are inflated so they will bounce high enough for the game to be viable.
- This game can only be played on firm surfaces because it will not be possible to play if the ball does not bounce high enough.
- Here are some key coaching points for a drop kick:
  - Drop the ball from a low height so that it lands on one of the pointed ends. It is important that the ball travels straight back up in the air after it bounces. This takes some practise as often beginners will drop the ball incorrectly, so it travels to the side after the bounce.
  - Do not throw the ball upwards; it should drop downwards when released.
  - Place the standing foot beside the ball and point it towards the target.
  - Use the laces to strike the ball.
  - Strike the ball just after it has touched the floor.
  - Keep an eye on the ball.
  - Take a high backswing and follow through with the kicking leg.
  - Lock the ankle of the kicking foot when striking the ball with the toes pointed down.

Variations

- **Easier/harder:** Change the size of the areas and the distance between them to change the difficulty level.
- **Large groups:** This game can be played in larger teams. Increase the size of the areas depending on the age or ability of the participants.
- **Sport-specific:** This game can be adapted for use in other passing and receiving and throwing and catching activities using similar rules. For example, players could chip or volley a soccer ball or throw a cricket ball.

Shield Tag
Ages 8 to 16

Equipment

- Cones
- Three rugby balls and two bibs (pinnies) per 12 participants

Game

Arrange the participants into groups of 12. Cone out an area of approximately 20 by 20 metres (22 by 22 yd) for each group. Choose two participants from each group to be chasers and have them put bibs on. The remaining participants are runners, and three of these should be given rugby balls.

When the game begins, the chasers try to tag the runners. However, they cannot tag runners who are holding balls. The runners try to avoid being tagged by running away from the chasers and dodging out of their way. The runners should also work together to pass the rugby balls to each other to avoid being tagged. Passes can be made in any direction, unlike in match play when participants can pass only to team-mates who are behind them (not between them and the goal line they are attacking). If a runner is holding one of the rugby balls, she should pass it to another runner if that runner is about to be tagged by one of the chasers.

If a chaser tags a runner, she gives that runner her bib and swaps roles. The new chaser may not move until she has put the bib on. Have them play for a set time (e.g., 2 minutes), and at the end of this time any participant who is a chaser has to perform a fun challenge (e.g., saying something funny or performing an animal impression). Participants should rest for a few minutes before starting the game again.

Safety Tips

- Warn the participants to be careful of collisions.
- Chasers should not tag too hard.
- If a runner has a rugby ball and is going to pass it to another runner, she should make sure the person she is passing to is looking at her before passing the ball.

Advice

- Instruct the runners to work together to avoid being tagged and to work cooperatively to pass the rugby balls to each other. Watch for runners keeping the ball for too long and not helping others.

- Encourage the participants to use correct rugby passing techniques. The most frequent technique they should use is the lateral (underarm) pass.

- Challenges should not be seen as a punishment. Make sure that no challenge is too strenuous or severe.

Variations

- **Easier:** To make the game easier for the runners, add more rugby balls, or play with only one chaser.

- **Game variation:** Have them play for a set time (e.g., 1 to 2 minutes). The chasers try to tag as many runners as possible in the set time. If the chaser tags a runner, the two do not switch roles, but the runner has to perform a fun challenge.

- **Harder:** Increase the number of chasers or remove one of the rugby balls to make it more difficult for the runners.

- **Harder:** If a runner drops a rugby ball thrown to her, she switches with one of the chasers.

- **Sport-specific:** This game can be adapted for use in other passing and receiving and throwing and catching activities using the same rules, such as cricket, basketball or netball.

Tadpole Pass

Ages 5 to 16

Key Skills and Fitness Components Developed

Skills

- Passing
- Receiving
- Running

Fitness Components

- Balance
- Coordination
- Reaction time
- Speed

Equipment

- One rugby ball per 12 to 18 participants
- Cones

Game

For the set-up of this activity, see the figure on this page. Arrange the participants into groups of 12 to 18; then separate each group into two equal teams. One team starts as the passing team, and the other team starts as the running team. One of the passers has the ball, and the remaining participants from his team form a circle around him. The passer in the middle of the circle is called the centre. The participants in the circle stand approximately 5 to 10 metres (5.5 to 11 yd) from the centre. Place a cone on the floor beside each of the passers standing in the circle. The cones should help the participants stand in the correct positions. The runners line up beside the circle with the front participant standing approximately 1 metre from the outside of the circle.

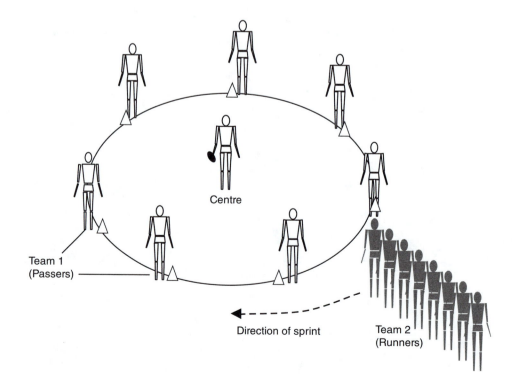

Centre

Team 1
(Passers)

Direction of sprint

Team 2
(Runners)

When the game starts, the centre passes the ball to a team-mate, who then passes it back. The centre then turns in a clockwise direction to the next player in the circle and throws the ball to and receives it back from him. This continues until the centre passes the ball to the first team-mate he passed to. This player then runs with the ball to the middle of the circle to switch roles with the centre. The new centre makes his first pass to the next person in the circle and continues passing in the same manner as the first centre. This continues until all of the passers have taken their turn as the centre.

At the same time that the passers start, the first runner in line sprints around the outside of the circle. When he gets back to the line, he tags the team-mate who is at the front of the line so he can run around the circle. Runners join the back of the line once they have sprinted around the circle. The runners score a point each time one of them completes a lap. The runners try to complete as many laps as possible before the passers have completed their passing task. Once the passers have finished, the teams swap roles. After each team has taken a turn to be the runners, the team that has run the most laps wins the game.

Safety Tips

- All passes should be aimed at the centre of the body. This should reduce the risk of receivers being hit in the face by balls passed to them.
- Use only a non-slippery surface.
- Runners should not pull or hold the passers as they run around them.

Advice

- Participants should practise the passing sequence in their teams before starting the game.
- Advise participants to give a target with their hands to indicate where they want the pass to be given.

Variations

- **Game variation:** Passers play according to the rules of Pass in Sequence (see page 144). There is no centre, and they pass around to each other in a specific order so they all receive and pass the ball once. They complete this sequence three times while the runners sprint around the outside.
- **Game variation:** Arrange the participants into teams of six to eight. The teams all set up as passers and race each other to complete the passing task. The team that is the first to complete the passing sequence so that all of them have taken their turn being the centre wins.

Cross the Area
Ages 8 to 16

Key Skills and Fitness Components Developed

Skills	Fitness Components
Attacking	Agility
Decision making	Balance
Defending	Coordination
Passing	Endurance
Receiving	Power
	Reaction time
	Speed

Equipment
- One bib (pinnie) per two participants
- Three rugby balls per 12 participants
- Cones

Game
Arrange the participants into groups of 12; then separate each group into teams of six. Number the teams 1 and 2, and have one team put bibs on. Cone out a rectangular area for each group approximately 30 by 20 metres (33 by 22 yd). Team 1 starts as the attacking team, and members line up on one of the shorter sides of the area. This is the start line. The opposite side of the area is the goal line. Attackers work in pairs with a rugby ball. Team 2 starts as the defending team, and members spread out inside the area.

When the game starts, the attackers attempt to run through the area to score a try. A try is counted if one of the pair touches the ball down, on or over the goal line. The pairs are allowed to pass the ball to each other, and the ball carrier should attempt to pass to his team-mate if he is about to be tackled. A point is scored for each successful try. Attackers are allowed to move only towards the goal line or in a sideways direction. They cannot move towards the start line. The defenders try to stop the attackers by tackling the ball carrier. If an attacker is tackled, the pair must return to the start line and attempt to score again. The attackers also return to the start if they score a try so they can attempt to score again.

If a participant passes the ball forwards to her partner or one of them drops the ball so it travels forwards (a knock-on), then they cannot score a point and should return to the start ready for their next attempt.

If a defender intercepts a pass or picks up a ball that has been dropped (but has travelled backwards), he gives the ball back to the attacking pair so they can score again. Whenever an attacker is returning to the start line, he should always do this outside the playing area; he must not run back through it.

Have them play for a set time (e.g., 2 to 3 minutes); then switch roles so Team 2 can attack. After both teams have attacked, the team with the most points win.

Safety Tips

- Full-contact tackling should not be incorporated into this game because there is a risk of two or more participants falling into each other if two attackers are being tackled close together. Attacking Run, in *Fun and Games* (page 122), is a similar game that can be adapted for use with full-contact tackling should you want to incorporate this.
- Warn the participants to be careful of collisions.
- Once they have started their attack, participants can move only towards the goal line or sideways; they must not move back to the start line. Although this rule is included in this game for safety reasons, it is something that beginners or younger participants do incorrectly during matches. This rule encourages them to run forwards and attack. Running back towards their own goal line during a match often means running past one of their own team-mates. Before the run, it would have been possible to pass to this team-mate, but after the run, passing to him would result in a forward pass (see the introduction to this chapter for more details).
- Allow recovery periods between rounds.

Advice

- Participants should pass the ball only backwards.
- You could mention a number of technical aspects to the attackers to improve their success rate. The ball carrier should
  - run fast,
  - draw the defender before passing,
  - keep checking to see where his (supporting) partner is,
  - use dummy passes to deceive the defender,
  - pass backwards if giving the ball to his partner, and
  - use side steps or body feints as well as changes of pace and direction to get past a defender without passing.
- The support player should
  - stay slightly behind the ball carrier,
  - not run too close to or too far away from the ball carrier, and
  - give a target with his hands to show where he wants to receive the pass.

Variations

- **Easier:** Make the game easier by reducing the number of defenders. For example, have only three defenders start in the playing area while the remaining three wait at the side. The defenders switch after the attackers have had half of their attacking time.
- **Easier:** As a slight variation of the previous one, have two rectangular areas side by side with a 5-metre (5.5-yd) gap between them. Have the goal lines at opposite ends and have half of the defenders in each of the areas. Attacking pairs attack in one of the areas, and then move to the other start line after this attempt. Pairs switch playing areas after each attempt.

(continued)

- **Easier/harder:** Modify the size of the area.
- **Game variation:** Participants are arranged in pairs and compete against all of the other pairs. Pairs score a point for each try. If a tackle is made, the participant who made the tackle and his partner switch roles with the attacking participant and his partner. The same applies if a defender forces an attacker to make a mistake (e.g., throws a forward pass or knocks on a pass when receiving it).
- **Sport-specific:** This game can be adapted for use in other passing and receiving activities using similar rules, such as soccer, basketball, hockey or netball. Allow passes forwards if playing this game in these sports.

Don't Drop It

Ages 8 to 16

Key Skills and Fitness Components Developed

Skills

· Catching

· Kicking

Fitness Components

· Balance

· Coordination

· Power

· Reaction time

· Speed

Equipment

One rugby ball and eight cones per eight participants

Game

Arrange the participants into groups of eight, and then separate each group into teams of four. Use cones to mark out a playing area for each team (see the figure on this page). The areas should be approximately 15 by 15 metres (16 by 16 yd). The distance between the two areas depends on the age or ability of the participants; a shorter distance is preferable for younger or less able participants.

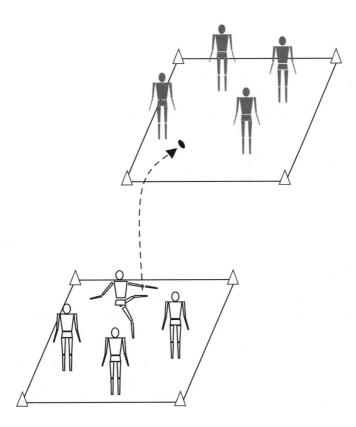

(continued)

One participant begins with the rugby ball as the kicker. She kicks the ball so it travels through the air (across the area between the teams) to bounce inside the opposing team's area. Members of the opposing team must try to catch the ball before it bounces in their area. However, they should let the ball bounce if it is not going to land in their area. The kicker scores a point if the ball bounces inside the opposing team's area. The opponents score a point if the ball does not land inside the area or is caught before it bounces. Teams take turns to kick the ball across to their opponents' area. Within each team, participants take turns to kick when it is their team's turn. Have them play for a set time (e.g., 5 to 10 minutes) or until one team has scored a set number of points (e.g., 15 to 20).

Safety Tips

- Warn participants to be careful of collisions.
- Ensure participants have completed a thorough warm-up before playing this activity because it involves ballistic kicking actions.
- Space the groups so participants aren't hit by stray rugby balls that other teams have kicked.

Advice

- Instruct participants to call out their names when they are going to catch the rugby ball so other team-mates do not go for it.
- Teach less able participants how to kick the ball correctly. Following are key coaching points for the kick:
  - Hold the middle of the ball, with one hand on the top of it and one on the bottom.
  - Hold the ball so that the longest axis of the ball is horizontal to the ground.
  - Drop the ball; do not throw it upwards prior to the foot strike.
  - Place the standing foot on the floor so it is pointing towards the target.
  - Use the laces to strike the ball.
  - Take a high backswing and follow through with the kicking leg.
  - Lock the ankle of the kicking foot when striking the ball with the toes pointed down.

Variations

- **Game variation:** This game can be played indoors on a badminton court. The kicker can throw or kick the ball over the net from the back of the court. This is a good variation for playing during a wet weather session.
- **Game variation:** A participant who drops the ball or is the closest to it when it bounces in her area is out. A player is also out if she kicks the ball so that it bounces outside of the opposing team's area. Participants stand to the side of their area when they are out. The game continues until all of the participants from one team are out, at which point the opposing team is awarded a point. Participants who are out rejoin the game for the next round. Have them play for a set time (e.g., 5 to 10 minutes); the team with the most points is the winner.

- **Harder:** Participants must use a drop-kick technique to play the ball across the area. See Reactor Bounce on page 146 for further information regarding the drop-kick technique.

- **Small groups:** Play according to the same rules as the game variation in which participants are removed from the game, but have only one participant stand in one of the areas; that person is the kicker. The remaining participants stand in the other area. The kicker keeps kicking the ball into the area until one participant is left; that participant scores a point and changes roles with the kicker. Have them play for a set time (e.g., 5 to 10 minutes); the participant with the most points wins.

Five Pass and Over
Ages 14 to 16

Key Skills and Fitness Components Developed

Skills	Fitness Components
· Attacking	· Agility
· Defending	· Balance
· Kicking	· Coordination
· Passing	· Power
· Receiving	· Reaction time
· Support play	· Speed

Equipment

- One rugby ball per 10 participants
- One bib (pinnie) per two participants
- Cones

Game

For the set-up of this activity, see the figure on page 159. Arrange the participants into groups of 20; then separate each group into teams of 10. Number the teams 1 and 2, and have one team put bibs on. Place cones to mark out a large rectangular area approximately 40 by 20 metres (44 by 22 yd) for each group. Use other cones to separate this large area into three zones. The two outer zones are attacking zones, and the zone between the attacking zones is the centre zone. The attacking zones are approximately 15 by 20 metres (16 by 22 yd), and the centre zone is approximately 10 by 20 metres (11 by 22 yd). Team 1 starts as the attacking team, with five participants standing in each of the attacking zones. Team 2 starts as the defending team and stands in the centre zone. Give a participant from Team 1 a rugby ball.

When the game starts, the participant with the ball passes it to one of his team-mates. All the attackers in this zone try to make five passes, after which, one of them kicks the ball over the heads of the defenders to one of their team-mates standing in the other attacking zone.

As soon as the attackers start passing the ball, two of the defenders move into the attacking zone where the ball is. The two defenders attempt to stop the attackers making five passes or the kick across by trying to intercept an attacker's pass, tackle an opponent in possession of the ball or block any attempted kicks. The attackers can continue to pass among each other after they have made the fifth pass if their kicks are blocked by a defender.

If the ball is caught after being kicked over the centre zone, the attacking team scores a point. The attackers in the zone where the kick has just been received try to make the set number of passes and then kick the ball back over to the other attacking zone.

Each time the ball is kicked into a new attacking zone, two new defenders move into this zone to prevent the attackers making the passes or kicking the ball over. The defenders who are in the zone where the ball was kicked move back to the centre area. If the

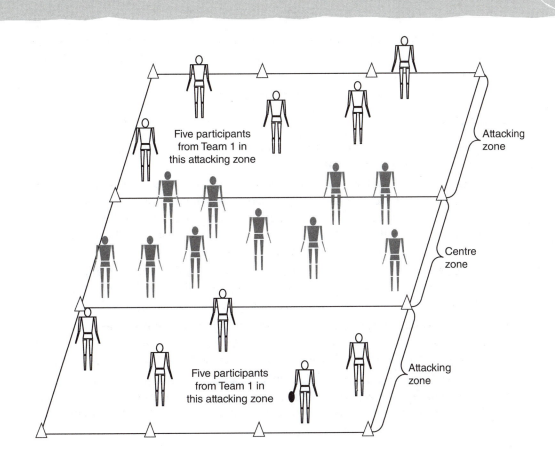

Five participants from Team 1 in this attacking zone

Attacking zone

Centre zone

Attacking zone

Five participants from Team 1 in this attacking zone

defenders prevent the attackers in one of the zones from making the set number of passes (by intercepting a pass) or the attackers drop the ball while passing it, the attackers start passing to each other again but they start counting the passes from zero.

If the attackers in one of the zones have three failed attempts to make the set number of passes, then possession is given to their team-mates in the other attacking zone. Once the ball has been kicked over the defenders, they cannot enter into the zone where the ball is until an attacker catches it or picks it up if one of them does not catch it. The defenders in the centre zone can try to block or catch any kicks across their area. Team 1 attacks for a set time (e.g., 5 minutes), trying to score as many points as possible. After the set time the teams swap roles. Once both teams have attacked, the team with the most points wins.

Safety Tip
Warn participants to be careful of collisions.

Advice
- This game is only suitable with participants who can kick the ball effectively.
- Make sure the outer areas are large enough.
- Defenders may enter into the attackers' areas only once an opponent has caught the ball. If the ball is kicked out of an area, the defenders must quickly return to the centre zone.

(continued)

- Attackers should not try to rush the kick after they have made the fifth pass. They should try to pass to a player in space who has time to kick the ball without it being blocked by an opponent.

- Defenders should take turns to enter into the attacking zones.

Variations

- **Easier/harder:** Change the number of defenders allowed into the attacking zone to change the level of difficulty.

- **Game variation:** Defenders start by sending one participant into the attacking zones, but when the attackers have scored three points, they are allowed to send in another defender. Continue adding defenders each time the attackers score 3 points to make the game more challenging for the attackers. This is similar to Make the Pass on page 132 in chapter 4 on hockey.

- **Game variation:** If the attackers drop the rugby ball or the defenders intercept the ball or catch a kicked ball in the centre zone, the teams switch roles. Have them play for a set time; the team with the most points wins.

- **Sport-specific:** This game can be adapted for use in soccer sessions. Participants must kick the ball to pass to team-mates when making the set number of passes. They should use a chipped pass to send the ball over the top of the defenders to team-mates in the other attacking zone.

- **Sport-specific:** This game can be adapted for use in other passing and receiving and throwing and catching games, such as basketball, cricket and netball.

Gladiator

Ages 8 to 16

Key Skills and Fitness Components Developed

Skills

- Attacking
- Defending

Fitness Components

- Agility
- Balance
- Coordination
- Endurance
- Power
- Reaction time
- Speed

Equipment

- One bib (pinnie) per two participants
- One rugby ball per participant
- Cones
- Five hoops per 12 participants

Game

Arrange the participants into groups of 12; then separate each group into teams of six. Number the teams 1 and 2, and have one team put bibs on. Team 1 start as the attacking team, and Team 2 starts as the defending team. Cone out a playing area for each group of approximately 30 by 30 metres (33 by 33 yd). Place five hoops on the floor in the area—one in the centre and the other four in a square of approximately 10 by 10 metres (11 by 11 yd) around the centre one (as shown in figure on page 162). Four of the defenders stand inside the playing area and start playing the game. The two other defenders stand outside the area waiting for their turn to join the action. Three attackers line up on the outside of one side of the area. The remaining attackers line up on the opposite side of the area. Place half of the rugby balls beside one line of attackers and the remaining balls beside the other line of attackers.

When the game begins, the attackers at the front of the two lines each pick up a ball and move into the area. They try to place the rugby ball inside one of the hoops without being tackled by one of the defenders. Five points are awarded if the ball is placed in the centre hoop, and three points are awarded for placing the ball in one of the outer hoops. The defenders try to stop the attackers from putting their rugby ball in the hoop by tackling them. If an attacker is tackled, she returns to her line, gives the ball to the team-mate at the front of the line and then joins the back of the line. If an attacker places her rugby ball inside one of the hoops, she leaves the ball there and returns to the back of her line. The next team-mate can go once the attacker has returned to the back of the line. Once an attacking team has managed to place all of its rugby balls in the hoops, team members can begin to score the equivalent number of points by retrieving any of the rugby balls. For example, if an attacker retrieves a ball from the centre hoop and returns with it back to her line without being tackled, she is awarded 5 points.

(continued)

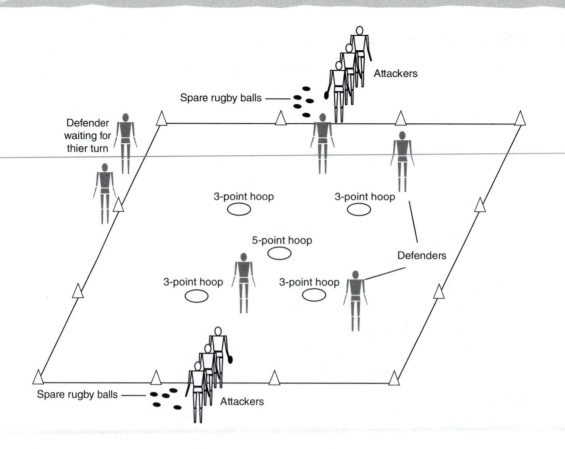

After a set time (e.g., 1 minute) the defenders who are waiting at the side of the area switch with two of their team-mates. This is repeated after another set time so that all the defenders on the side of the area have taken a turn. At this point the teams switch roles so Team 2 can take its turn to attack. Once both teams have taken their turns to attack, the team with the most points wins.

Safety Tips

- Use tag or touch rules for tackling (see the chapter introduction for more details). Full-contact tackling should be incorporated only when participants have been taught the correct techniques.
- Warn participants to be careful of collisions.
- Allow recovery periods between rounds.
- Warn attackers to be very careful not to clash heads with each other when trying to place a rugby ball in the same hoop.

Advice

- Participants should place the rugby balls in the hoops and not throw them. They must place the ball inside the hoop so that it stays there. If the ball does not stay in the hoop, then no points are awarded.

- Attackers should try to dodge, sidestep, swerve and use changes of pace to get past the defenders.
- Attackers should carry the rugby ball in both hands.

Variations

- **Easier:** Make the game easier for the attackers by allowing them to enter into the area whenever they like. They do not have to line up. Ideally, you should have more rugby balls per group if playing this variation.
- **Easier:** Make the game easier for the attackers by having only two defenders working at the same time. Defenders swap in and out every minute.
- **Game variation:** Attackers work in pairs to try to place the rugby balls in the hoops. The attackers can pass the ball to each other. The defenders can tackle the attackers only when they are in possession of the ball.
- **Harder:** Make the game harder for the attackers by taking away some of the hoops.

Key Skills and Fitness Components Developed

Skills	Fitness Components
· Decision making	· Agility
· Passing	· Balance
· Receiving	· Coordination
· Tactical awareness	· Power
	· Reaction time
	· Speed

Equipment

- One bib and one rugby ball per two participants
- Cones

Game

Arrange the participants into groups of eight; then separate each group into two teams of four. Number the teams 1 and 2, and have one of the teams put bibs on. Using cones, mark a playing area of approximately 45 by 15 metres (49 by 16 yd) for each group. Use other cones to split the area into three zones, with the two outer zones being approximately 15 by 15 metres (16 by 16 yd). Team 1 stands in one of the outer zones, and Team 2 stands in the other. Each team should be given two rugby balls, but they are only needed when the team is defending. The area between the two teams is the centre zone (see the figure on page 165).

A participant from Team 1 attacks while all of the participants from Team 2 defend. A participant attacks by moving across to the other team's zone and trying to tag one of the defenders. Two of the defenders start with their team's rugby balls, which the defenders can pass between each other. A defender with a rugby ball in his hand cannot be tagged. The attacker tries to tag one of the defenders who isn't holding a ball. Defenders are not allowed to have possession of the ball for longer than 10 seconds at a time. The defenders are allowed to move around their zone, but they must stay inside of it.

Once an attacker has tagged an opponent, he has to run back to his own zone as quickly as possible. If he successfully gets back to his zone, he scores a point. Once an attacker has tagged a defender, the defenders can prevent the attacker from scoring a point by tagging him with a ball. Defenders can move into the centre zone to tag the attacker if they have a ball, but they can only move into this area once a team-mate has been tagged. To tag an opponent, the defenders must touch him with one of the rugby balls. A tag counts only if the attacker is touched on the back or arms with the ball. It should not be pushed into the front of his body, at his head or in his face. Defenders must hold the ball while tagging; they are not allowed to throw it.

After the first participant has attacked, the teams switch roles and one participant from Team 2 becomes the attacker. Teams then alternate between attacking and defending, but within each team, participants take turns to attack. Have them play for a set time (e.g.,

5 to 10 minutes) or until all the participants have had a set number of turns being the attacker (e.g., three turns each). The team with the most points wins the game.

Safety Tips
- Warn participants to be careful of collisions.
- Attackers should not tag the defenders too hard.
- Defenders should not tag too hard with the rugby ball. Defenders must not throw the rugby ball at attackers to tag them. The rugby ball must be in the defender's hand when he tags the attacker.

Advice
- Ask questions to check understanding after explaining the rules.
- The size of the areas depends on the age or ability of the participants. Smaller areas and a shorter distance between them is preferable for younger or less able participants.
- If attackers are struggling to tag one of the defenders, allow them only 30 seconds to try. If they do not tag an opponent in 30 seconds, the team defending is awarded a point and the teams switch roles.

Variations
- **Easier/harder:** Make the game easier for the attackers (and harder for the defenders) by allowing the defenders to have only one ball.
- **Easier/harder:** Change the size of the areas to change the level of difficulty of the game.
- **Game variation:** Teams are allowed to send two attackers across. Once an attacker has tagged a defender, the defenders can tag either of the attackers, so both attackers should return to their zone. Attackers should call out 'tag' when they have made the tag so their team-mate knows to run back to the area.
- **Game variation:** Defenders cannot move when they are in possession of one of the rugby balls, until a tag has been made. Defenders can move with the ball after a tag.

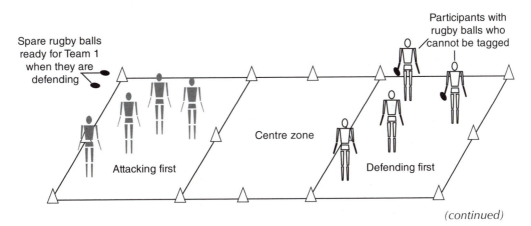

Spare rugby balls ready for Team 1 when they are defending

Participants with rugby balls who cannot be tagged

Centre zone

Attacking first

Defending first

(continued)

- **Game variation:** Only play this game with sponge rugby balls. Defenders are not allowed to leave their zone. They can tag an attacker with the ball when he is in his area, but once the attacker is in the centre zone, the defenders can throw the ball so that it hits the attacker below the waist. The defenders must use an underarm action to throw the ball and must keep it low (i.e., below the waist).

Rugby Golf
Ages 5 to 16

Key Skills and Fitness Components Developed

Skills
- Catching
- Decision making
- Kicking
- Passing

Fitness Components
- Balance
- Coordination
- Power
- Reaction time
- Speed

Equipment
- One rugby ball per two participants
- Hoops
- Cones

Game

This game is based on golf, so an understanding of how to play that game is helpful. A large space is required to play this game; an area at least the size of a soccer, hockey or rugby field (pitch) is advisable. The participants work in pairs to complete the rugby golf course in as few passes as possible. Set up a number of 'holes' for participants to play. Use cones to mark out tee boxes approximately 3 by 3 or 5 by 5 metres (3.3 by 3.3 or 5.5 by 5.5 yd), from which participants start each hole. The target (also termed the hole in golf) is a hoop placed between 30 and 50 metres (33 and 55 yd) from the tee box. Number the holes in the order the participants should play them. Arrange the holes so that the tee box from one hole is close to the target from the previous hole so the participants can easily move from one hole to the next.

To play rugby golf, the participants work in pairs taking turns to kick or pass the ball to each other moving from the tee box until one participant receives it while standing in the hoop. The hitter starts in the tee box with a ball. His partner is a catcher and moves towards the target. The catcher should move to a distance where it is possible for his partner to kick or pass (throw) the ball to him without it bouncing. The hitter kicks or passes the ball to his partner. If the catcher catches the ball before it bounces, the hitter moves past his partner close to (or in the target) and they switch roles. The new hitter kicks or passes the ball to his partner so that he can catch it before it bounces.

If the catcher is close enough to the target to be able to stand in the hoop, he should do this because the goal is for one of them to catch the ball while standing in the hoop to finish the hole. The pair should try to do this in as few passes as possible. If the catcher drops the ball or the kick is not close enough for the catcher to receive it, the hitter must take the kick or pass again from the same place. The catcher can move to catch a ball that has been kicked or passed to him. Participants keep score of how many shots they take on each hole and add up their shots throughout the game. The pair scoring the fewest shots wins.

(continued)

Safety Tips

- Provide adequate space between the holes and between the target of one hole and the next tee box.

- Do not allow more than two pairs to play the same hole at the same time.

- Similar to golf, if a participant takes a wayward kick so that the ball travels towards another player on the course, he should shout 'Fore!' This warns participants that another ball may be heading towards them so they can dodge out of the way. Alternatively, they can cover their heads if they cannot see the ball coming towards them.

- Ensure participants are warmed up before playing this activity because it involves ballistic kicking and passing actions.

Advice

- If you have a large group, start participants at different holes so there is not a build-up of pairs waiting to play certain holes. Participants complete the holes in the same order and finish their round when they have completed every hole.

- Depending on the time you have to set up the course and the size of your area, try to have at least one hole for every two pairs.

- Advise the pairs not to be too ambitious when choosing the distance between them because continually missing overly ambitious throws or kicks will quickly run up their score.

- Vary the difficulty of the holes so all of the players are challenged.

Variations

- **Easier/harder:** If there is a wide range in ability between the pairs, some can be given handicaps. The handicap is the number of shots a participant can take off at the end of a round. For example, if playing 18 holes, a lower-ability pair may be given a handicap of 18. This means they take 18 shots off their total at the end of the round. Vary the handicap depending on the number of holes participants have to play. As a general rule, participants with a moderate ability should be allowed to take off a shot every two or three holes, and lower-ability participants should be allowed to take off one shot, or up to two shots, every hole. In golf, a handicap is usually based on past performances, so if you keep track of your groups' scores, you can give them handicaps based on these scores. For example, a team that finished two shots higher than the winners would have a handicap of 2 the next time you played the game.

- **Easier/harder:** Change the distance between the tee box and the target to change the level of difficulty.

- **Harder:** Make the holes more difficult by having trees or other obstructions between the tee box and the target. The participants can decide to kick or pass over the obstruction or around it.

- **Game variation:** Use cones to mark out a 'green' around the target. Participants have to kick the ball until it is on the green. Once on the green they can only throw it.

- **Game variation:** Play match play rules. Award a par for each hole, which represents how many shots the pair should take to complete it. Shorter holes have a par 3, medium-sized holes have a par 4 and longer holes have a par 5. Participants are awarded points depending on how many shots they take compared to the par for a hole.
  - Zero points are scored for taking two or more shots over the par (e.g., taking 6 shots on a par 4 hole).
  - One point is scored for taking one shot over the par (this is called a bogie in real golf).
  - Two points are scored for taking the same amount of shots as par for the hole (this is called par in real golf).
  - Three points are scored for taking one shot less than par for the hole (a birdie).
  - Four points are scored for taking two shots less than par for the hole (an eagle)—for example, a hole-in-one on a par 3 hole.
  - Five points are scored for taking three shots less than par for the hole (an albatross). This could be a hole-in-one on a par 4 hole or two shots on a par 5 hole.
- **Sport-specific:** This game can be adapted for use in other passing and receiving games, such as soccer, netball and hockey. Play according to the same rules when playing in soccer sessions, but netball participants can only throw the ball to pass it. When playing in hockey sessions, the participants can only hit and receive the ball using the stick, and the catcher, or receiver, who has to control the ball must do so without moving after the hitter has passed to them.

six

Soccer Games

The following activities relate to soccer and comprise a mixture of games, warm-up activities and skill practices. Collectively, they can develop passing, dribbling, heading, shooting and goalkeeping skills, among others. The majority of the activities in *Fun and Games* (2005) were aimed at younger participants. *More Fun and Games* includes some activities for younger participants but the majority are aimed at older and more able participants.

If you are unfamiliar with some of the soccer terms in this chapter or the rules of soccer, you should consult relevant coaching manuals, such as *Coaching Youth Soccer* by the American Sport Education Program in conjunction with Sam Snow, director of coaching education for US Youth Soccer, or gain soccer coaching qualifications to improve your knowledge.

When you coach soccer, use the correct size of soccer ball for the participants' age and ability level. The English Football Association (FA) recommends that

- under-eights use a size 3 ball,
- under-elevens use a size 4 ball and
- over-elevens use a size 5 ball.

However, these are only recommendations; you should choose your ball size based on the size, maturity level and ability of your participants. Participants with poor strength or low ability should use smaller soccer balls than those recommended for their age.

Ensure that soccer balls are inflated to the correct pressure; balls that are too soft are harder to control and kick, and balls that are over-inflated can cause pain and injury if kicked too hard. Also, participants can be hurt if someone kicks an over-inflated ball hard at them from a close range.

If you use portable goals for any of the activities, they should be pinned or weighted down to prevent them toppling forwards. The goals should be sized correctly, according to the age and experience of the players. The FA recommends that children under the age of 10 use goals that are 3.6 by 1.88 metres (12 by 6 ft). Older participants should use regulation size soccer goals, which are 7.32 by 2.44 metres (24 by 8 ft).

Participants should wear shin guards during activities that involve tackling. They should also wear the correct footwear for the surface they are training on (e.g., soccer boots or cleats if playing on wet grass).

When leading activities that require goalkeepers (e.g., Volley Game on page 198), try to use participants who are trained in that position. It is advisable to give all participants some basic handling and catching training and to teach them how to use diving saves correctly before they take on the goalkeeper's role. This will reduce the risk of injury when they take their turn in goal. You may also want to teach basic goalkeeping skills to all of your team players in case your regular goalkeepers are unavailable and one of them has to fill this position for a match!

If you are knowledgeable about the key factors, or coaching points, of soccer skills, try to mention these regularly during these activities. For example, during a game where dribbling is involved (e.g., Dribble Chase in *Fun and Games,* pages 150-151), you should remind participants to

- keep the ball in close control,
- use different parts of both feet to move the ball and
- keep looking around for space and defenders after touches of the ball.

Try to give participants individual feedback that will help them improve because this will speed up their learning and result in greater confidence. In a few of the activities in this chapter, key factors of the skills are provided in the Safety Tips or Advice sections. When the key factors are included in the Safety Tips section, mention these to participants before participants play the games. This can help to reduce injuries. When key factors are given in the Advice section, the intention is to help you improve the competence and skill level of your participants. Therefore it is not necessary to tell them this information before they play. However, research, reading and taking a relevant soccer coaching qualification or course is advised if you do not have much knowledge about soccer techniques.

Reference

American Sport Education Program. 2006. *Coaching Youth Soccer.* Champaign, IL: Human Kinetics.

Ball Collide
Ages 8 to 16

Key Skills and Fitness Components Developed

Skills
- Decision making
- Passing
- Receiving

Fitness Components
- Agility
- Balance
- Coordination
- Power
- Reaction time
- Speed

Equipment
- Cones
- One bib (pinnie) per two participants
- Three soccer balls per 10 to 14 participants

Game

Arrange the participants into groups of 10 to 14; then separate each group into two equal teams. Number the teams in each group 1 and 2, and have one team put bibs (pinnies) on. Cone out a large playing area of approximately 20 by 20 metres (22 by 22 yd) for each group.

Team 1 starts with one of the balls, which they must pass to each other to try to make a set number of consecutive passes (e.g., 15). As they pass they should count up (starting from zero) each time a pass is made so that the opponents know how many they have completed. Team 1 scores a point each time the players complete the set number of passes. They have a set time (e.g., 3 minutes) to score as many points as possible. If the ball rolls or is passed out of the area, the team must start counting passes from zero once the ball is back in the area. Although participants will play most passes along the floor, they can use a chip pass in the air to play the ball to team-mates.

Team 2 is given the other two soccer balls, which team members can pass around the area trying to hit Team 1's ball. If Team 2 hits Team 1's ball with one of its own, the pass count returns to zero. However, any completed points are kept. If a participant from Team 2 kicks one of the team's balls out of the area, one of them should collect it, so they can kick it again. After the set time, stop the game; then have the teams switch roles. After Team 2 has taken a turn at trying to score points, the team with the most points wins.

Safety Tips
- Warn participants to be careful of collisions.
- Watch carefully for participants hitting the ball too hard or too high.

(continued)

- Ensure that the participants know why they must keep the ball low and how to do this. Give them these tips:
  - Keep your head over the soccer ball as you strike it; do not lean back.
  - Use the inside of your foot to pass the ball.
  - Hit the ball just above its centre.

Advice

- Advise the participants who are trying to collide a soccer ball against the opponents' ball not to kick or pass the ball too hard in case it misses. If they kick it too hard the ball will travel for a long distance out of the area. Their opponents would have a great advantage if they had only one ball to avoid.
- This game can be played outdoors, but it works better indoors because missed shots do not travel as far. If playing outdoors, try to find a space where there is a fence or wall close by so that balls kicked out of the area do not travel too far. The corner of your soccer pitch would be a good choice if a fence surrounds the outside of two sides of the playing area.

Variations

- **Easier:** Make the game easier for the team trying to make passes by reducing the number of passes they have to make (e.g., 10) or by taking away one of the opponents' balls.
- **Game variation:** All the participants in Team 1 have soccer balls. Team 2 has two balls. If Team 2 collides one of its balls against any of Team 1's balls, the ball that has been hit is removed from the game. If a participant's ball is hit and removed, team-mates can pass to that person, so all the participants in Team 1 can work together to prevent their other balls being hit. Time how long it takes for Team 2 to hit all of Team 1's soccer balls, or continue for a set time (e.g., 3 minutes) and count how many balls have been removed. Teams should then swap roles and try to beat the opposing team's performance.
- **Game variation:** All the participants in Team 2 have soccer balls, whereas Team 1 passes around only one soccer ball. Participants from Team 2 dribble their ball around, and when they are in close range, try to kick it at Team 1's ball. Team 1 scores a point for every five passes its members make, but loses a point each time an opponent's ball hits their own. Have them play for a set time and then switch roles. The team with the most points at the end of the game is the winner.
- **Harder:** Make the game harder for the team trying to make passes by increasing the number of passes team members have to make (e.g., 20) or by giving their opponents more soccer balls.
- **Harder:** Make the game harder for either team by restricting the number of touches each participant can have before he must pass the ball on—for example, a participant can touch the ball only twice before a team-mate does.
- **Smaller groups:** With a group of six to eight participants you could play in pairs. One pair starts with a ball and tries to score points by making a set number of consecutive passes (e.g., five). Call this pair the passers. The remaining participants

work in pairs, each pair with one ball, trying to pass theirs against the passers' ball (call these pairs colliders). The passers continue for a set time (e.g., 2 minutes) and score a point each time they make the set number of passes. The colliders score 3 points each time they hit the passers' ball. Each pair should have a turn being the passers, and when each of them has taken a turn, the pair with the most points wins.

- **Sport-specific:** This game can be modified for use in basketball, netball or rugby. Use similar rules, but players must pass and catch balls with their hands. All passes must be low (bounce passes are advisable for basketball and netball). Participants cannot move when they have possession of the ball, but they can run when they do not have it. When a participant tries to throw the ball at an opponent's, the hit must be mid-air. They should not throw the ball at an opponent's ball when the opponent is holding it. Participants can only have possession of the ball for 3 seconds before they must pass it to a team-mate.

One Bounce

Ages 11 to 16

Key Skills and Fitness Components Developed

Skills

- Decision making
- Passing

Fitness Components

- Agility
- Balance
- Coordination
- Power
- Reaction time
- Speed

Equipment

- Cones
- One soccer ball per two participants

Game

Arrange the participants into pairs with one ball between them. Cone out an area of approximately 10 by 10 metres (11 by 11 yd) for each pair. Within each pair, participants play a competitive game against each other. One participant begins with the ball in her hands and starts a rally by kicking it up into the air. The ball must travel above a specified height (e.g., above 1.8 m [6 ft] or maybe as high as the taller of the two players) and then bounce inside the area. The opposing player must get to the ball before it bounces a second time and kick it back into the air (without catching it). Again, the ball must travel above the specified height and bounce inside the area. Participants continue the rally, taking turns to kick the ball. A participant wins a point if her opponent kicks the ball so it lands outside the area, does not kick the ball high enough or does not get to the ball before it bounces twice. Have pairs play for a set time (e.g., 3 minutes) or until one of them has scored a set number of points, such as 10.

Safety Tips

- Provide a space of at least 5 metres (5.5 yd) between each of the pairs' playing areas.
- Warn participants to be careful of collisions when retrieving stray soccer balls.

Advice

- Ensure that the soccer balls are inflated so they will bounce high enough for the game to be viable.
- Use only firm surfaces because it will not be possible to play if the ball does not bounce high enough.
- Participants can only kick the ball; they cannot use other parts of their bodies.

Variations

- **Easier:** With younger or less able participants, allow them to have two or three touches to play the ball.

- **Easier:** With younger or less able participants, allow two bounces before they must play the ball.

- **Game variation:** Play in teams of two or three. Make the area bigger depending on participants' age or ability level.

Weighted Pass
Ages 5 to 10

Equipment

- Cones
- One soccer ball per participant

Game

Use this activity to develop the correct weighting (or power) for short passes. For the set-up of this activity, see the figure on this page. Use cones to mark a passing line, behind which the participants line up with their soccer balls. Use cones to mark out a scoring zone in front of the participants. The area between the passing line and the scoring zone and the area past the scoring zone are no-score zones. The scoring zone should be between 5 and 10 metres (5.5 and 11 yd) wide, and the distance from the passing line should be dependant on the age and ability of the participants.

When the game starts, the participants have to pass their soccer balls so they roll into, and stop in, the scoring zone. A point is scored for each successfully weighted, or powered, pass that stops in the scoring zone. Any ball that does not reach the scoring zone or rolls past it will land in a no-score zone, and the participant will not receive a point for that pass or kick. Participants collect their balls and dribble back to the passing line.

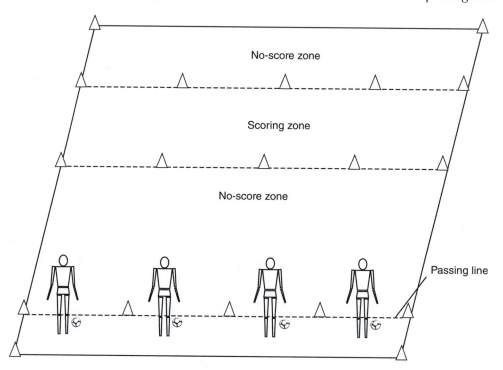

No-score zone

Scoring zone

No-score zone

Passing line

Each participant has 10 attempts to pass the ball into the scoring zone. The participant who scores the most points after all have taken their 10 passes wins the game.

Safety Tips

- Participants should not pass their ball if someone is in front of them, close to the passing line. They should wait until this participant has moved out of the way before kicking their ball.

- A participant should watch for other balls being passed when they run out to collect their ball and when they dribble it back in.

- Warn participants to be careful of collisions.

Advice

- The ball must stop completely in the scoring zone to earn a point.

- This game cannot be played on fast-rolling surfaces (e.g., in sports halls or on AstroTurf).

- Space participants appropriately.

Variations

- **Easier/harder:** Change the size of the scoring zone to make the game easier or harder.

- **Easier/harder:** Change the distance between the passing line and the scoring zone to make the game easier or harder.

- **Game variation:** Participants work in pairs or teams and line up behind the passing line; the front participant in each pair has a ball. Once they have taken their pass at the scoring zone, participants collect the ball and pass it back to the next participant before joining the back of the line. When the participants have each taken a set number of passes (e.g., 5 to 8), the pair scoring the most points wins.

- **Game variation:** Participants play for a set time (e.g., 2 minutes) and race to see how many points they can score. After each kick, they quickly collect their balls and dribble them back to the passing line before taking their next kick. They must make sure the ball has stopped in the scoring zone before they count it as a point.

- **Game variation:** Play with a circular target with three scoring zones similar to an archery target. The centre is worth 5 points, the next outer ring is worth 3 points and the largest ring is worth 1 point. No points are awarded if the participant misses the target completely.

- **Game variation:** This game can be adapted to long-range, chipped passes. Participants are set up in pairs. Pairs are set up facing their partner with a passing line in front of them and the scoring zone in between them. The rules are similar, but the participants try to power their kicks so that the ball's first bounce is in the scoring zone.

- **Harder:** Participants can use only their non-dominant foot to pass the soccer ball.

- **Sport-specific:** This game can be adapted to hockey using similar rules.

Chipping Game
Ages 11 to 16

Key Skills and Fitness Components Developed

Skills	Fitness Components
· Decision making	· Balance
· Goalkeeper catching skills	· Coordination
· Receiving	· Power
· Soccer chip pass	· Reaction time
	· Speed

Equipment

- Cones
- One soccer ball per two participants

Game

Arrange the participants into teams of four, and cone out a playing area for each team (see figure on page 181). There should be two 10-by-10-metre (11-by-11-yd) areas, with a distance of 15 to 25 metres (16 to 27 yd) between them. Two of the participants from each team stand in one of their team's areas, and their team-mates stand in the other area. The distance between the two areas depends on the age or ability of the participants; a shorter distance is preferable for younger or less able participants. The aim of this game is to chip the ball across to the team-mates in the other area so that they can catch it.

One participant tries to chip the ball (from inside his area) to his team-mates in the other area. If one of them catches the ball before it bounces, the team gains a point. The passer must chip the ball from inside his area, and the catcher must have both feet inside his area for a point to be awarded. Regardless of whether the ball is caught, it should be placed on the ground inside the area for one of the participants in this area to chip across to the other area. Team-mates take turns to chip pass when the ball is in their area. Have them continue for a set time (e.g., 3 minutes), after which, the team with the most points wins. Alternatively, have them play until one team has scored a set number of points (e.g., 10).

Safety Tips

- Warn participants to be careful of collisions.
- Ensure participants have completed a thorough warm-up before playing this activity because it involves ballistic kicking actions.
- There should be a large gap between groups, so there is less risk of participants being hit by stray passes from other groups.
- To avoid collisions, instruct participants to call out their names when they are going to catch the soccer ball so team-mates do not go for it at the same time.

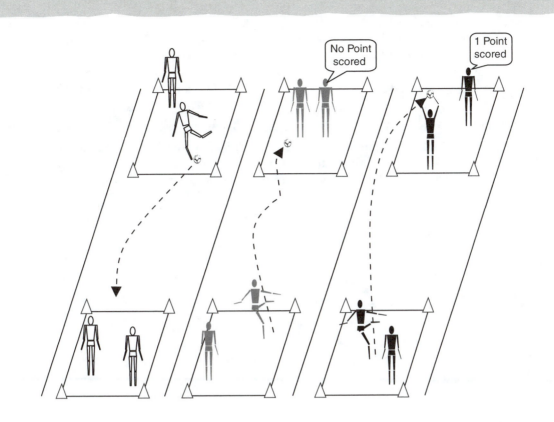

Advice

- Use this game only with participants who are competent at chipping the ball.
- Here are key coaching points for chipping the ball:
    - Take a run-up and place the non-kicking leg beside the ball so the foot is pointing towards the target area.
    - Use the instep of the foot to strike the ball and contact it below its centre.
    - Lean back during the kicking motion.
    - If you are not getting enough power behind the chip, take a high back lift, especially at the hip joint, and follow through after striking the ball.

Variations

- **Easier:** Participants are allowed to catch the ball before it bounces or after it has bounced once.
- **Easier/harder:** Change the size of the areas and the distance between them to change the level of difficulty.
- **Harder:** The ball must be controlled or received by one participant and caught by his team-mate. The controlling touch must be played to the team-mate so that he can catch it without the ball touching the floor. This first touch must not be with the hands or arms, but participants can use their feet, thighs, chest or head to

(continued)

control or pass the ball. For example, one participant can use a cushioned header to control the ball to his team-mate for him to catch it. Both the control and the catch must occur inside the pair's playing area. For extremely advanced participants, you can add more touches or controls before they have to catch the ball.

- **Large groups:** This game can be played with more participants per team. Depending on the age or ability of the participants, make the area bigger if required.

- **Sport-specific:** This game can be adapted for use in other passing and receiving and throwing and catching activities using similar rules. For example, participants could kick a rugby ball across to team-mates, or throw a cricket ball.

Coconut Shy
Ages 5 to 10

Key Skills and Fitness Components Developed

Skills	Fitness Components
· Dribbling	· Balance
· Passing	· Coordination
· Receiving	· Speed

Equipment
- One soccer ball per participant
- Cones

Game
This game develops the correct accuracy and weighting (power) of a soccer pass. Arrange the participants into teams of four. Use cones to mark out a coconut shy lane and a passing line for each group (see figure on page 184). The participants in each team line up behind the passing line; the one at the front (the passer) has a soccer ball. Place three cones on the floor in a triangular formation approximately 10 metres (11 yd) in front of each of the teams. Balance the soccer balls on top of each one. These are coconuts like the ones found in Coconut Shy, a game usually played at fairgrounds. The distance between the coconuts and the passing lines depends on the age or ability level of the participants.

When the game starts, the passers pass their balls at their teams' coconuts, aiming to knock one off its cone. Regardless of whether they hit a coconut, the passers run to their balls, collect them and dribble back to the passing line. If a passer manages to knock off one of the coconuts, she leaves the coconut where it is, unless it is blocking the other coconuts. If it is blocking the other coconuts, she should move it out of the way, preferably behind the other coconuts. The passer leaves the ball on or behind the passing line ready for the next passer in line and joins the back of her team's queue, to wait for her next turn to be the passer. The next passer repeats the process of passing at the coconuts, collecting the ball and then dribbling it back for the next participant. Participants can knock off more than one coconut with each pass. This happens quite often when the front coconut is hit; either the coconut or the passed soccer ball can ricochet into the back ones.

The game continues until one team has knocked all of its coconuts from the cones. This team wins a point. All the teams return their coconuts back onto the cones, then line up so the fun can start again. Have them play for a set time (e.g., 3 to 5 minutes) or until one team has scored a set number of points (e.g., 5 to 8 points) to decide who wins.

Safety Tips
- Warn participants to be careful of collisions.
- Have participants wait until there are no other participants in front of them when they take their shots.
- Instruct participants to watch the other balls kicked by other teams' passers when they are collecting their own. They should dodge any stray passes hit by the opposing teams' passers.

(continued)

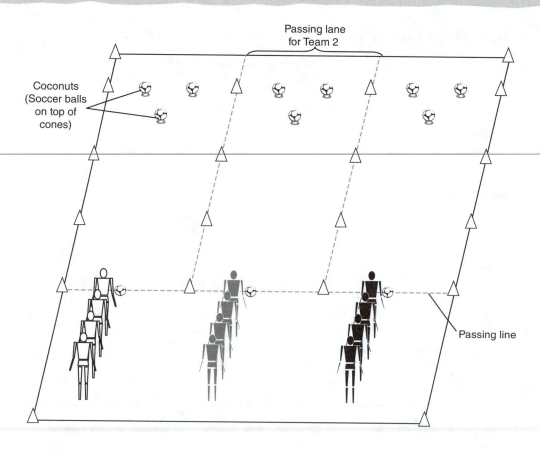

Advice

- If playing outdoors, participants will quickly learn not to kick the ball too hard because it will take a long time to retrieve if it travels a long way past the coconuts. Participants should focus on accuracy and the correct weighting of the pass.

- If playing this game on a fast-rolling surface (e.g., in a sports hall or on AstroTurf), set up in front of a wall, fence or other suitable barrier to stop participants' balls from travelling too far. However, coconuts knocked off their cones by soccer balls rebounding off the barrier do not count; they must be hit directly from the pass. Players should replace coconuts onto their cones if they are knocked off by rebounding balls.

- If a participant knocks off a coconut when she is dribbling the ball back, she must replace this onto the cone before continuing.

- Do not play this game in very windy conditions because the coconuts will be blown off the cones.

Variations

- **Easier/harder:** Change the difficulty level by changing the distance of the cones from the passing line.

- **Harder:** Participants can only kick the ball with their non-dominant foot.

- **Small groups:** The game can be played individually or in pairs. However, it can be very tiring, so play each round only for a short time (e.g., a maximum of 2 minutes), unless one participant has knocked off all of her coconuts. Provide participants with enough rest between rounds.

- **Sport-specific:** This game can be adapted to other sports that involve passing by using relevant techniques (e.g., basketball, netball, hockey or rugby).

Key Skills and Fitness Components Developed

Skills

- Decision making
- Controlling the ball
- Passing
- Receiving

Fitness Components

- Balance
- Coordination
- Power
- Reaction time
- Speed

Equipment

- Cones
- One soccer ball per two participants

Game

This game uses the badminton scoring system, so some of the terminology used here is taken from that game. Arrange the participants into groups of four; then separate each group into teams of two and give each group a soccer ball. Cone out a playing area for each group (see figure on page 187). There should be two 10-by-10-metre (11-by-11-yd) areas, with a distance of 15 to 25 metres (16 to 27 yd) between them. One team stands in one of the areas, and its opponents stand in the other. The distance between the two areas depends on the age or ability of the participants; a shorter distance is preferable for younger or less able ones. One participant (the server) begins with the ball.

To start a rally, the server kicks the ball into the opponents' area. The ball must travel so it rolls through or bounces inside the opponents' area. The server gets only one chance to do this. If the ball does pass into the opposing team's area, both opponents must take a touch to get the ball back across to the serving team's area. Because team-mates must both take a touch of the ball (either to control it or kick or pass it), one should control the ball and the other should pass it back. A rally continues with teams playing the ball back and forth until one team makes a mistake. A team gains a point if the opponents

- do not each take one touch before playing the ball back over (e.g., only one opponent takes a touch or one of them takes more than one touch),
- do not control and pass the ball from inside their own area or
- kick the ball so it does not land in or roll through the opposing team's area.

The server serves again if his team wins a rally, and he continues to serve if his team keeps winning rallies, or points. If a rally is lost, then service passes to the opposing team for one of them to serve. Team-mates take turns serving when they win back service from opponents (remember they keep serving if they win a rally when they start serving). The game continues for a set time (e.g., 3 minutes) or until one team has won a set number of points (e.g., 15).

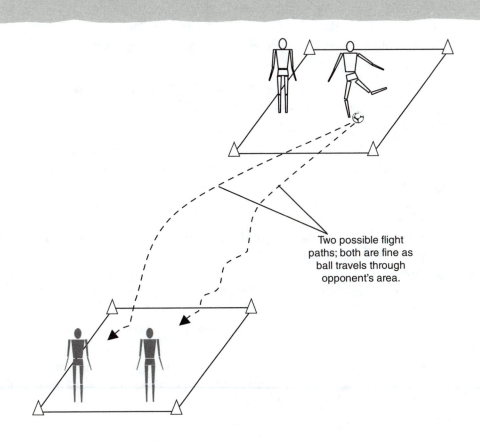

Two possible flight paths; both are fine as ball travels through opponent's area.

Safety Tips

- Warn participants to be careful of collisions.
- Ensure participants have completed a thorough warm-up before playing this activity because it involves ballistic kicking actions.
- There should be a large gap between groups, so there is less risk of participants being hit by stray passes from other groups.

Advice

- Advise participants to call out their names when they are going to control the ball so that their team-mate can move out of the way.
- Participants should control, or cushion, the ball in front of their team-mates so it is easy for them to run onto to strike it. If a participant calls to receive the ball played across from the opponents, their team-mate should move towards the back of his area so he can play the ball in front of him.
- Chipped passes are more difficult to control, so participants should be encouraged to use this technique to play across to opponents.

(continued)

- Here are some key coaching points for striking the ball powerfully:
    - Take a run-up before kicking the ball.
    - Place the standing foot beside the ball and point it towards the target.
    - Use the instep or laces to strike the ball.
    - Keep an eye on the ball.
    - Take a high backswing and follow through with the kicking leg.
    - Lock the ankle of the kicking foot when striking the ball with toes pointed down.

Variations

- **Easier/harder:** Change the size of the areas or the distance between them to change the level of difficulty.
- **Large groups:** This game can be played with 3 or 4 participants per team. Depending on the age or ability of the participants, make the area bigger if playing in larger teams.
- **Harder:** The ball can only bounce inside the area. It cannot be kicked along the floor so that it rolls into the area.
- **Harder:** Participants are allowed to control or pass the soccer ball with only one of their legs or feet. For example, all passes and controls must be played with the right thigh and foot.
- **Small groups:** This game can be played individually.
- **Sport-specific:** This game can be adapted for hockey using the same rules.

Passing Forwards

Key Skills and Fitness Components Developed

Skills

· Attacking and defending skills

· Passing

· Receiving

Fitness Components

· Agility

· Balance

· Coordination

· Endurance

· Power

· Reaction time

· Speed

Equipment

• One bib (pinnie) per two participants

• One soccer ball per eight participants

• Cones

Game

Use this game to develop passing and receiving skills. It is also a good game to develop the tactics of passing the ball forwards when attacking, as well as to teach how to move and lose a marker when passing up field. It is also a great game for teaching players how to stop forward passes when they are defending. For the set-up of this game, see figure on page 190. Arrange the participants in groups of eight, and separate each group into teams of four. Use cones to mark out each group's area, which should be approximately 20 by 20 to 25 by 25 metres (22 by 22 to 27 by 27 yd). Use the cones to mark out the side boundary lines and three mini-goals on the other sides. Number the teams 1 and 2, and have one team put bibs (pinnies) on. Each team should nominate two target players and two outfield players. The target players from each team stand on the ends where their team-mates will be attacking.

When the game begins, the target players can move sideways along the lines they are standing on, but they cannot move into the playing area and they cannot stand in the mini-goals. The aim of the outfield players is to score by passing the ball though any of the mini-goals that they are attacking. The ball must roll along the floor through a mini-goal to be counted as a score. Participants in the outfield role can pass to each other, but to score a goal, they must pass the ball to a target player. At that point he or a team-mate should look to make a forward run to receive the ball back from the target player to score. *The ball must be scored with one kick, pass or touch after it has been played back from one of the target players.* The target players are limited to taking only two touches any time they have possession. When a ball is passed to them, they can pass it back into play to either of their outfield team-mates, but they cannot pass the ball to the other target player on their team.

If a goal is scored, the outfield opponents (the participants who were defending) receive the ball in front of the mini-goal where the goal was scored. They then try to

(continued)

189

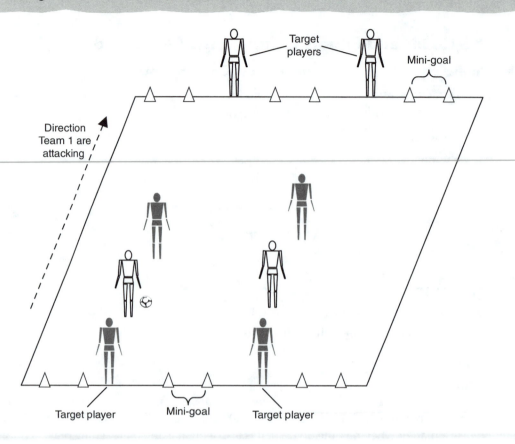

Target players

Mini-goal

Direction Team 1 are attacking

Target player   Mini-goal   Target player

score by playing up to their target players and making a forward run to receive the ball back. Have them play for a set time (e.g., 3 minutes) and keep count of their scores. The target players and the outfield players then switch roles. Again, have them play for the set time, after which the team with the highest combined score wins.

Safety Tips

- Warn participants to be careful of collisions.
- Provide adequate space between groups.
- This game can be very tiring, so don't let the outfield players play for too long before switching to the target player role.

Advice

- Have a few spare soccer balls behind the target players to start the game quickly if the ball being used is kicked out of play. Collect the balls at the end of the set time before starting the next game.
- Demonstrate how a goal is scored so the participants can see this happening.
- Ask questions after explaining the game to check understanding.
- Try to encourage the participants to look to pass forwards as often as possible. It helps if the target players are moving laterally so they are always available for a pass.

- Participants who pass the ball forwards to the target player should power, or weight, the pass correctly so it is easy for their team-mate to control.
- Participants who have passed to one of their target players should sprint forwards and lose their opponents to receive the ball back.
- If your focus is on improving defending, encourage the participants who are closing down the player in possession of the ball to make a run that cuts off a forward pass. They should also track the opponent they are marking to prevent him from scoring once he has played the ball up to the target player.

Variations

- **Easier:** To make the game easier, increase the number of target players or allow the target players to have more touches (or do both).
- **Easier:** Allow outfield players to use two touches to score once they have received the ball back from the target player.
- **Game variation:** Teams have five participants. Each team still has two target players, but three participants play the outfield.
- **Harder:** Limit the number of touches the outfield participants can take (e.g., a maximum of two).
- **Harder:** Allow only the target player to have one touch to play the ball back into play.
- **Sport-specific:** This game can be adapted for use in hockey sessions using similar rules.

Key Skills and Fitness Components Developed	
Skills	**Fitness Components**
· Control	· Agility
· Heading	· Balance
· Passing	· Coordination
· Volleying	· Power
	· Reaction time
	· Speed

Equipment

One tennis court and one soccer ball per 8 to 12 participants

Game

This game has similar rules to those of tennis and volleyball. Because it is ideally played on a tennis court, it can be a good game to play when the fields are too muddy for soccer and the courts are too wet for tennis. Arrange the participants into groups of 8 to 12; then separate each group into two teams. Each group should play on a tennis court, and teams should stand on opposite sides of the net. See figure on page 193 for the set-up of where participants stand at the start of the game. There should be an equal number of participants playing at the front and back of their side of the court. One participant is given the ball to start as the server. The server stands behind the baseline on the right-hand side of the court. The participants on the server's team who are at the front of the court should stand to the side until the ball has been kicked, and then move into position for the rest of the rally.

Similar to tennis and volleyball, soccer tennis involves participants playing rallies. In this game, the winner of a rally is awarded one point. The server starts a rally by kicking the ball over the net. The server must let the ball bounce on the floor before she kicks or serves it, meaning that it is played as a half-volley. However, after the kick, the serve must then travel straight over the net to bounce in the opponents' half of the court. A server has only one chance to get the serve right. If she kicks the ball into the net or it does not bounce in the opponents' half of the court, the opposing team wins the rally, as well as service. Unlike the serving rule in tennis (which stipulates that the ball must land in the service box), the ball can bounce anywhere in the opponents' half of the court. The team receiving the serve does not have to let the ball bounce; players can play it straight back over the net if they wish.

Members of the opposing team can take as many or as few touches as they like to get the ball back to their opponents' side, but they must not let the ball bounce twice in their half. Participants are allowed to use any part of their bodies except their arms and hands to play the ball. Their aim is to set up or use a volley or header to get the ball back over the net again and in the opponents' court. Teams continue to play the ball over the net until one of them wins the rally. A team wins a rally if the opponents let the ball bounce twice on their side, play the ball into the net or kick the ball over the net but outside the court.

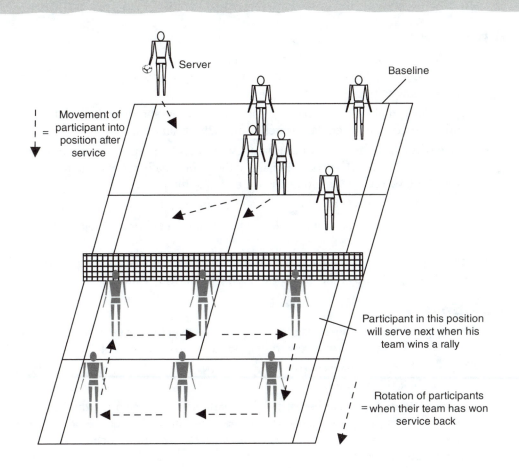

Server

Baseline

Movement of
participant into
position after
service

Participant in this position
will serve next when his
team wins a rally

Rotation of participants
= when their team has won
service back

The server continues to serve if her team wins a rally. If her team loses a rally, the opposing team takes service. Participants rotate positions in a clockwise direction (in a similar way to volleyball) when their team wins service. The participant who was at the front right of the court (looking at the net) should have moved to the back right to become the new server. This ensures that all participants have a chance to play at the front and back of the court and that they all take turns to serve. Have them play for a set time (e.g., 5 to 10 minutes) or until one team has scored a set number of points (e.g., 15 to 21) to decide the winner.

Safety

- Warn participants to be careful of collisions with opponents when playing balls close to the net. Don't allow them to reach over the net to head or kick the ball; they must stay on their own sides. A team loses a rally if one of the participants reaches over the net to play the ball.

- Participants should always keep an eye on the ball to avoid being hit during the game.

- To avoid colliding with their own team-mates, participants should call out their names loudly and as early as possible if they are going to play the ball. This allows other participants to move out of their way.

(continued)

Advice

- The ball must be inflated and bouncy enough for the game to be viable. If playing outdoors on grass, ensure that the area is not too muddy, or the ball will not bounce high enough.

- The court can also be set up using cones to mark out the boundary of the court and played over a soccer tennis net (or something similar).

- Have participants rotate positions so they all spend an equal amount of time at the front and back of the court. Playing at the front usually requires more heading of the ball, whereas more volleying is needed at the back.

- Instruct participants to work as a team to get the ball back over the net.

- Watch for participants trying to dominate the play; encourage them all to work as a team.

- Try to group your participants by ability. If you have lower ability groups, then have them play one of the easier variations in the next section.

Variations

- **Easier:** If participants are struggling to get the ball over the net when serving, allow them to use an underarm throw from a position closer to the net.

- **Easier:** Allow participants two or three bounces of the ball when the ball is played over to their side of the net.

- **Harder:** Restrict the number of touches participants have to get the ball back over. For example, team-mates have to get the ball back over the net in fewer than five touches, but the same participant isn't allowed to touch the ball more than twice consecutively.

- **Smaller groups:** This game can be played with fewer numbers on each team. Participants must have a high ability, and you may still need to restrict the court size (e.g., play in pairs on half a court).

Throw, Head, Catch
Ages 11 to 16

Key Skills and Fitness Components Developed

Skills
- Catching
- Decision making
- Heading
- Throwing

Fitness Components
- Agility
- Balance
- Coordination
- Endurance
- Power
- Reaction time
- Speed

Equipment
- One bib (pinnie) per two participants
- One soccer ball per 12 participants
- Co2nes

Game

Arrange the participants into groups of 12, and then separate each group into two teams of six. Number the teams 1 and 2, and have one team put bibs (pinnies) on. For each group, cone out a large rectangular playing area. Team-mates work together to try to score points during the game. To score a point, team-mates must pass the soccer ball around inside the playing area using the specific throw, head, catch sequence five times.

To start the game, give one of the participants the ball. This participant should hold the ball in their hands. The participants must *throw* the ball to a team-mate for him to *head* it. After the ball has been headed, it must be caught (*catch*). A point is scored when a team has repeated this sequence five times. Once a point has been scored, the team in possession can continue to try to score another point. To prevent a team scoring, the opposing team tries to gain possession of the ball. To gain possession of the ball, the opponents must participate appropriately in the throw, head, catch sequence. For example:

- If a participant from Team 1 has thrown the ball, a participant from Team 2 must head it to a team-mate to gain possession of the ball.
- If a participant from Team 1 has headed the ball, a participant from Team 2 must catch it to gain possession of the ball.

After a header, a team-mate can catch the ball without a bounce or after it has bounced once. If the ball bounces twice (or more) after a header, the opponents gain possession. A team can also gain possession of the ball if an opponent throws a ball that is not headed by a team-mate. If a team gains or regains possession of the ball from its opponents, its members must start their throw, head, catch sequence from zero. When participants have the ball in their hands, they cannot move with it. Participants can move around the area when they do not have possession of the ball. If the ball is thrown or headed out of the

(continued)

playing area, the opposing team gets the ball, which it must throw into play from where the ball left the area. Have teams play for a set time (e.g., 5 to 10 minutes) or until one team has scored a set number of points (e.g., 10).

Safety Tips

- Warn participants to be careful of collisions, especially when they are competing against an opponent when trying to head the soccer ball.
- When jumping for a header, a participant should swing her arms up for lift, but also to position them so they are protecting her head. However, she should be careful not to elbow an opponent in the face or head when she is doing this.
- Participants should call out their names when they are going to head or catch the ball if other team-mates are in close proximity. This should ensure that participants from the same team do not collide when challenging for the ball.
- Have younger participants practice throwing and heading the ball first so their throws are not too hard. You can also encourage participants to use a slower, looping underarm action to throw the ball.

Advice

- Demonstrate the throw, head, catch sequence to the group before starting the game.
- Clearly explain to (and show) participants that when the opposing team has the ball, they must follow the throw, head, catch sequence to gain possession.
- Ask questions after explaining the game to check understanding.
- To head the ball participants should do the following:
    - Use their forehead to head the ball.
    - Keep their eyes open and focused on the ball.
    - Lean back before heading the ball.
    - Use a powerful neck movement.
    - Follow through with the head and neck movement after heading and ensure that the head and body are facing the intended target area.

Variations

- **Easier:** After a team-mate has headed the soccer ball, participants are allowed to catch it after two or three bounces.
- **Easier:** Opponents can intercept the ball only after a header (remember this must be with a catch). They are not allowed to compete for headers after one of the opponents has thrown the ball.
- **Easier/harder:** Change the number of throw, head, catch sequences a team must make before scoring a point.
- **Game variation:** Add two goals. Team 1 attacks one of the goals, and Team 2 attacks the other. Participants can score a point by heading the ball through the goal they are attacking or by making the throw, head, catch sequence five times consecutively.

- **Harder:** Participants cannot head the ball back to the team-mate who threw the ball to them; they must head it to another team-mate.
- **Harder:** Possession changes to the other team if the ball is not caught (after a header) before it bounces.
- **Harder:** Participants must throw the soccer ball using the correct throw-in technique. The ball must be thrown with both feet on the ground as the ball is released. The ball must start, or be taken, behind the head before throwing. It must also be released above (and not in front of) the head.

Volley Game
Ages 11 to 16

Key Skills and Fitness Components Developed

Skills
· Goalkeeping
· Throwing
· Volleying

Fitness Components
· Agility
· Balance
· Coordination
· Power
· Reaction time
· Speed

Equipment
- Two goals per 10 participants
- One soccer ball per participant
- Cones

Game

Arrange the participants into groups of 10; then separate each group into teams of five. Set up two goals for each group. Each team in a group tries to score as many goals as possible into one of these goals in a set period of time (e.g., 2 minutes). Place cones around each goal to mark a goalkeeper's area (see the figure on this page). Each team has five soccer balls, but tries to score with only one ball at a time; the spare balls are placed to the side of the area to be used if the ball being played with is kicked out of play. A participant from each team is nominated to start as the goalkeeper (see information in Safety Tips regarding goalkeepers). The goalkeepers stand in the goal that the opposing team is going to shoot into and tries to save or stop any volley shots that they have.

When the game begins, participants try to score as many goals as possible using volley shots. A volley shot is one in which a player kicks the ball after receiving it in the air and before it bounces. When playing the game with beginners, allow them to throw the ball to a team-mate to set them up for a volley. With more advanced performers, only kicked passes can be used to set up a team-mate. Participants must set each other up for the volley; they cannot throw or chip, kick or flick the ball up for themselves. Participants

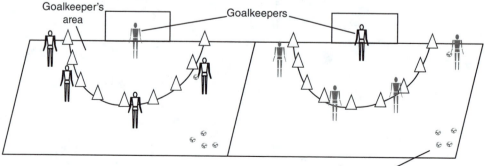

Goalkeeper's area   Goalkeepers

Spare soccer balls

are only allowed to enter into the goalkeeper's area to retrieve a ball. No shots can be taken from inside the area, and volleys cannot be set up from inside it. The goalkeeper must stay inside the area. Because there will be lots of volley shots at the goals, try to set the goals up in front of a wall or fence so balls do not travel too far if they miss the goal. Teams keep score of how many goals they score. After the set time, change the goalkeeper for each team, then start the fun again. Repeat this process until all participants have taken a turn in goal. The team with the most combined goals at the end of the game wins.

Safety Tips

- As mentioned in the chapter introduction, before going in goal, participants should receive some goalkeeper coaching before playing in this position for safety reasons. This should include relevant catching and diving techniques.

- The size of the goalkeeper's area should be relevant to the age or ability of the group. Larger boxes are preferable for older or more able groups so volleys are not taken from close range. The goalkeeper should have time to react to the shot.

- Participants use only one soccer ball at a time.

- Create a suitable gap between each goal so participants are not hit by stray volleys from other groups or teams. For the same reason, do not set groups up so their goals are behind each other. Set them up side by side or so participants are shooting away from a central point.

- Participants collecting stray soccer balls should keep their eyes on the game so they do not get hit by other team-mates' shots.

Advice

- It is crucial that the participants set up the volleys correctly. Tell the participants to throw the ball using an underarm action and to aim for their team-mates' knees. They must not throw the ball too hard.

- If possible, set up the goals with a fence close behind them so that missed shots do not travel far. If this is not possible, have more participants on a team and ask them to collect the ball after their shots.

- Here are key coaching points for the side and front volley techniques:
  - Go for accuracy before power (hit the target) and try to keep shots low.
  - Use the laces to strike the ball.
  - Keep an eye on the ball.
  - Lock the ankle of the kicking foot.
  - Place the standing foot so it is pointing towards the goal.
  - **Side volley:** Swing the leg above the ball before contact and strike down on it to keep it low. The body and leg should be swivelled through at least 180° during the volley, and it is essential that the leg is swivelled before contacting with the ball.
  - **Front volley:** Let the ball drop close to the ground before striking it. Try to keep the toes pointed down throughout the skill. Have a backswing and when swinging the leg forward to play the volley, bend the knee slightly and maintain this bend throughout the kick and follow-through.

(continued)

Variations

- **Easier:** Allow younger or less able participants to throw the ball up to themselves to set up a volley.

- **Easier:** Allow participants to shoot using a half-volley. This is when a shot is taken after the ball has bounced once. Do not allow participants to shoot if the ball has bounced more than once. A half-volley that is scored earns 1 point, whereas a volley that is scored earns 2 points.

- **Harder:** With older or more able participants, add a rule that volleys must be set up using a chipped pass. The ball cannot be thrown to set up the volley.

- **Game variation:** Participants must kick or cross the ball using chipped or longer passes. Set up crossing areas using cones where the ball must be chipped from. Allow teams to score from inside the semi-circle as well, but only using headers. Volleys must be scored from outside the area.

- **Game variation:** This variation is good if you have only one goal, a smaller group or 2 or more participants whose specialist position is goalkeeping. Participants (apart from the goalkeepers) are arranged into two teams that compete against each other. The goalkeepers compete against the other goalkeepers, but not against the two volleying teams. One team stands behind the goal and collects the balls, while the other team tries to score. One of the goalkeepers starts in goal, trying to save volley shots from the team trying to score. A goalkeeper stays in goal until a team has scored and then switches with another goalkeeper. If a goalkeeper saves three shots in a row, she gains a point and switches with another goalkeeper. After a set time (e.g., 3 minutes) the teams swap roles and the other team tries to beat the first team's score to win the game. The goalkeeper who has the most points also wins her competition.

seven

Tennis and Badminton Games

The activities in this chapter relate to tennis or badminton and include a mixture of skill practices, warm-up activities and games. Collectively, they can be used to develop most tennis and badminton shots, footwork, decision making and tactical awareness.

Apart from Two Shuttle Down (page 208) which is predominately played in badminton sessions, these activities are written up for use in tennis sessions. However, the majority of these can be adapted easily for badminton and may not need modifications to make them suitable. Some activities require modifications to make them suitable, and if it is possible to adapt an activity to badminton, the information for this is found in the Variations section.

Most activities can be played indoors using 'short tennis' equipment. For indoor sessions use plastic rackets and sponge balls when instructing younger participants. For outdoor sessions use rackets that are an appropriate size and weight for the participants. Provide younger or less able group members with rackets with smaller handles, if available, to give them more success. Younger or less able players should also use less bouncy tennis balls so they have more time to get into position during the activities.

In this book, I use the term 'side' to refer to the areas of the court on either side of the net. When playing a singles' tennis match, opponents will stand on opposite sides of the net. When I use the term 'half', this refers to the left and right half of the court. If a line is drawn from the centre lines to the baselines on each side of the court, participants could play a singles match on half a court (e.g., one participant on either side of the net, using the side line and the centre [and chalk] line) as the side boundaries for their game. The diagram in Two Shuttle Down (page 209) shows pairs of participants playing against each other on half a court.

In tennis or badminton sessions, you may sometimes have more participants than you can accommodate because of the limited amount of court space. Thus, a number of participants might have to sit out of the action at any one time, waiting for their turn on court. Because children learn best when they are enjoying themselves and have lots of opportunities to practise, the activities in this chapter aim to involve participants more frequently. Participants will not be off court for longer than a few minutes. With more involvement, your group will enjoy the session more.

Catching Game
Ages 8 to 13

Key Skills and Fitness Components Developed

Skills

· Catching

· Ground strokes

· Volleying

Fitness Components

· Balance

· Coordination

· Power

· Reaction time

· Speed

Equipment

- One tennis ball and racket per participant
- One tennis court per 8 to 12 participants

Game

This game can be used to develop various tennis strokes. For the set-up of this activity, see the figure on page 204. Arrange the participants into groups of 8 to 12. Each group works on its own court. Half of the group starts as hitters. The hitters line up behind the baseline on one side of the court, each of them with a tennis racket. The remaining participants stand on the opposite side of the net. One of them is a server and stands beside the net just off the court with the tennis balls. The others are catchers who spread out in their side of the court trying to cover as much area as possible.

The aim of this activity is to be the last hitter in the game. The first hitter moves onto the court, and the server throws him a ball. If you want your players to work on a particular shot, the server should throw the ball so the hitter can use that technique to play the ball across the net. The hitter tries to play the ball so it travels over the net and lands on the other side of the court. If the hitter plays a successful shot, he remains a hitter but moves to the back of the hitting line ready for another turn. If the hitter hits an unsuccessful shot, he moves over to the other side to become a catcher. As hitters move to the other side of the net, they should place their rackets down off the court so other participants do not step on or trip over them.

An unsuccessful shot is one that lands outside the court, doesn't clear the net or is caught by a catcher before it bounces. If the latter occurs, the participant who caught the ball switches roles with the hitter. The participant who caught the ball should give the ball to the server; then pick up a tennis racket and join the back of the hitting line. The next hitter moves onto the court, and the process is repeated.

As the game continues, the number of hitters should decrease as shots are hit into the net or out of the court (although any participant who is a catcher can become a hitter by catching a ball hit by a hitter). The last participant hitting wins the round and scores a point. Set the game up again, but the participants switch their starting positions from the last round (i.e., the catchers are hitters and vice versa). Each time a new round starts, there should be a new server so that all participants have a turn at this role. Have them play for a set number of rounds (e.g., 10 minutes) or until one participant has scored a set number of points (e.g., 3 to 5).

(continued)

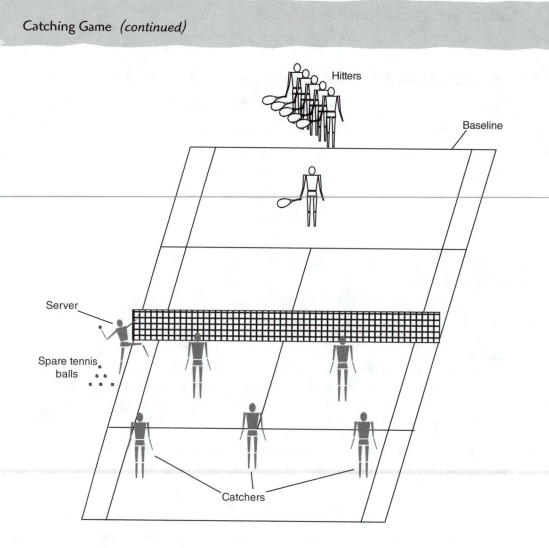

Safety Tips

- Warn the catchers to be careful of collisions. They should call their name if they are going to catch a ball, so other catchers can move out of their way.

- Do not allow participants to hit volley shots close to the net or smashes because they may hit the ball too hard.

- Participants who need to place their rackets down should do so safely out of the way of the game until they become hitters again.

- Ensure that no loose tennis balls roll onto the court when participants are playing. Ideally, a basket or bucket should be placed beside the server to store the tennis balls. Participants picking up a ball should place it inside the basket rather than try to throw it in.

- Participants should watch the game and keep their eyes on the ball so they can dodge any stray shots hit towards them. However, when they are catchers, they should watch the game so they can catch any balls hit towards them.

Advice

- If the serve is not accurate, allow the hitter to have another turn to strike the ball.
- Catchers are allowed to catch the ball while standing off the court. This means that if the hitter hits a ball that is going to land off court, a catcher can run off court to catch it.
- The server can feed the ball in various ways so that participants work on a number of different shots.
- With younger or less able participants, you may want to serve so balls land in the correct place, enabling hitters to use the correct hitting technique.

Variations

- **Easier:** Make the game easier for the catchers by allowing them to catch the ball after it has bounced once. The catch must be taken with one hand if it bounces.
- **Game variation:** Hitters start with 2 points. They continue hitting until they lose both of their points; then they become catchers. If a catcher becomes a hitter (after catching a ball), he moves to the other side but has only 1 point.
- **Game variation:** Arrange the participants into two teams of six. Members of the hitting team take turns to serve to each other (from the net). Hitters must strike the ball using the specified shot that they are trying to develop. The hitters have 30 serves and should take turns to hit so that they have five shots each. The hitting team scores a point when a hitter plays a successful shot, and the catching team scores a point if the shot is caught, does not clear the net or lands outside the court. Once all of the hitters have taken their shots, the teams swap roles. The team with the most points when both teams have hit wins.
- **Game variation:** Within each group the participants play against each other, scoring points throughout the game. Half of the group are hitters, and the other half are catchers. When hitting, participants are each given five serves; then the hitters and the catchers swap roles. One point is awarded for every successful shot, and one point is awarded for every catch. Participants get two opportunities to hit (10 serves in total), and after they have all had the set number of serves, the participant with the most points wins.
- **Smaller groups:** If playing with groups of four or five, play with similar rules to the previous variation, but participants take turns to hit. The remaining participants are the catchers, apart from the one who starts as the server. A point is scored for each successful shot or catch. Participants swap roles once the hitter has received and hit their 5 serves. The participant with the most points after each participant has been the hitter three times wins. With groups of four or five, you may want to serve the ball, have one participant hit and have the remaining participants catch.
- **Sport-specific:** This game can be adapted for use in badminton sessions. Group sizes should be smaller, and you may want to use the individual version outlined previously. With more able participants, each catcher should be given a hoop to stand inside. Catchers are not allowed to step out of their hoops to catch the shuttle, or birdie. If you play this game with beginners allow them to play the smash shot, but if doing this, do not allow the catchers to stand between the service line and the net before the hitters have played the shot. Catchers can move forwards after the shot has been played but not before.

Ball Familiarisation
Ages 5 to 10

Key Skills and Fitness Components Developed

Skill
Basic racket control

Fitness Components
Coordination and other components are dependent on the skills chosen during the activity.

Equipment
One tennis ball and racket per participant

Game
This is a good activity for developing competence in hitting a tennis ball in a variety of ways. It is also useful as part of a progressive warm-up and can be used with younger or less able participants at the beginning of each session. Each participant has a tennis racket and tennis ball. Participants spread out and should not work within 5 metres (5.5 yd) of another participant. The participants then complete the skills that you choose, trying to do their best at each one. Choose skills that will challenge them and develop their ability to hit the ball in a variety of ways. This will help to develop their timing and coordination. Most activities can be modified so the participants become familiar with using both sides of the racket to hit the ball.

Following are some examples of the skills the participants can perform:

- Hitting the ball up in the air continuously (participants can use only one side of the racket or alternate touches between the forehand and backhand sides of the racket).
- Bouncing the ball on the floor by hitting it in a downwards motion with the racket (again, this could be with just one side or alternating between the two).
- Bouncing the ball as in the previous example, but participants walk or jog around the area as they bounce the ball.
- Hitting the ball up in the air continuously while moving around the area.
- Balancing the ball on the racket head and then throwing the ball straight into the air before catching it on the racket head.
- Hitting the ball up in the air continuously but putting spin on it each time. This should be done by slicing the racket under the ball when striking.
- Keeping the ball in the air by gently hitting it and then leaving it to try to get another participant's ball when you call 'change'. Participants should try to get to another ball before it bounces too low or stops bouncing.

Safety Tips
- Warn participants to be careful of collisions, especially when retrieving stray tennis balls.
- Space participants so you don't have too many on one court.

Advice

- Younger or less able participants tend to grip the racket at the top of the grip or even where the head joins the handle, which should be avoided. Demonstrate the correct grip before starting the activity, and ensure that all participants are using this grip.

- Use your imagination to design skill challenges or ask participants to think of their own. Make them fun and appropriate for the ability of the group.

- Participants should not use their non-dominant hand to play this game.

- Increase the difficulty of the activities as the participants become more accomplished.

Variations

- **Game variation:** Have participants play this game competitively by asking them to keep score of their best attempts and compare their results. For example, the participants have to hit the ball into the air continuously, but must alternate which side of the racket is used to hit the ball into the air. Participants count how many shots they play before the ball drops on the floor or they do not alternate between sides when hitting it. The participant who scores the most on each activity is awarded a point, and the one who scores the most points once all the activities are completed wins.

- **Game variation:** Some of these activities can be played in pairs using one ball. For example, if one participant hits the ball twice, bouncing the ball on the forehand, then backhand side of the racket, he can pass the ball to his partner with the second hit. The partner needs to repeat the process of hitting the ball with the forehand, then backhand side of the racket, and then pass the ball back with a backhand hit. Participants continue to play the ball back and forth until the ball bounces on the floor or one participant takes too few or too many touches.

- **Sport-specific:** This game can be adapted to badminton, but only a few of the challenges can be performed individually. It may be better to think of familiarisation activities that involve a partner or working in groups of three.

Two Shuttle Down
Ages 8 to 16

Key Skills and Fitness Components Developed

Skills
- Catching
- Decision making
- Throwing

Fitness Components
- Agility
- Balance
- Coordination
- Power
- Reaction time
- Speed

Equipment
One shuttle per participant and one badminton court per four participants

Game
This is a throwing game that is appropriate for badminton sessions. It is a good activity to use towards the end of a warm-up to work on an overarm throwing action (this type of action is needed for smashing and clearing shots when playing badminton) or develop tactical knowledge. Arrange the participants in pairs and give each participant a shuttle. Each pair works on half a badminton court, and participants stand on opposite sides of the net (see the figure on page 209).

When a rally begins, both participants throw their shuttles over the net onto their opponent's side of the court. The shuttle must land in the playing area. They should try to throw the shuttle to a place on the court where the opponent is not standing. The aim of the game is to throw the shuttles over the net into their opponent's side of the court so that both shuttles are touching the floor (on the opponent's side of the net) at the same time. Doing so earns the participant a point. For example, if a participant throws the shuttle over the head of her opponent while the opponent throws her shuttle straight at her, she may be able to catch and throw the second shuttle onto her opponent's side (before the opponent picks up the first one) so both shuttles are on the floor at the same time. Participants are not allowed to pick up both shuttles at the same time, so if they have one shuttle in their hand, they must throw it over the net before picking up the next one. If a shuttle lands outside the playing area or does not travel over the net, the opponent wins the rally and gains a point. After a point is won or lost, participants play another rally with each of them starting with a shuttle. Participants cannot reach over or past the net to throw or drop their shuttles on their opponent's side of the court. Have them play for a set time (e.g., 3 minutes) or until one participant has won a set number of points (e.g., 10).

Safety Tips
- If a shuttle lands on another pair's court, participants should wait until this pair has finished the point before collecting the stray shuttle.
- Ensure participants have completed a thorough warm-up before carrying out this activity because it involves ballistic movements.

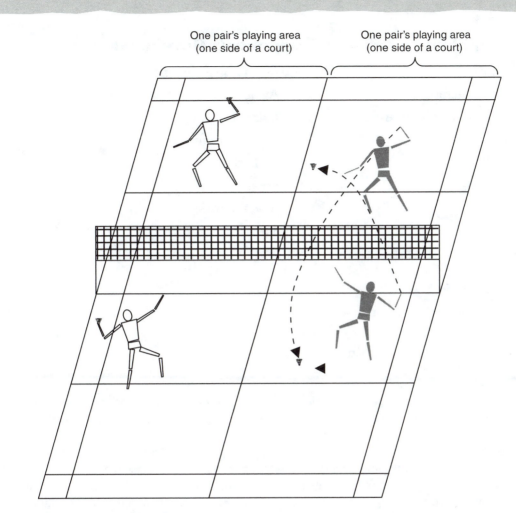

One pair's playing area (one side of a court)

One pair's playing area (one side of a court)

Advice

If participants are trying to throw the shuttle to the back of the court, they should use an overarm throwing action.

Variations

- **Game variation:** Participants have four shuttles each, which they place on the floor on their side of the net. Participants throw the shuttles over the net, but can pick up only one shuttle at a time. Have them play for a set time (e.g., 30 to 45 seconds); then halt the game and count how many shuttles are on either side of the court. The participant with the fewest shuttles on her side wins the game.

- **Game variation:** Participants are in teams of two competing against another pair. Play with four shuttles, and participants must have three shuttles on the floor on the opponent's side of the net to win a point.

- **Sport-specific:** This game can be adapted for use in tennis sessions. Use an alternative to shuttles (e.g., soft bean bags) and play on a restricted area on the court. For example, a pair may play on half a court.

Cooperative-Competitive Rally
Ages 8 to 16

Equipment

- One tennis racket per participant
- One tennis ball per two participants
- One court per four participants

Game

In badminton and tennis (and other similar sports), participants can benefit from working cooperatively when trying to develop particular shots. For example, if working on the forehand drive in tennis or the overhead clear in badminton, participants can play these shots to each other and keep a rally going so they can refine their technique. This is a good activity for developing cooperation when playing rallies, but with a twist.

Arrange participants in pairs and give each pair a ball. Set up each pair to work on their own half of a court. One participant stands on one side of the net, and her partner stands on the opposite side. The two then play a cooperative rally, hitting the ball to each other and trying to keep the rally going. If working on a particular shot, tell the participants to play the ball across the net so their partners can return the ball using the specified shot.

The participants should count how many shots they play and try to keep the rally going for as long as possible. The rally continues until one participant makes a mistake. This could be hitting the ball into the net or hitting it so it bounces outside of the court. When a rally ends, the participant who did not make the mistake wins the rally and is awarded points to equal the score of the shots achieved in the rally. For example, if they played 12 shots before one participant hit the ball into the net, their partner is awarded 12 points. The participants compete against each other to win the longest rally. Rally scores are not added up throughout the game, but participants work to win a rally after playing progressively more shots. For example, if the participant who had 12 points (from earlier example) won the next rally after five shots, their best score would still be 12. They would not add the two scores together.

After each rally has ended, the participants start a new one, counting the shots from zero. Participants can beat their own score only by playing a rally that continues for more shots than their current best score. The following examples show how the scores are counted over the first few rallies:

- Rally 1: The pair plays 6 shots before player 1 hits the ball into the net. Current score: player 1 = 0 points; player 2 = 6 points
- Rally 2: The pair plays 10 shots before player 2 misses the ball. Current score: player 1 = 10 points; player 2 = 6 points
- Rally 3: The pair plays 5 shots before player 2 hits the ball out of the court. Current score: player 1 = 10 points; player 2 = 6 points
- Rally 4: The pair plays 13 shots before player 1 hits the ball into the net. Current score: player 1 = 10 points; player 2 = 13 points

The participants play for a set time (e.g., 3 to 5 minutes); this is termed a round. At the end of a round, rearrange the participants into new pairs for a new round. The two participants with the highest scores work together, the participants who had the third- and fourth-highest scores are paired, and this arrangement continues with the subsequent lower-scoring participants. After another round, switch the participants again using the same highest-to-lowest pairing system. After three or four rounds, rank the participants according to their scores from the final match to determine their positions. The participant with the highest score is the winner.

Safety Tips
- If a tennis ball rolls onto another pair's court, participants should wait until the pair has finished the rally before collecting the stray ball. They should also shout a warning if they believe a player has not seen the ball and may step on it. If a pair have stopped playing a rally because another pair's ball comes onto their court (for safety reasons or because this ball prevents them from keeping their own rally going), when they start the next rally they can start counting from the number of shots before they had to stop the previous rally.
- Ensure participants have completed a thorough warm-up before playing this activity because it involves ballistic movements.

Advice
- Demonstrate and talk through the scoring system before the participants start to play.
- Ask questions to check understanding after explaining the rules.
- If one participant has a higher score than his partner, he may be tempted to repeatedly make mistakes early in the rally so his partner cannot beat him. This can happen in the final round when participants are competing against their partner for the final finishing rank. To prevent this, if the participant who is leading loses three rallies in a row, then the leader switches scores with his partner.
- With some groups it may be useful for the participants to count out loudly so you can monitor how many shots they have played.
- This is a good game to use to learn the ability levels of your participants if you want to group them by skill level. At the end of the game you should be able to gauge how well they play by their scores throughout the rounds and their finishing ranks.
- If there is a wide range in ability within your group, you may want to start the activity with the participants paired according to skill level.

(continued)

Variations

- **Game variation:** Participants work in pairs to score the highest total of consecutive shots in one rally. Play for a set time (e.g., 5 to 10 minutes). All of the pairs' best rallies, or scores, are compared, and the pair with the highest number is the winner.

- **Game variation:** Participants work in pairs to keep a rally going for a specific number of shots (e.g., 10) and score a point each time they achieve this. Participants can keep the rally going if they reach the target number of shots, so if they played 22 shots they would be awarded two points. Have them play for a set time (e.g., 5 to 10 minutes); the pair that scores the most points is the winner.

- **Game variation:** This variation should be used to develop the lob shot. Participants are in groups of four and then separated into teams. Two participants are hitting while the other two catch. The catchers do not have rackets, and they stand within a metre of the net, one on each side of it. The participants who are hitting count up how many shots they play during a cooperative rally. They should use lob shots to hit over the catchers. Catchers who catch a ball switch positions with the hitter who hit it. The participant hitting gains the score of the shots played before the ball was caught.

- **Game variation:** It is possible for a pair of participants to play one round against each other to determine a winner. However, if one participant has a higher score than his partner, he may be tempted to repeatedly make mistakes early in the rally so his partner cannot beat him. To prevent this, remind the participants that if the participant who is leading loses three rallies in a row, he must switch scores with his partner.

- **Harder:** Pairs play on full courts.

- **Harder:** Participants can use only a specific shot to hit the ball (e.g., a volley shot). Participants stand in the court in a specific place to be able to hit this particular shot. For a rally of volley shots, they should stand close to the net.

- **Sport-specific:** This game can be played in badminton sessions using the same rules.

Lob It
Ages 11 to 16

Key Skills and Fitness Components Developed

Skills
- Lob
- Smash
- Volley shot

Fitness Components
- Agility
- Balance
- Coordination
- Power
- Reaction time
- Speed

Equipment
- One racket and tennis ball per participant
- One tennis court per eight participants
- Chalk

Game
For the set-up of this activity, see the figure on page 214. Arrange the participants into groups of eight; then separate them into two teams of four. Number the teams 1 and 2. Team 1 starts as the hitting team, and team 2 starts as the receiving team. Each group work on its own court, and teams start on opposite sides of the net. One of the hitters starts as a server, another starts on court as the striking hitter and the remaining participants from this team line up behind the baseline, waiting for their turn. The striking hitter stands on court and the server should stand off-court by the net with the tennis balls.

Using the chalk, draw a line on the floor on the receivers' side of the court halfway between the net and the service line, from doubles sideline to doubles sideline. Two of the receivers start on the court between the chalk line and the net. The other two receivers start off the court, and while they are waiting to play, they collect any of the tennis balls that are hit out of the game on their side.

When the groups are set up, the server throws a tennis ball for the striking hitter to play a lob shot. The striking hitter tries to hit the ball over the top of her on-court opponents so it lands inside their side of the court. If she is successful with the lob shot, she scores a point for her team. If she strikes the ball into the net or out of the court, the opposing team is awarded a point. The receivers can also win a point if either of them smashes (or volleys) the ball back into the hitters' side of the court. This can happen if the hitter hits a poor lob shot that does not travel high enough over the receivers. The receivers can move back to the service line to play a return, but they cannot move until the hitter has struck the ball.

The hitters rotate positions after each hit; the striking hitter moves to the net to become a server, and the server joins the back of the hitting line. The participant who was at the front of the hitting line moves onto the court to become the striking hitter. The receivers who are off-court switch with their on-court team-mates after their opponents have

(continued)

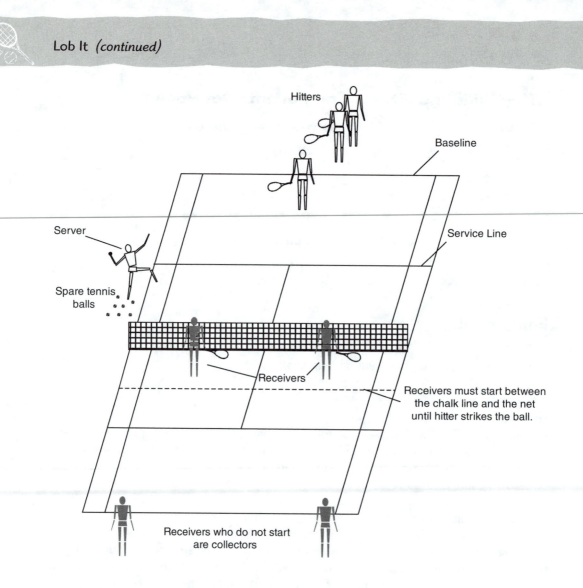

Hitters

Baseline

Server

Service Line

Spare tennis
balls

Receivers

Receivers must start between
the chalk line and the net
until hitter strikes the ball.

Receivers who do not start
are collectors

taken half of their shots. After each hitter has taken a set number of hits (e.g., 5 to 10), the teams swap roles, and after both teams have hit, the team with the most points wins.

Safety Tips

- Receivers who are collecting the tennis balls should keep their eyes on the play so that they are not hit by any stray shots.
- Make sure the hitters who are waiting for their turn stand well back from the baseline.
- Ensure participants are suitably warmed up before playing the game because it involves ballistic movements.

Advice

- If the wind is making it too difficult to hit the lob from one side of the net, participants should switch sides so hitters play from the other side. If it is very windy, you may not be able to play this game.

- Make sure the server throws the ball in the right place for the hitter to play the lob shot.
- Receivers should not move until the hitter has struck the ball.
- Receivers should return to their starting positions quickly after each point to speed up the game.
- Older and more able participants should be taught how to play the lob with topspin.

Variations

- **Harder:** Participants have to play the backhand lob shot.
- **Harder:** Make the game harder for hitters by allowing the receivers to move to the back of the court to return any lobs. The receivers should still not be allowed to move until the hitter has struck the ball.
- **Game variation:** The participants continue to play the point if the receivers manage to return the hitter's lob shot. The receivers are still not allowed to move to the back of the court until the first lob shot has been taken. However, after the hitter's shot, they can move anywhere they like on their side of the court. The server should have a racket which they pick up, then join the play after serving so the point becomes a doubles rally or match. After each point the participants set up in the starting positions for the next one.
- **Game variation:** If a participant hits a winning lob, she continues to be the hitter. If she loses the point, the teams switch roles. If a hitter wins 3 points in a row, she is awarded 2 bonus points for the team but rotates out of the position so there is a new hitter. Have them play for a set time (e.g., 10 minutes), after which, the team with the most points wins.
- **Game variation:** This game can be adapted for developing forehand and backhand ground strokes. The server throws the ball to the relevant place for the hitter to play the correct ground stroke. The hitter must hit the ball below a specified height, trying to pass the opponents. The opponents should try to play a volley shot to win the point.
- **Sport-specific:** This game can be adapted for use in badminton sessions using the same rules. The striking hitter can be served the shuttle so she can play an overhead clear from the back of the court or a lob shot from the front of the court.

Speed Drop
Ages 5 to 16

Key Skills and Fitness Components Developed

Skills
· Catching
· Footwork

Fitness Components
· Agility
· Reaction time
· Speed

Equipment
- One tennis ball per three participants
- One court per 12 participants
- Cones

Game

The set-up of this activity is shown in the figure on page 217. Arrange the participants into groups of three. One participant is a server and has a ball. The remaining participants are runners who will be competing against each other. Two groups work on either side of the court. However, the groups do not work together; each group works on its own half. Each group places two cones on the baseline, one in the corner and the other approximately 50 centimetres (20 in.) from the centre of the court. The server stands approximately 2 to 5 metres from the baseline, towards the net. One of the runners stands on the baseline. The other runner stands a few metres behind the baseline to wait for his turn.

To start the game, the server holds the ball out to the side at shoulder height, and the runner on the baseline starts sidestepping along the baseline moving from cone to cone at a slow-to-moderate pace. After a few seconds the server drops the ball so it lands on the ground directly under where he was holding it. The runner has to react quickly and attempt to catch the ball before it bounces twice on the floor. The runner then gives the ball back to the server so the other runner can take his turn. The runners take turns to react and catch the ball dropped by the server. If the runners both succeed in catching the ball, the server takes one step towards the net to make it more difficult for the runners to catch the ball. If a runner doesn't make it to the ball before it bounces twice, he is allowed one more attempt to catch the ball with the server at that distance. The game continues until one of the participants cannot react and run fast enough to catch the ball before it bounces twice. The participant winning is awarded 2 points. If they both fail at the same distance, they are awarded a point each. The game is repeated with each of the runners taking two turns as the server. After each of the participants has served twice, the participant with the most points wins.

Safety Tips
- Ensure participants have completed a thorough warm-up before carrying out this activity because it involves ballistic movements.
- Groups who are working on the same baseline should not place their cones too close together in the middle of the court.

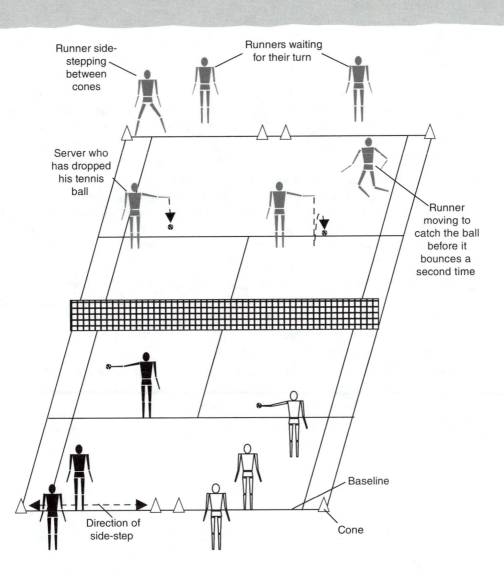

Runner side-stepping between cones

Runners waiting for their turn

Server who has dropped his tennis ball

Runner moving to catch the ball before it bounces a second time

Baseline

Direction of side-step

Cone

- Runners should stay on their feet at all times. Instruct them not to dive when they attempt to catch the ball.
- The server may want to move out of the runner's way once he has dropped the ball.

Advice

- Tennis balls must have adequate bounce. Do not use old tennis balls that have lost some of their springiness.
- Ensure that the runner does not move towards the ball until the server has dropped it.
- Carry out this activity on hard, bouncy surfaces.
- Group participants by ability so they are all challenged during the game.

(continued)

Variations

- **Game variation:** Runners catch the ball on a racket instead of using their hands.

- **Game variation:** The server holds two tennis balls, one in each hand. He holds both arms out to the side and drops one of the balls. The runner tries to catch the ball while the server throws the other ball over the runner's head to bounce on the floor behind him. The runner attempts to turn and catch the second ball before it bounces twice on the floor. The runner scores a point for each ball caught.

- **Harder:** The runner has a racket and must hit the ball after the server drops it. It is important that the server steps out of the way after they have dropped the ball, so they don't get hit by the hitter's racket when he swings for the ball. The ball must bounce once, and the shot must travel over the net and into the court to be counted as a successful attempt. Only two groups can work on one court for this variation. Each group should work on its own half of the court.

- **Sport-specific:** This activity can be adapted for use in rugby or soccer sessions, using relevant sports balls. The various deviations of the bounce of rugby balls makes this variation even more entertaining. In soccer sessions this is particularly good for coaching goalkeepers. If they are playing on a suitable surface (e.g., grass), allow the participants to dive to catch the ball.

- **Sport-specific:** This game can be adapted for use in badminton sessions. The server holds up, then drops a shuttle, or birdie, and the runner has a racket. The runner tries to catch the shuttle on the racket before it touches the floor.

Team Catch

Ages 8 to 16

Key Skills and Fitness Components Developed

Skills
- Catching
- Volleying

Fitness Components
- Balance
- Coordination
- Reaction time
- Speed

Equipment
- One tennis racket per participant
- One tennis ball and court per six participants
- Chalk

Game
For the set-up of this activity, see the figure on this page. Arrange the participants into teams of six. Each team works on its own court and starts with one hitter and four catchers; the remaining participant waits at the side of the court to be the next hitter. Use the chalk to draw out a hitting area on one side of the court. This should be approximately 2 by 2 metres and be drawn between the service line and the net in the centre of that side of the court. The hitter stands in this area with a racket. The catchers place their rackets down at the side of the court, next to the waiting hitter, and then stand on the other side of the net, approximately 1 metre from it. Give two of the catchers a tennis ball each.

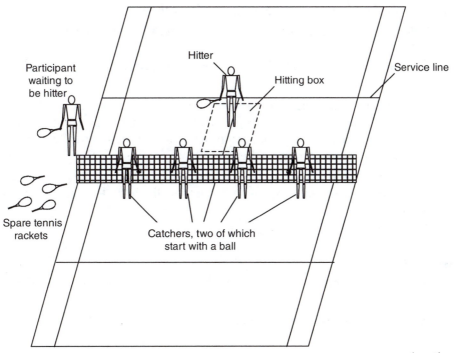

(continued)

When the game starts, one of the catchers throws her ball to the hitter so she can play a volley shot. The hitter volleys the ball to one of the catchers so that she can catch the ball before it bounces. The catchers alternate throwing to the hitter so the same ball is not hit twice in a row. The hitter continues hitting volleys to the catchers until each one of them has caught the ball. The hitter may not hit a ball to a catcher who is holding one, and the hitter cannot hit the ball back to the catcher who threw it.

The minimum number of volleys that a hitter can take would be four. For example, four volleys occur in the following throwing-volleying-catching sequence: (1) Participant 1 throws the first ball, which is caught by participant 2; (2) participant 3 throws the second ball, which is caught by participant 4; (3) participant 2 now throws the first ball, which is caught by participant 1; and (4) participant 4 now throws the second ball, which is caught by participant 3.

If a catcher drops a ball, it doesn't count as a catch so the hitter must hit another ball to this catcher. When all of the catchers have caught a volley, the team gains a point and the participants rotate positions in the following pattern:

- The participant waiting at the side of the court becomes the hitter.
- The catcher nearest the rackets picks one up and waits to be the next hitter.
- The hitter moves off the court, places her racket down and then becomes a catcher in the position farthest from the spare rackets.

The team continues to rotate positions each time all of the catchers have caught a volley. Have them play for a set time (e.g., 8 to 10 minutes). The team with the most points at the end wins.

Advice

- Demonstrate this activity before allowing the participants to play, and ask questions to check understanding after explaining the rules.
- Catchers should not pass the ball to each other. They can only throw balls to the hitter.
- Catchers should not reach over the net to catch the ball. It must pass over the net before they can catch it.
- You may find that some hitters just lob the ball to the catchers. This is not advisable if the team wants to win the game. Hitting the ball with slightly more power so that it travels with a flat trajectory will result in quicker volleys (as long as team-mates are competent catchers) and more points scored before time runs out.
- The server should throw the ball in the right place for the hitter to play a volley shot. The throw should be quite hard to enable the hitter to play with the correct technique.
- The hitter should return to the ready position after each shot.

Variations

- **Easier:** Participants are allowed to hit the ball back to the participant who threw it to them.
- **Easier:** Allow the hitter to play the ball if it bounces before the shot.

- **Game variation:** The hitter hits for a set time (e.g., 1 minute). A point is awarded for every volley caught. After the set time the participants rotate positions. This continues until all team members have hit. After all participants have hit, add their scores together to give the team score. The team with the most points at that point wins the game.

- **Game variation:** Participants play in groups of five. They play individually against the other members of the group. There should be one hitter and four catchers. The catchers should have a ball each, and they take turns throwing to the hitter. The catchers on the right half of their side of the court throw the ball to the left of the hitter (so a right-handed hitter would use a backhand volley). This is repeated on the other side, but those catchers throw the ball to the hitter's right (so a right-handed hitter would play a forehand volley). The hitter hits the ball back to the catcher who threw the ball to them. The hitter scores a point for each catch taken; the catcher who catches it also scores a point. Participants hit for 1 minute; then rotate. Once everyone in the group has had a turn as the hitter, the participant with the most points wins.

- **Harder:** Hitters can only play volleys using either the forehand or the backhand.

- **Large groups:** If you have a limited number of courts, this game can be played without hitting the ball over the net. This version also makes the game easier so could be used with less able participants.

- **Sport-specific:** This game can be adapted for use in badminton sessions using relevant badminton techniques such as overhead clears, drop shots and net play. Place four hoops on the ground for the catchers to stand in. Catchers can catch a shuttle only when they have both feet in their hoop.

Top Square

Ages 8 to 16

Key Skills and Fitness Components Developed

Skills

- Basic hitting skills
- Decision making
- Footwork

Fitness Components

- Agility
- Balance
- Coordination
- Reaction time
- Speed

Equipment

- One tennis racket per participant
- One tennis ball per four participants
- Chalk

Game

Arrange the participants in groups of four. For each group use chalk to mark out an area approximately 7-by-7 to 10-by-10 metres (7.7-by-7.7 to 11-by-11 yd); then divide this area into four smaller squares. Starting in one corner and working in a clockwise direction, number the smaller squares 1 to 4. One participant stands by each of the corners so that each participant has his own square. Give the participant standing by square 1 (the top square) the ball.

To start a rally, the participant by square 1 serves the ball into one of the other squares. During the service and for all other shots, the ball should not be hit with a downwards motion, because it must travel upwards after it has been struck. The ball should be played gently and must travel above a specified height (e.g., 1 metre). If the ball bounces in a participant's square, he has to hit it into an opponent's square before it bounces a second time. The rally continues until someone makes a mistake. This can occur if a participant

- hits the ball so it does not bounce in an opponent's square,
- does not hit the ball upwards or above the specified height, or
- does not hit the ball before it bounces a second time if the first bounce was in his area.

Participants are allowed to step in the square, but should return to the outside of the square after they have hit the ball. If a participant is hit with the ball while standing in the square, he loses the rally and moves back to square 4 (see further information later in this game for more details on how participants move when playing this game). The aim of the game is to get to square 1 and stay there. If any of the participants who are standing by square 1, 2 or 3 make a mistake, they move back to square 4. The other participants move to the next available square. The following examples show how participants move after one of them has made a mistake:

- If the participant in square 4 makes a mistake, all participants stay by their squares; no one moves.
- If the participant in square 3 makes a mistake, he moves to square 4. The participant in square 4 replaces him in square 3.
- If the participant in square 2 makes a mistake, he moves to square 4. The participant in square 4 moves to square 3, and the participant in square 3 moves to square 2.
- If the participant in square 1 makes a mistake, he moves to square 4. The participant in square 4 moves to square 3, the participant in square 3 moves to square 2 and the participant in square 2 moves to the top square (square 1).

The game continues for a set time (e.g., 5 minutes). At the end of this time, the participant in square 1 is the winner. Change the groups; then start the game again.

Safety Tips
- Participants must hit the ball with an upwards swing of the racket and must not strike too hard.
- If the ball bouncing in a participant's area is moving towards another participant, he should be careful not to hit the other participant when he swings. The other participant should move out of the way to allow him to swing his racket.

Advice
- Make the size of the area and the height the participants have to play the ball relevant to the age or ability of the group.
- Participants should not catch the ball on their racket heads when they are hitting it.
- Creating a 'net' with any suitable objects makes the game more realistic. For example, you could push gym benches together across the centre lines to create a net between the opponents' squares.
- More able participants who can put spin or slice on the ball should try to do this to deceive opponents.

Variations
- **Easier/harder:** Make the squares bigger or smaller to change the level of difficulty.
- **Easier/harder:** Change the height the participants have to play the ball to change the level of difficulty.
- **Game variation:** The squares are not numbered, and participants continue to play from the same square throughout the game. Participants start with 10 points; if one of them makes a mistake, he loses a point and the other participants all gain a point. Have them play for the set time, after which the participant with the most points is the winner.
- **Game variation:** Participants in a group do not play competitively within their group, but work together against the other groups. They must hit the ball into the squares in a certain sequence. For example, the first sequence could be 4, 3, 2 and 1. Participants must hit the ball so it bounces in the squares in this order. Each time they complete the sequence, they earn a point, and they continue hitting

(continued)

223

until they make a mistake, after which they start counting from zero. Have them play for a minute and keep their best score. For example, if they hit the ball in the sequence three times they would score three points. If they did not manage to hit the sequence four times then their best score would be three. Change the sequence; then start again.

- **Sport-specific:** This game can be adapted for use in soccer sessions. Participants kick the ball into opponents' squares.
- **Sport-specific:** This game can be modified for use with a bigger ball (e.g., a basketball); participants hit it with their hands.

eight

Volleyball Games

The activities in this chapter relate to volleyball and include some games and some skill practices. Collectively, they can be used to develop serving, spiking, volleying and digging skills. Many of the games in this section are for use with older children who are experienced at playing; however, only a few modifications are needed to adapt these for use with younger children. Information about how to adapt a game to make it more suitable for beginners or younger participants is found in this introduction and in the Variations section of each game.

You are provided with a basic summary of the rules of volleyball and the techniques used in the game here, but I encourage you to attend a volleyball coaching course to further your knowledge. For more information about the rules of volleyball, visit the International Federation of Volleyball website (www.fivb.com).

Volleyball teams are allowed 12 players, but only six play on court at any one time. Teams set up with three players at the front of the court and three at the back. Players at front of the court can play the ball anywhere on the court. Players at the back of the court can play the ball from the back of the court without restriction. They can also play the ball from the front of the court; however, back-court players must contact the ball while they are in the air, having jumped from the back. Attack lines on both sides of the court 3 metres (3.3 yd) from the net separate the front from the back.

To start a rally, one player serves the ball over the net from behind the end line. When the ball has passed over the net, players from the opposing team can touch, or play, the ball three times before it must travel over the net. If a block is made at the net, the team is still allowed to touch the ball three times. A participant cannot play the ball for two consecutive touches (unless the first is a block). The rally continues with teams hitting the ball over the net so it lands in the opponents' half of the court.

If one team touches the ball four times, does not play the ball over the net or hits the ball over the net so it lands out of the opposing team's court, the team loses the rally and the opposing team is awarded a point and the service. A player continues to serve if his team wins a rally, but service changes to the opponents if his team loses the rally. When a team wins the right to serve, the participants from that team rotate positions in a clockwise direction (looking at the team from the net). The participant who was standing at the front of the court on the left-hand side of the court (again, looking at the team from the net) moves to the back of the court and serves the ball. To win the game, a team must win a specific number of points (e.g., 15 to 25). A team needs to win two of three games to win the match.

Participants are allowed to use any part of their bodies to play the ball, but the main skills used in volleyball are the following:

- **The serve:** A rally starts with a serve. The server uses either an underarm or overarm action and must strike the ball from behind the end line (sometimes called the baseline). The server throws or drops the ball out of one hand, hitting it with the other so that it travels over the net across to the opponents' side of the court through the air. She should not bounce the ball before hitting it.

- **The dig (or bump):** The dig is usually used when receiving a serve or spike. Before hitting the ball, the player takes a low, wide stance with both arms extended. She uses her forearms to dig (pass) the ball and extend her legs if she needs extra power or height. The ball is usually played to the team-mate standing in the centre of the court at the front, called the setter. The setter usually plays a volley pass to set up a team-mate so she can spike the ball.

- **The volley (or set):** The volley is an overhead pass. To play a volley, a player positions herself under where the ball is dropping so it would land on her head if she did not volley it. He bends his legs and positions both hands above his head, as though he were going to catch the ball above his head. She makes a ball shape with his fingers and thumbs. As he contacts the ball, the player extends his legs and arms. The arms push the ball away and are fully extended after hitting the ball. As mentioned, the volley is usually played to set up a team-mate so she can spike, or smash, the ball into the opposing team's half.

- **The spike (or smash):** To set a team-mate up to spike the ball, ideally a player should pass to her so she can run and jump to hit the ball close to the net, making contact with the ball when it is above the net. A spike shot should be hit with an overarm 'throwing' action at the highest point of the jump. If the shot is executed well, the ball should fly downwards into the opposing team's half of the court.
- **The block:** One or more of the players at the front of the court can try to block the ball after an opponent has hit a spike shot. They jump up, extend their arms and put their hands close together to form a barrier. If they can get their hands above the net and in line with the flight of the ball, they can block it from coming onto their side of the net.

The International Federation of Volleyball (FIVB) recommends that children under the age of 13 play mini-volleyball. Mini-volleyball has a number of adapted rules to make the game easier. The biggest difference between this version and regulation volleyball is that participants can catch the ball. With younger participants all three touches can be caught. As the participants' ability improves, allow them to catch the ball only during the first and second touches. The final progression for mini-volleyball is to allow only the second touch to be a catch. Mini-volleyball is played with up to four players on the team on a smaller court. The court should be up to 6 by 13 metres (6.6 by 14.2 yd), which is about the size of a badminton court. The net should be lowered so it is easier for participants to play the ball over the net. Have one of the participants, who is of average height, stand with their arms straight up in the air next to the net. The top of the net should be set so it is level with this participant's hands. After the participants have played for a while, decide whether the net height is appropriate, and lower or raise this depending on their ability. Playing games with fewer participants on a team increases the amount of touches they each have, thereby promoting faster learning and more enjoyment. Mini-volleyballs are softer and hurt less to play with, so they are recommended for use with children.

Catch and Throw
Ages 8 to 13

> ## Key Skills and Fitness Components Developed
>
> **Skills**
> - Catching
> - Decision making
> - Digging
> - Throwing
>
> **Fitness Components**
> - Agility
> - Balance
> - Coordination
> - Power
> - Reaction time
> - Speed

Equipment

One volleyball and court per 6 to 12 participants

Game

This game is good for introducing the dig shot to beginners. Arrange the participants into groups of 12; then separate them into two teams of six. Each group works on one court, and teams stand on either side of the net. Three participants are at the front of the court, and three are at the back.

A participant throws or serves the ball over the net to start a rally. One of the participants receiving the service moves to a position to catch the ball before it bounces or after one bounce. He tries to stay facing the net and attempts to catch the ball in front of him in a digging position (see figure on page 229). If he does this correctly, he should have his feet on the floor just wider than the width of his shoulders and be able to catch the ball with both hands so that he can immediately throw the ball back over the net. Participants should use an underarm throwing action to send the ball over the net. The rally continues with participants from opposing teams catching the ball in a digging position and throwing it over the net. If a participant fails to throw the ball over the net, or throws it out of the court, the opposing team wins a point. The team that wins a point always serves for the next rally. Participants rotate positions when their team wins service back from their opponents. Participants rotate in a clockwise direction, and the participant who moves to the back left (looking from the net) serves. Play continues for a set time (e.g., 5 minutes) or until one team has scored a set number of points (e.g., 15).

Safety Tips

- If a participant is going to play the ball, he should position himself in line with the ball when it is travelling towards him. Once he is in line, he should move forwards or backwards to ensure that it bounces into his hands and does not rebound off the floor so hard that it hits him in the face.

- Participants should look at the ball at all times to avoid being hit by stray shots. This is particularly important for participants standing at the front of the court when a team-mate is throwing the ball from the back. Participants should call out their names if they are going to play the ball so that team-mates can move out of their way.

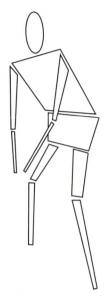

Advice

- Ask questions to check understanding after explaining the rules.
- Use the progressions (found in the Variations section) to make the game more difficult as participants' skill levels improve. The aim is to get the participants to play a dig shot after the bounce, and then eventually without the bounce.

Variations

- **Easier:** Participants are allowed to catch the volleyball after it bounces twice on the floor.
- **Easier:** Play with more participants on a team to make the game easier.
- **Easier:** When a participant is playing the ball from the back of the court, his/her team-mates who are standing at the front of the court should help to get the ball over if the shot they play is not going to travel over the net. They should do this by volleying, digging or tapping the ball so it passes over the net.
- **Game variation:** Participants play a normal game, so teams are allowed up to three touches or hits to play the ball over the net. However, after the ball has been hit over the net to a team's side, the first participant to play the ball can choose to catch the ball in the digging position then throw it to a team-mate rather than hitting it. This can be before a bounce or after it. Further touches to get the ball over the net should be made using correct volleyball techniques.
- **Harder:** Participants must catch the volleyball in the digging position before it bounces.
- **Harder:** Participants must dig the ball back over the net. They can do this before or after the ball has bounced once.

Catch, Pass, Spike

Ages 8 to 16

Key Skills and Fitness Components Developed

Skills

- Catching
- Decision making
- Digging
- Serving
- Spiking
- Throwing
- Volleying

Fitness Components

- Agility
- Balance
- Coordination
- Power
- Reaction time
- Speed

Equipment

One volleyball and court per 12 participants

Game

Use this activity to develop team play and the ability to set up and execute the spike shot during volleyball match play. One of the most effective ways of winning a rally when playing volleyball is through setting up a team-mate at the net to spike (smash) the ball hard into the opponents' half of the court. Beginners frequently hit the ball over the net using a dig or volley shot, but this is not a successful tactic when playing against opponents with a higher skill level. Participants must be familiar with using two touches, or passes, to set up the spike (smash) shot.

This game is played with the same scoring and serving rules as a normal volleyball match, but participants are allowed to catch the ball when taking their first two touches. Arrange the participants into groups of 12; then separate them into two teams of six. Each group works on one court, and teams stand on either side of the net. Three participants are at the front of the court, and three are at the back.

One participant starts a rally by serving the ball over the net. After the ball has been hit over the net (and on all subsequent occasions during the rally), teams try to set up spikes at the net using two catch-and-pass touches. The first participant to play the ball should catch it in a digging position—with two hands, below the waist and with the palms facing upwards. She should then throw the ball to one of her team-mates so she receives it above her head in a volleying position. Ideally this should be one of the participants at the front of the court (by the net); this participant is called the setter. The setter throws the ball up from above her head for one of the other team-mates playing at the front of the court to spike it down into the opponents' side. A point is scored for winning each rally. Groups play until one team has won a set number of points (e.g., 15) or for a set time (e.g., 10 minutes) to decide the winner.

Safety Tips

- Warn participants to be careful of collisions when collecting stray balls.
- Participants should call out their name when they are going to play the ball so that team-mates can move out of the way.

Advice

- Allow teams to practise the passing sequence before putting it into a competitive game.
- If the participants cannot serve very well, then either have them throw the ball over the net or serve the ball yourself, if you can do so effectively.
- The participant who is going to spike the ball should be in a position to run forwards and jump, so the ball is hit close to the net. Without a run-up, participants frequently do not get enough height to spike the ball over the net and down into their opponents' side.
- Set the net height so that the majority of participants can spike the ball downwards into the opponents' side of the court.

Variations

- **Easier:** After a team has served or hit the ball over the net, allow the opponent who makes the first catch to do so after the ball has bounced once.
- **Easier:** Allow the setter to move with the ball once he has caught it. This should make it easier for him to set up a team-mate to spike the ball close to the net.
- **Game variation:** Play with Skittle Knock-Down rules (see page 247). Teams take turns to receive a set number of serves (e.g., 24). Set up skittles on the other side of the net. The team receiving the serve tries to use the catch-pass-spike sequence to knock over the skittles.
- **Harder:** Participants can use only one catch each time the ball is played into their half. For example, if the first participant to touch the ball catches it, then the next team-mate may not. Similarly, if the first participant plays a dig or volley shot, then the next participant may catch it.
- **Harder:** As an alternative to the previous variation, state which of the touches must be caught. To work on digging, allow participants to catch the second touch. To develop setting and volleying, allow them to catch the ball after it has been played over the net.

Dig It, Volley It
Ages 8 to 16

Equipment
One volleyball per six participants

Game
Arrange the participants into groups of six. Participants from each group stand in a circle between 1 to 3 metres apart, creating a circle with a 6- to 8-metre diameter (6.6 to 8.7 yd).

One of the participants throws the ball using an underarm action to one of the other participants so he can use a dig shot to play the ball. The participants continue to play the ball to each other using dig shots until the ball bounces or is hit out of the circle.

If a participant hits a poor dig shot that prevents the group from keeping the rally going (e.g., too high, low or hard), he kneels down in his position in the circle. Kneeling participants are allowed to use dig shots, but most of their shots will be volleys. If a kneeling participant makes another poor shot, he sits on the floor. The game continues with participants kneeling, and then sitting after each mistake they make. If a sitting participant makes another mistake, the game restarts, and participants are awarded points as follows:

• Sitting participants are awarded 1 point.

• Kneeling participants are awarded 2 points.

• Standing participants are awarded 3 points.

Have them play for a set time (e.g., 10 minutes) or a set number of rounds (e.g., 5 to 10). The participant with the most points at the end wins.

Safety Tips
• On very hard floors (e.g., concrete) participants should have something to kneel on when they have to, such as a gym mat or something similar.

• Leave a suitable gap between the groups. This should reduce the risk of miss-hit volleyballs rolling into other groups' areas.

Advice
• Try to group the participants by ability. If some of the participants in each group have a lower ability than the rest, they may lose confidence and not enjoy the game if they are constantly making mistakes when others in the group are not.

• Reinforce the key factors of digging and volleying. If some participants are making mistakes frequently, try to improve their skill level by giving them feedback on their performance.

- Remind participants to keep their own scores and to remember to keep adding their scores from each of the rounds.

Variations

- **Easier:** Allow the participants to play the ball after one bounce to keep the game going.

- **Game variation:** Play in teams. Within the groups separate the participants into two teams of three. Participants stand in the circle with an opponent on either side of them. Participants can pass, or play, the ball to any participant in the group, but should try to play the majority to the opponents. After each round team-mates add their scores together. For example, if a sitting player makes a mistake and his team-mates are both sitting, then the team score for that round is 3 (each participant scores 1 point). If the opponents were all still standing, then that team's score would be 9 (each participant scores 3 points). The team with the most points at the end of the set time wins.

- **Game variation:** Participants start the game with 10 points. Participants stay standing and do not kneel or sit after a mistake but they lose a point, whereas the rest of the participants in the group gain one. The game continues for a set time, and the participant with the most points at the end is the winner.

- **Sport-specific:** Adapt this game for use in throwing and catching games, such as cricket and rugby. Participants must catch the ball before throwing it to other group members. Make the circle slightly bigger and add a rule that participants cannot pass the ball to either of those standing on either side of them.

How Many Touches?
Ages 11 to 16

Key Skills and Fitness Components Developed

Skills
- Digging
- Serving
- Spiking
- Volleying

Fitness Components
- Agility
- Balance
- Coordination
- Power
- Reaction time
- Speed

Equipment
- One ball per six participants
- One court per 12 participants

Game

Use this game to develop good individual play as well as the ability to play as a team. Arrange the participants into groups of 12; then separate groups into teams of six. Each team is on one side of a court. One team starts as hitters. Their opponents start as servers and line up on the end line with a ball each.

The first server serves the ball over the net. As soon as he hits the ball, he calls out the number of touches the opponents must take to play the ball back over (one, two or three). For example if the server calls out 'two', one opponent must play the ball to a team-mate, who must hit it over. If the server calls out 'three', the opponents must take three touches to play the ball over. If three is called, participants must adhere to volleyball match play rules, which state that one participant can play the ball twice but not consecutively.

A point is scored every time a team uses the correct number of touches to hit the ball back over the net to land in the serving team's court. The servers take turns to serve the ball over the net for the hitters to play back. Regardless of whether the opponents are successful or not, after the opponents have played the ball, the server collects it and joins the back of the line. Hitters are awarded a point if the server does not serve the ball over the net or it doesn't land on their side of the court. The hitting team receives a set number of serves (e.g., 24); then the teams switch roles. The team with the most points when they have both hit wins.

Safety Tips
- Participants should call out their names if they are going to play the ball so that team-mates can move out of their way.
- Servers should keep an eye on the ball being served if they are collecting their own.
- Do not allow servers to serve if there is a stray ball on the opponents' side of the court because the hitters may trip over it.
- Have hitters roll the ball under the net rather than kick it when giving it back to a server.

234

Advice

- Make sure the server gives the call early.
- If a participant can serve powerfully using an overarm action, she must call out 'two' or 'three'.
- Servers must allow opponents to reposition after the last service before serving.
- If a server is struggling to hit the ball over, allow her to move closer or to throw the ball over the net to serve.

Variations

- **Easier:** After the server has called 'two' or 'three', allow the first participant to catch the ball so he can throw it to a team-mate.
- **Easier:** Servers stand close to the net and must throw the ball gently over it to make it easier for the hitters.
- **Game variation:** The server doesn't call out a number as they serve. The hitters must take one touch for the first service, two for the second and three for the third. They repeat this sequence for the remaining serves they receive.
- **Game variation:** The server moves onto court after hitting the ball. If he catches the ball before it bounces after the opponents hit it over the net, the hitters are not awarded the point.
- **Game variation:** Two teams play a competitive rally against each other. The server calls the number of touches the receiving team must take, and then serves the ball. As the receiving team plays the ball, a nominated team member calls the number of touches the serving team must take after the receivers have hit the ball over to them. The rally continues until one team does not take the required number of touches.
- **Harder:** On the server's side of the court use chalk to split the playing area into fourths. Draw a line on the court from the net to the end line halfway between the right and left sidelines. Draw a second line from the right to the left sideline halfway between the net and the end line. Give each section a letter from A to D; these are target areas for the hitters to aim at. Section A is the front left section (looking from the serving team's end line), section B is the front right, section C is the back right and section D is the back left.

  While throwing the ball over the net, the server calls out the number of touches the opponents must take and the letter of the section the team must play the ball into. For example, if the server calls 'three D', the team must take three touches with the third participant playing the ball to land over the net and into section D. Three points are scored if the ball passes over the net and lands in the correct area, but one point is scored if it passes over the net, and lands in one of the other areas.

Into the Setter
Ages 8 to 16

Key Skills and Fitness Components Developed

Skills
- Digging
- Directional passing
- Serving
- Team play
- Volleying

Fitness Components
- Agility
- Balance
- Coordination
- Power
- Reaction time
- Speed

Equipment
- Two volleyballs and one court per nine participants
- Spots or chalk

Game
One of the most effective ways of winning a rally when playing volleyball is through setting up a team-mate at the net to spike (or smash) the ball hard into the opponents' half of the court. One way that is used frequently to set up a spike is for the participant who has the first touch to play the ball to their team-mate who is standing at the front centre of their court (the setter). The setter usually volleys the ball up for other team-mates to spike into the opponents' court. This game develops the ability to pass the ball to the setter. Arrange the participants into teams of nine, with each team working on their own court. The teams compete against other teams when the game begins. Within each team three participants stand on one side of the court and start as servers. The remaining participants stand on the court on the other side of the net in the positions they would normally stand to play in a volleyball match—three at the front of the court and three at the back. The participant who stands in the middle of the court at the net is the setter. Rubber spots should be placed on the floor to mark out a square approximately 1 metre squared around the setter. Chalk could be used to draw out this box if spots are not available.

Each server has a volleyball, and they take turns to serve (throw). The first server throws the ball over the net using an overarm action. As the servers throw the ball over the net, the servers may need to stand close to the net so that they can get the ball over. The ball should not be thrown to the setter. The participant who receives the serve tries to pass the ball to the setter so that she can catch it before it bounces. A point is scored if the team manages to do this. The setter must keep both or one foot inside the area she is standing in at all times. The team tries to score as many points as possible in a set time (e.g., 3 minutes). After the team has scored 3 points, the participants receiving service rotate positions in a clockwise direction. Every 60 seconds the servers should switch with three of their team-mates so all participants have a turn to serve. Teams count how many points they score in the set time, and the team with the most points is the winner.

Safety Tips

- Participants should ensure that no stray volleyballs are on the court during play. After a ball has been served, participants should roll it back to the server under the net before getting into position for the next serve.
- Participants should call out their names when they are going to play the ball so that team-mates can move out of the way.
- Warn participants to be careful of collisions.
- Do not use cones as an alternative to spots because the setter will stand on them and on most floors they will slide, increasing the risk of injury.

Advice

- The setter must have at least one foot inside her area at all times for a point to be scored.
- Remind servers to vary who they are throwing the ball to so that all participants are involved in the game. With older or more able participants, servers should use the correct serving technique from behind the end line.
- The server should quickly collect her ball if it rolls onto another team's court. She should also yell a warning to the participants on that court so that they are aware of the ball and are less likely to trip on it.

Variations

- **Game variation:** On the receiving side of the net, have each of the participants at the front of the court stand in a hoop and number them 1 to 3. As the ball is thrown over the net, the server should call out the number of one of the participants at the front. If the participants play the ball to the correct team-mate at the front of the court, then 1 point is scored if that person catches the ball.
- **Harder:** The setter has to catch the ball above her head. A point is scored only if she does this.
- **Harder:** The servers use correct serving techniques rather than throwing the ball over the net.
- **Small groups:** Participants work in teams of six, with two of them being servers. The remaining participants should stand on the other side of the net to receive the serves. One should be the setter at the front of the court and the others should stand at the back.

Line Volley
Ages 14 to 16

Equipment
One ball per four participants

Game
Use this game to develop the ability to play the volley shot in a forwards and backwards direction. The setter frequently uses the volley shot to set up a team-mate at the net to spike the ball. Being able to set up team-mates in front and behind a setter can help to deceive opponents and win more points. Arrange the participants into teams of three. Within each team, the participants stand in a line with a gap of approximately 3 to 5 metres (3.3 to 5.5 yd) between them. Number the participants 1, 2 and 3. The participant in the centre should be number 2. The participants at the ends of the line (numbers 1 and 3) should face number 2. Number 1 should be given a ball and number 2 should face them.

Number 1 throws the ball to number 2 so he can volley it. The participants try to continuously volley the ball to each other in the following sequence:

- Number 2 passes the ball to number 1.
- Number 1 passes back to number 2.
- Number 2 passes the ball backwards to number 3; then turns around to face him.
- Number 3 passes back to number 2.
- Number 2 passes back to number 3.
- Number 3 passes back to number 2.
- Number 2 passes the ball backwards to number 1; then turns around to face him.

One point is scored each time the participants complete the sequence. The participants continue passing the ball in the sequence until the ball drops to the floor or one of them doesn't use a volley technique to pass the ball. If this occurs, one of the participants at the end of the line switches with the centre participant. The participants take turns being in the centre. Have them play for a set time (e.g., 5 minutes). The team with the most points at the end of the set time wins.

Safety Tips
- Set a gap of at least 5 metres (5.5 yd) between teams.
- Warn participants to be careful of collisions when collecting stray balls.

Advice

- Allow the participants to practise the passing sequence by throwing and catching the ball before starting to time the activity.
- To help the centre participant remember his role in the sequence, have him repeat his actions: forwards (pass), backwards (pass), turn.

Variations

- **Easier:** Participants at the ends of the lines throw and catch the ball instead of volleying it.
- **Easier:** The participants on the ends of the lines use other techniques to play the ball to the centre participant.
- **Easier/harder:** Change the distance between the participants to change the level of difficulty.
- **Game variation:** Change the sequence of the volleys. One of the participants at the end of the line throws the ball to the centre participant, who volleys it backwards to the participant behind him. The participant receiving this pass plays a long volley pass to the participant on the other end (over the head of the centre participant). The sequence is completed when the ball is played back to the centre participant.
- **Sport-specific:** With older or more advanced soccer players, this activity can be carried out using headers.

Key Skill and Fitness Components Developed

Skill
Spiking

Fitness Components
- Balance
- Coordination
- Power
- Reaction time

Equipment

- One volleyball per two to four participants
- A wall or something similar

Game

This activity requires a wall to hit the ball against, so it is ideally played indoors. Arrange the participants into teams of two to four, and have each team line up about 10 to 15 metres (11 to 16 yd) from a wall.

The first participant in each team is given a ball, which they should spike towards the wall before joining the back of his team's line. He should hit the ball hard into the ground so it bounces up to hit the wall (before it bounces again) and rebounds back towards the other participants (see the figure on this page). The next participant in the line repeats the process of spiking the ball and then joining the back of the line. The aim

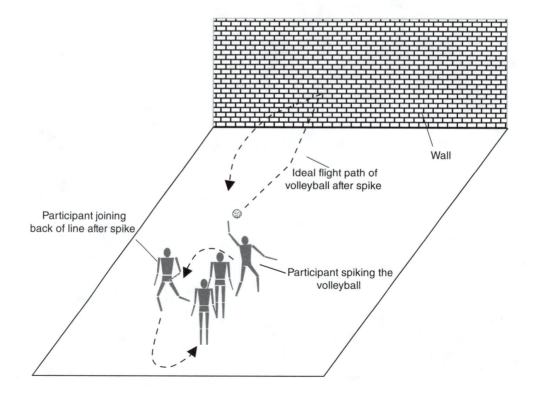

Wall

Ideal flight path of volleyball after spike

Participant joining back of line after spike

Participant spiking the volleyball

is to see how many times the participants can keep the spiking sequence going. A point is scored each time a new participant can spike the ball to keep the sequence going. If a team cannot continue their rally, then they will set up and start again. Teams should keep score of their best rally sequence. Play for a set time (e.g., 5 minutes), with the team having the longest spike rally sequence winning.

Safety Tips

- Allow rest periods for participants to recover.
- After spiking the volleyball, participants should quickly move out to the side and then to the back of the line.
- The participant standing behind their team-mate who is spiking should be well out of the way.

Advice

- Volleyballs need to be inflated so they are bouncy enough to rebound high after they are hit against the floor and wall.
- Participants need to have a good spiking technique and be able to hit the volleyball hard enough so it will rebound back with enough height for the next participant in the line to hit.
- Encourage participants to work cooperatively to keep the sequence going.

Variations

- **Game variation:** Participants work in groups of four to six. Within each group, participants play against each other. They all start with 10 points. Participants responsible for the rally breaking down lose a point, and the other participants in the group gain a point. Have them play for a set time (e.g., 3 to 5 minutes). The participant who has the most points at the end of the set time wins the game.
- **Game variation:** Participants work in groups of three to four. Within each group, participants play against each other. They all start with 5 points, and those who are responsible for the rally breaking down lose a point. Once a participant has lost all of her points, she is out of the game. The participant who still has points remaining when all the others are out wins the game.

Key Skills and Fitness Components Developed

Skills

- Digging
- Running
- Volleying

Fitness Components

- Agility
- Balance
- Coordination
- Endurance
- Reaction time
- Speed

Equipment

- Two volleyballs per 10 to 12 participants
- Cones

Game

This is a good activity for use as part of a progressive warm-up. It can also be adapted into a challenging team game (see the Variations section for instructions on how to modify the rules). Arrange the participants into groups of 10 to 12 and for each group, use cones to set up two 10-by-10-metre (11-by-11yd) areas, with a distance of 10 metres (11 yd) between them. Number the areas 1 and 2. Within each group, half of the participants should stand in area 1 and the other half in area 2. One participant in each area has a volleyball. The participants in each area should form a circle. The aim of the activity is for the participants in each group to work together to keep the two balls in the air.

When the activity begins, the participants with the balls hit them into the air to another person in their area. After hitting the ball, participants will run across to the other area to help keep that ball in the air. Participants should use volleyball techniques to play the balls. If a ball drops onto the floor, one of the participants picks it up and hits it into the air to continue the game. The aim is to keep both volleyballs in the air for as long as possible. As the warm-up progresses, move the groups farther apart so they have to run farther and therefore faster between touches. This also makes the activity more challenging.

Safety Tip

Warn the participants to be careful of collisions, particularly when they are running across the space between the two areas.

Advice

- Show the group how to play by asking them to catch and throw the ball instead of hitting or passing it. Once they understand how to play, they can only use volleyball techniques to pass the ball.
- Encourage participants to try to give passes that other group members will find easy to hit and keep the rally going. Instruct them to work cooperatively. If a ball

is hit out of a group's area, unless it is retrieved quickly, there will be a build-up of participants waiting to hit this ball and too few participants keeping the other ball going. If you see this happening, stop the game and restart it when there are an equal number of participants in each of the smaller groups.

- This activity is best played once the group has some experience of using the volley and dig passes. With beginners allow a bounce between hits (see the Variations section).

Variations

- **Easier:** Allow the ball to bounce between hits if the participants are struggling.
- **Easier:** Allow the participants to play the ball twice before moving to the other group.
- **Game variation:** With groups of 12 to 18, cone out three 10-by-10-metre (11-by-11-yd) areas in a triangular arrangement. There should be a distance of 10 metres (11 yd) between each of the areas. An equal number of participants should stand in each of the areas. Once the game has started participants move in a clockwise direction to the next area after hitting a ball.
- **Game variation:** Make this into a competitive team game. Use the same set-up as the original version but each group is a team. Each team begins with a set number of points (e.g., 20). Teams lose a point each time one of their volleyballs touches the floor. Have them play for a set time (e.g., 3 minutes), and the team with the most points left at the end wins the game.
- **Smaller groups:** With smaller groups, reduce the number of participants in each area but also the distance between the areas to approximately 5 metres (5.5 yd).
- **Sport-specific:** This activity can be adapted to badminton, tennis and soccer. Participants use relevant sports skills to keep the ball in the air. When playing this game in badminton and soccer sessions, it is important that participants are watching the person hitting the shuttle (or ball), and do not get too close to them, otherwise they may be hit by their racket.

Key Skills and Fitness Components Developed

Skills
- Catching
- Decision making
- Digging
- Serving
- Spiking
- Throwing
- Volleying

Fitness Components
- Agility
- Balance
- Coordination
- Power
- Reaction time
- Speed

Equipment

One volleyball and court per 12 participants

Game

This is an activity that develops teamwork and the ability to play the various passing techniques in a variety of directions. Arrange the participants into groups of 12; then separate the groups into teams of six and number the teams 1 and 2. Each group works on its own volleyball court, and teams stand on opposite sides of the net. Each team is arranged with three participants at the back of the court and three at the front; number them 1 to 6. The participant standing at the back of the court on the right-hand side of the court is number 1; the remaining participants are numbered up, working in an anti-clockwise direction (see the figure on page 245).

The participant numbered 1 from Team 1 serves or throws the ball over the net for Team 2 to play back over. As the serve travels over the net, the server calls out three numbers (between 1 and 6). The same number should not be called twice, and the first number called should be the number of the participant to whom the ball is travelling. The next two numbers could be any of the other numbers, but it is preferable to call the numbers of the participants at the front of the court because generally the ball is played to these participants during a rally in a match situation. For example, if the ball is served to the participant standing at the back left of the court (looking at the team from the net), the call could be '1, 3, 4'. Points are awarded for getting the ball back over the net so it lands in the opponents' court, as follows:

- Three points are awarded if the participants successfully pass the ball in sequence and play the ball over the net and into the opponents' court.
- Two points are awarded if the team takes three shots and the correct participants play the ball but not in the correct order.
- One point is awarded if the participants return the ball over the net but take fewer touches, or if participants who have not had their number called play the ball.
- No points are awarded if the team fails to return over the net and into the opponents' court.

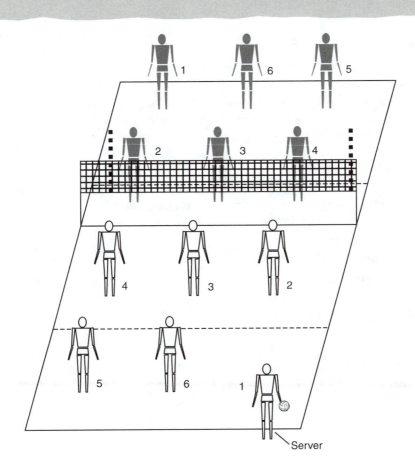

Server

Team 1 does not return the ball to Team 2 if that team successfully plays the ball over the net, although this is a progression for more able participants (see the Variations section). After a service, participants from Team 1 rotate positions in a clockwise direction. The new server will throw or serve the ball over and call out the three numbers. Team 1 has a set number of serves (e.g., 6 to 12), at which point the teams switch roles. Participants do not rotate positions when they are receiving the set number of serves, but they will rotate one position when their team switches from being servers to receivers. Play for a set time (e.g., 10 minutes) or until each team has had a set number of serves (e.g., 30), with the team scoring the most points at the end winning.

Safety Tips

- Participants should call out their names when they are going to play the ball so that team-mates can move out of the way.
- Warn participants to be careful of collisions when collecting stray balls on other teams' courts.

(continued)

Advice

- Make sure the server gives the call early enough and that calls are loud and clear.
- Make sure the server calls out the correct first number (the number of the opponent who the ball has been thrown to). If she does not do this, the receiving team gains 3 points if they return the ball back across the net and into the serving team's court, regardless of the order and number of touches they take.

Variations

- **Easier:** The participants can 'catch and throw' one, two or three of the hits or passes. For example, the participants can catch and throw the first and second hits but the third hit must be played using correct volleyball shots or techniques to hit the ball over the net.
- **Game variation:** Call out the names of the participants instead of their numbers.
- **Game variation:** The serving team can call out two or three numbers. Play to the same rules as the original version if three numbers are called, but if only two numbers are called, the two participants who are given these numbers can play the ball over to get it over the net.
- **Harder:** If the team receiving the serve plays the ball over the net, the rally continues with the receiving team calling out three numbers for the serving team. The teams continue to call out numbers as they hit the ball over until the rally ends.

Skittle Knock-Down
Ages 11 to 16

Key Skills and Fitness Components Developed

Skills

· Spiking

· Volleying

Fitness Components

· Balance

· Coordination

· Power

· Reaction time

Equipment

- One volleyball per two participants
- Six to eight skittles or targets; large cones, 'kwik' cricket wickets or large empty plastic drink bottles could be used as targets
- A volleyball court per 8 to 12 participants

Game

Arrange the participants into teams of 8 to 12, with each team on a separate court (see the figure on page 248). On one side of each court set up six to eight skittles or targets. These could be any suitable object, such as large cones or large, empty plastic water bottles. Participants try to knock over the targets by setting each other up for spike shots at the net. The participants hit from the opposite side of the net to the side where the targets are set up, and the volleyballs must travel over the net. Half of the team are hitters and line up approximately 5 metres (5.5 yd) from the net. One or two participants act as a setter, standing close to the net with the volleyballs. The remaining participants are collectors, and their job is to ensure that the setters have a constant supply of volleyballs to set up the spikes for the hitters.

When the game begins, a setter throws the ball up for the first hitter to run up and spike. The hitter tries to spike the ball to knock over one of the targets. Once he has taken his turn, he returns to the back of the hitting line. The collectors retrieve the volleyballs after the hitters have spiked the ball. The setters continue to set up the hitters for a set time (e.g., 30 to 60 seconds), after which the participants switch roles, with the collectors and the setters becoming hitters, two of the hitters becoming setters and the remaining hitters becoming collectors. The teams try to knock over all of their targets in the quickest time possible. The first team to knock over all of their targets wins. Alternatively, if the teams haven't knocked over all of their targets by the end of a set time (e.g., 5 minutes), then the team that has knocked over the most wins. Set up the targets again and start the game again.

Safety Tips

- Collectors should watch when the hitters are striking the volleyballs so they can dodge any shots that are hit towards them.
- Ensure that no loose balls roll onto other courts or in front of the hitters when they are taking their turn to spike. Ideally, a basket or large container should be

(continued)

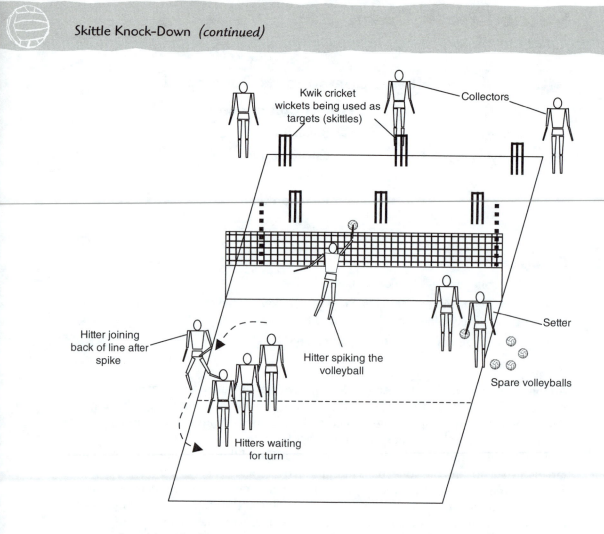

Kwik cricket wickets being used as targets (skittles)

Collectors

Setter

Spare volleyballs

Hitter joining back of line after spike

Hitter spiking the volleyball

Hitters waiting for turn

placed beside the setters to store the volleyballs. Collectors should place balls inside the basket rather than throw balls towards it.

- Depending on the layout and size of your gymnasium or sports hall, you may want to alternate the direction in which the teams are hitting.

Advice

- Setters must throw accurately so that the hitters have a chance to strike the ball close to the net.
- Set the net at a height that is not too high, yet is still challenging for the participants.

Variations

- **Easier:** Lower the net slightly to make it easier for the hitters to get the ball over it.
- **Game variation:** Create teams of six and number them 1 and 2. Team 1 starts as the hitting (attacking) team, and team 2 starts as the defending team. The hitters have three participants spiking and three setting. The setters play the ball for their team-mates to spike and knock over the skittles. The defenders choose three participants to be blockers at the net, and the remaining three collect the volleyballs

for their opponents while their team-mates are working. They also pick up any of the targets that have been knocked over. After a set time hitting (e.g., 30 to 60 seconds), participants within each team swap roles. After the participants from team 1 have each taken two turns spiking (e.g., 2 by 60 seconds), the teams swap so that team 2 becomes the hitting team and team 1 defends. The team knocking over the most targets after both teams have hit wins.

- **Small groups:** Participants work in small teams (e.g., two to four in each team). Teams work on the same court, and both hit from the same side of the net. However, one team hits from the right side of the court, and the opposing team hits from the left. The targets are set up on the other side of the net, and when the game starts, both teams try to knock them over. Participants take turns to set team-mates up for spikes. After a spike, the participant who has hit the ball collects it and becomes a setter. The setter then takes her turn to spike. Count how many targets each team knocks over, continuing until all the targets are knocked over. The team that knocks over the most targets wins the game.

- **Sport-specific:** This game can be adapted for use in tennis sessions with advanced performers. Choose large objects as the skittles/targets, (e.g., a set of 'kwik' cricket wickets) as it will be too difficult to hit smaller ones (e.g., large drink bottles). Participants can practise a number of hitting techniques including the volley, smash and ground strokes.

nine

Cool-Down Games

A cool-down is the practice of exercising at a low intensity after a coaching session or game has ended to help to return the body to a resting state more rapidly. The games in this chapter are good for use in cool-down sessions after intense activity. However, most can also be adapted for use during a warm-up or modified for use as skill practice.

A cool-down after high-intensity exercise is important for adults and older children (those who are experiencing or have finished their growth spurt) for many physiological reasons. Although not all of these reasons are applicable for younger children, it is good to get them in the habit of cooling down so that when they are older they will know how to do so effectively.

A cool-down normally includes jogging and moving around in a variety of ways for a few minutes followed by stretching, but this can be boring, especially if it happens the same way at every session. This is the last thing a participant wants to do, particularly after a hard coaching or training session. This chapter offers a variety of activities that participants will enjoy playing so that they will enjoy cooling down and not see this as something that is monotonous or boring.

Following are types of intense activities that should be followed with a cool-down:

- Running a 400- or 800-metre race
- Playing an intense game, such as squash, soccer, hockey or basketball (depending on the role or position in the game)
- Playing a tag game or something similar

How to Cool Down

A good cool-down incorporates dynamic exercises performed at a low speed or intensity. Because most of the activities in this book involve running and sprinting, jogging-based activities are ideal for cooling down afterwards because this will help the recovery in the muscles that have been used during the session. The cool-down should include exercises that work the same muscles that were used during the activities, so gentle sidestepping and other similar exercises may be appropriate. Participants should steadily decrease the speed of the movements in a cool-down to a very slow jog or fast walk towards the end. Ball work could be included in the cool-down, but this must not involve ballistic actions. Younger children do not need to cool down for as long as older people do. Approximately 3 minutes of dynamic exercise is suitable for younger children before they perform a few stretches during a cool-down. Older participants should cool down for between 10 and 15 minutes. They should spend approximately two thirds of a cool-down performing dynamic exercises, and stretches should be focused on the muscles that have been used most during the session.

Stretches and flexibility work can be included in the cool-down, either interspersed within the dynamic exercise or at the end of it. Dynamic and ballistic stretches should be avoided, and static stretches should be held for a longer period of time than during a warm-up (e.g., 20 to 40 seconds). If participants performed lots of sprinting and turning during the main phase of the session, or if the session was longer than usual, they are likely to suffer some delayed onset muscle soreness, or DOMS (see more details on this topic later in this introduction to the chapter). If this is the case, stretching work should be avoided and carried out at a later time (e.g., at least 6 hours later). It is important that participants not stretch excessively during the cool-down because this may also cause DOMS. Ideally, muscles should be returned to their pre-exercise resting lengths during a cool-down, although too much pain or discomfort should not be experienced while stretching.

Benefits of Cooling Down

The term *cool-down* (also sometimes called a *warm-down*) reflects the early belief that its purpose was to gradually lower body temperature after vigorous activities. Today, we have a more thorough understanding of the benefits to cooling down, and these are given here. Some of the processes are quite complicated, so do not worry if you do not fully grasp all of the information. The most important thing to know is how to perform a cool-down; however, if you are a teacher or coach, it is important that you have some understanding as to why a cool-down is important in case your participants ask why they have to perform one.

Before an exercise session, only small amounts of blood flow through capillaries in the working muscles, but during exercise, lots of blood is pushed through to deliver oxygen and other nutrients. The muscles take oxygen from the blood and release carbon dioxide, a waste product of energy production, into the blood. After blood passes through the muscles, it returns to the heart and then to the lungs to release the carbon dioxide and pick up more oxygen. When performing dynamic exercises in a cool-down, such as jogging, the muscles contract (get bigger in the centre) and relax (get smaller). When the muscles contract, they squeeze the veins and push the blood back towards the heart, when they relax the veins can fill with more blood. This is known as the 'muscle pump action', and this mechanism increases the amount of blood returning to the heart and pushed through to the lungs.

If exercise stops abruptly, the muscle pump action does not work, so blood accumulates in the muscles. This is called blood pooling. When less blood returns to the heart, it means less blood can be pushed to the lungs and around the body. A resultant drop in blood pressure can cause a person to feel dizzy and faint because of an inadequate blood (and oxygen) supply to the brain. A cool-down can help to prevent feeling dizzy and faint because it maintains the muscle pump action and keeps a steady flow of blood returning to the heart so it can be pushed to the lungs and then on to the head and body.

During intense sprinting and similar activities waste products such as carbon dioxide and lactate (usually called lactic acid) are produced in the working muscles and a build-up within the muscles and blood occurs. Although some of these are not particularly harmful or fatiguing, others can be. For this reason it is necessary to deal with them quickly and effectively. Because lactate can accumulate in the muscles and blood and cause muscle fatigue, it needs to be removed after intense activities. Lactate can be dealt with in the liver and other tissues but this requires oxygen so the speed that lactate is removed from the muscles and blood depends on how effectively a person can take in and deliver oxygen to the body's tissues. A suitable cool-down can help maintain blood pressure and deliver blood around the body.

Many believe that a cool-down prevents delayed onset muscle soreness (DOMS), which is the soreness and pain experienced in the muscles after exercise. It is caused by slight damage to the muscle's structure and is sometimes not felt until 24 to 48 hours after exercise. In some cases it may take over a week to ease. However, there is debate about whether a cool-down can prevent DOMS because damage may already have occurred during exercise. Despite the fact that a cool-down may not prevent DOMS, because it provides other benefits, it should always be performed if the session has incorporated intense activity towards the end. Performing a cool-down can help the body to recover faster, which means that the body will be prepared for the next session sooner.

Active Recovery

Active recovery is the term used to describe exercises that are used to recover after intense periods of work within a session. Your performers may benefit from active recovery when one intense game follows another. A few minutes of low-intensity dynamic exercise can help them speed up their recovery between the games. Some of the games in this chapter are useful for incorporating active recovery into coaching sessions.

Cone Visit

Ages 5 to 16

Key Skills and Fitness Components Developed

Skills

- Decision making
- Running

Fitness Components

- Coordination
- Flexibility (if stretches are added)

Equipment

A minimum of one cone per participant. If possible, you should have an equal number of a variety of colours, ideally four to six. For example, if you have 25 participants, you should have five cones in each of the following colours: red, blue, white, green and yellow.

Game

Scatter the cones around the playing area. Try to place them so that cones of the same colour are not too close to each other. Ask the participants to stand next to one of the cones. The colour of the cone they are standing beside is the colour of the cones they will be working to first. Ask them to jog to the cones of the same colour as the one they started beside.

You can ask the participants to do a variety of exercises and move to different colours to vary the activities. Here are some examples:

- Moving to cones of the same colour: Jog forwards to one cone and backwards to the next.

- Moving to cones of the same colour: Sidestep leading with the right foot to one cone and then with the left foot to the next cone.

- Moving to cones of the same colour: Jog to three different cones then perform a static stretch for 20 seconds at the next. Repeat this process a number of times.

- Alternating between moving to a cone of one colour and a cone of a different colour: Do heel flicks to one colour and high-knees running to the next.

- Alternating between moving to a cone of one colour and a cone of a different colour: Skip forwards to one colour and then backwards to the next.

Safety Tip

Choose exercises that are appropriate for a cool-down and ensure that participants are working at a moderate-to-low intensity.

Advice

- To facilitate setting this activity up quickly at the end of a session, ask the participants to help by getting a cone each, finding a space in the area and placing the cone on the floor.

- Ask the participants to collect the cones at the end of the activity.

Variations

Sport-specific: This game can be suited to activities that involve dribbling a ball, such as hockey, soccer and basketball. Participants dribble the ball to the cones in various ways and using a variety of skills. For example, they could dribble a basketball with their left hand to one cone and then with their right hand to the next.

Count Up
Ages 8 to 16

Key Skills and Fitness Component Developed

Skills	Fitness Component
· Decision making	Flexibility (if stretches are added)
· Running	

Equipment
Cones

Game
Arrange the participants into groups of 6 to 10 and cone out a playing area for each group of approximately 15 by 15 metres (16 by 16 yd). Participants move around inside their group's area performing activities that are suitable for a cool-down. As they are moving, one of them starts the game by calling out the number 1. Any of the participants can start their group's game by calling out number 1. The remaining participants try to count up from 1 until they have all called out a number (e.g., one participant calls out '2'; then another calls out '3', and so on). Once a participant has called out a number, he does not call out another; he just continues performing the exercises that are part of the cool-down. The game continues until all the participants have called out a number except for one participant, who performs a fun challenge. The challenge should be something fun, such as saying something funny or performing an animal impression.

Stop the game if two participants call out a number at the same time or if one of them calls out a number out of sequence (e.g., a participant calls out '5' before someone has called out '4'). Participants who make these mistakes must also perform the fun challenge. After participants have performed their fun challenge, have them start the game again.

Safety Tip
Warn the participants to be careful of collisions.

Advice
- Ask questions to check understanding after explaining the game, and reiterate that participants call out only one number.
- If a number of groups are playing this game at the same time, leave a suitable space between their areas so that participants do not get confused by the numbers being called out by participants in other groups.
- Challenges should not be seen as a punishment. Make sure that no challenge is too strenuous or severe.

Variations
- **Game variation:** Participants must call out a letter of the alphabet.
- **Small groups:** In groups of four or five, participants must call out two numbers, but they cannot call out two numbers in a row.
- **Sport-specific:** In games that involve passing (e.g., basketball, hockey, netball, rugby or soccer), participants pass a ball as they move around the area.

Down the Gears
Ages 5-8

Key Skill and Fitness Component Developed

Skill

Running

Fitness Component

Flexibility (if stretches are added)

Equipment
Cones

Game
This is a good activity to teach younger participants about pacing and working at various intensities. Using cones, set up a race track and a pit lane. The race track should be similar to a motor racing track (i.e., have some bends but finish in the same place as it starts) so participants can complete laps. The participants move around the track to complete five laps. They start at a moderate-to-fast jog (fifth gear) in the first lap and get progressively slower with each lap until they are jogging or walking (first gear) during the final lap. Explain that they are to change down a gear at the end of each lap. At the end of the five laps, the participants enter the pit lane to perform their stretches.

Safety Tips
- Warn the participants to be careful of collisions.
- Choose exercises that are appropriate for a cool-down, and ensure that participants start working at a moderate intensity, working down to a low intensity by the last lap.

Advice
- The race track should be long enough that it takes the participants approximately 2 to 3 minutes to finish the final two or three laps.
- Make sure participants' last few laps are at the correct intensity or speed.
- Participants should not race each other around the track. Explain that the race has already been won.
- If possible, make the route interesting by having the participants move around trees or similar objects.

Variations
- **Game variation:** Participants work in pairs. While one participant is completing a lap, her partner stretches in the pit lane. Once the participant jogging has finished her lap, she moves into the pit lane and switches roles with her partner. The participants must both complete five laps, moving down the gears at the end of each lap. You can call this 'Le Mans Cool-Down'.
- **Sport-specific:** For sports that require dribbling skills (e.g., soccer, hockey or basketball), participants can dribble a ball around the track.

Four Square

Ages 5 to 16

Key Skills and Fitness Components Developed

Skills

- Decision making
- Dribbling
- Passing
- Receiving
- Running

Fitness Components

- Balance
- Coordination
- Flexibility (if stretches are added)

Equipment

- Four balls per 12 to 20 participants
- Cones

Game

This is a good activity for use as a cool-down, but it is also good for use as part of a progressive warm-up or a skill practice. Because participants are passing a ball to each other, this cool-down is particularly applicable for use when coaching any ball game. For the set-up of this activity, see the figure on this page. Use cones to mark out four areas of approximately 10 by 10 metres (11 by 11 yd). The areas should be arranged in a square formation with a distance of 10 metres (11 yd) between them. Arrange the participants in four groups with equal numbers in each. Each of the groups stands in their own area.

Once you have explained how to play, participants move around their area passing the ball to each other. Everyone should be moving around at an intensity suitable for a cool-down. You could give a number of commands to vary the activities, such as the following:

- **Pass clockwise:** The participants pass the ball to each other within their area, but when you call 'pass clockwise,' the participants in possession of the balls pass

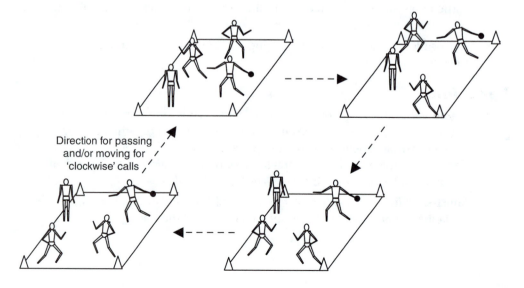

Direction for passing and/or moving for 'clockwise' calls

them to the next group in a clockwise direction. The passer stays in the same group; only the ball moves to the next square.

- **Pass anti-clockwise:** Like 'pass clockwise', but the ball is passed in an anti-clockwise direction.
- **Pass and follow (clockwise or anti-clockwise):** This command is the same as the previous one but the participant who passes the ball follows it into the next group either clockwise or anti-clockwise depending on the call.
- **Cross pass:** Like 'pass clockwise' except that the ball is passed to the group diagonally across the area.
- **All change:** Participants leave the balls they were passing in their areas and move to different areas. They should not all move to the same area, but separate and move to different ones. Once all participants are in new areas, they continue to move around the areas passing the balls to each other. There should be an equal number of participants in each area.

To make the game more interesting, have participants perform a fun challenge if they make a mistake when one of the instructions is called. For example, if they are supposed to pass the ball in a clockwise direction and a participant passes it the other way, he has to perform the fun challenge. Add some periods of stretching into the activity or have participants stretch at the end of it.

Safety Tips
- Choose exercises that are appropriate for a cool-down, and ensure that participants are working at a moderate-to-low intensity.
- Warn the participants to be careful of collisions.

Advice
- Add one or two instructions at a time so the participants become familiar with them.
- Ask questions to check understanding after explaining the game.
- Challenges should not be seen as a punishment. Make sure that no challenge is too strenuous or severe.
- This activity is also good for use as part of a progressive warm-up. The set-ups for a number of the games in this book and in *Fun and Games* involve participants working in groups of three to five in small 10-by-10-metre (11-by-11-yd) areas, so these games can be played with few changes to the set-up straight after the warm-up (e.g., groups of five could play Crossover, see page 12 in chapter 1).

Variations
- **Large groups:** Make the areas bigger and have more participants in each area.
- **Large groups:** If you have more than 25 participants in the group, separate them into two groups and set up two Four Square areas.
- **Small groups:** Have three areas in a triangular shape. It is not possible to call 'cross pass' with this variation.

Name the Stretch
Ages 5 to 13

Equipment

- Cones
- Chalk if playing on a hard surface

Game

Arrange the participants into groups of five to eight. Use cones to mark out an area of approximately 6 by 6 to 10 by 10 metres (6.6 by 6.6 to 11 by 11 yd) for each group. Choose one participant in each group to be the leader. The leader stands a few metres away from the outside of her group's area. The remaining participants move around inside the area performing the cool-down exercises as instructed by the leader. The leader performs the exercises on the spot or around the outside of the area. The chosen exercises should be of a low intensity, such as jogging, sidestepping, skipping or marching.

After 2 to 3 minutes of cool-down exercises, the leader turns away from the group and calls 'stretch'. The other participants stop moving around the area then choose and perform a static stretch. After approximately 10 to 15 seconds the leader calls out the name of a stretch and then turns around to face the group. If any of the participants are performing that stretch, they switch roles with the leader.

The new leader stands outside the area and chooses an exercise for the group to perform. On this and subsequent occasions the leader should have the group exercise for only 30 to 45 seconds before turning away and calling 'stretch'. If a leader chooses a stretch and then turns around to find none of the participants performing that stretch, she continues to be the leader. A participant can be a leader for a maximum of three times before she must choose a new leader if none of the participants match her choice of stretch. If two participants are both performing the named stretch, the leader continues leading the game.

Safety Tips

- Warn participants to be careful of collisions.
- Ensure that participants are working at a correct intensity when they are moving around their area. They should not be working too hard because this will prevent an optimal recovery from the previous games and activities.
- Participants should use correct techniques when carrying out the stretches.

Advice

- Ensure that the first leader should have participants perform moving exercises for 2 to 3 minutes before calling 'stretch'. On subsequent occasions the leader should call 'stretch' after only 30 to 45 seconds.

- With younger participants you may want to time how long they are working during the active part of this game.

- Participants need to know 5 to 10 of the major stretches. Teach a number of stretches before playing the game if the group has little experience of stretching.

- Some groups may need to be reminded of the names of the stretches before starting.

Variations

- **Easier:** Give the leader laminated cards that have the names and pictures of common stretches on them. The leader picks one of the cards and turns around to show this to the group after 10 to 15 seconds of stretching. Participants should finish their stretches before the new leader calls out the next exercise.

- **Harder:** If a participant is performing the stretch the leader calls out, she must name the muscle she is stretching before becoming the leader. If she cannot name the muscle, she does not change with the leader.

Inner Circle
Ages 5 to 16

Key Skills and Fitness Components Developed

Skills

- Dribbling
- Passing
- Receiving
- Running

Fitness Components

- Balance
- Coordination
- Flexibility (if stretches are added)

Equipment

- One ball per two participants
- Cones

Game

Because this is a passing and dribbling activity, it is suited for a cool-down after any sport that requires these skills. You can modify this activity in a number of ways to maintain participants' interest and motivation.

For the set-up of this activity, see the figure on page 263. Use cones to mark out two circles: an inner one and an outer one. If there are 16 participants in the group, there should be eight cones in the inner circle and eight cones in the outer circle. The inner circle should be approximately 10 to 15 metres (11 to 16 yd) in diameter. There should be an equal spacing between each of cones with approximately 3 metres (3.3 yd) distance between each of them. Each cone in the outer circle should be aligned with a cone in the inner circle, approximately 10 metres (11 yd) from it. A participant stands beside each of the cones, and each participant in the inner circle has a ball.

To start the activity, participants in the inner circle pass their ball to the participant in the outer circle who is standing next to the cone that is in line with their own. The participants in the outer circle pass the ball back; then move in a clockwise direction to the next cone (in the outer circle). When the participant who started with the ball receives it back, he dribbles to the centre of the circle, turns with the ball and returns to the cone where he started. All of the participants in the outer circle should have moved on one cone and be waiting to receive the next pass. This sequence continues for a few minutes, repeating the process as follows:

- The participants on the outside pass the ball and move around the circle in a clockwise direction to the next cone.
- The participants in the centre receive the ball, dribble into the middle and then return to the cone where they started before passing to the next participant in the outer circle.

After a few minutes the participants swap roles so those in the outer circle move to the inner circle and vice versa. After playing for another few minutes, the participants stop and carry out some stretches (if required). Restart the activity, but have the participants in the outer circle move in an anti-clockwise direction. For different progressions, see the Variations section.

262

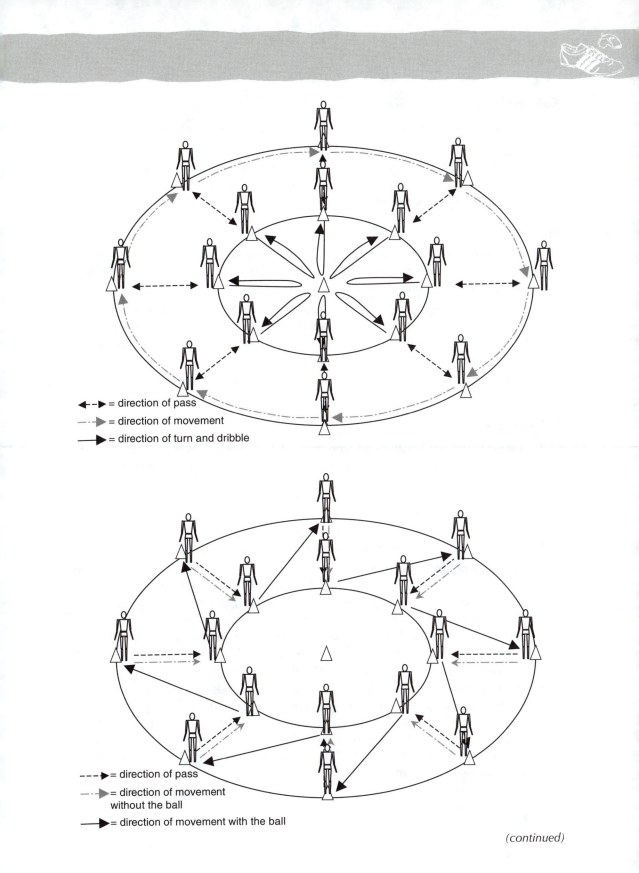

◄-►- = direction of pass

---►- = direction of movement

━━► = direction of turn and dribble

----►= direction of pass

---►= direction of movement
without the ball

━━►= direction of movement with the ball

(continued)

Safety Tips

- Participants in the inner circle should be careful not to collide with each other when they dribble into the middle of the area.

- Participants should work at a low intensity throughout this activity.

- If stretches are included between periods of activity, ensure that participants are using the correct techniques.

Advice

- With younger or less able participants you may want to walk through the activity step by step until they are familiar with it. When they understand their role fully, ask them to speed up slightly.

- If any of the participants make a mistake, the whole activity can come to a halt. Try to keep a close watch for this happening. If there seems to be a problem, stop the activity and ask the participants to perform a stretch before returning to their start positions.

- Participants should use correct stretching techniques and hold stretches for an appropriate length of time.

Variations

- **Game variation:** See the figure on page 263. In this variation participants in the outer circle begin with the ball. They pass the ball to the participant in the inner circle and then follow the pass and move to the inner circle. Meanwhile, the participant who receives the pass dribbles the ball to the next *outer* cone in a clockwise direction and the process continues. On command the group can change direction. They still pass (and follow) from the outer circle to the inner circle, but they should dribble to the next outer cone in an anti-clockwise movement.

- **Game variation:** Participants in the outer circle begin with the ball. They pass the ball to the participant in the inner circle, who passes the ball back. The participant in the outer circle stops the ball next to the cone she is standing beside. Participants in the inner circle then move to the next cone in a clockwise direction, and those in the outer circle move to the next cone in an anti-clockwise direction. The participants in the outer circle pass the ball that has been left at the cone they have moved to, to the participants across from them in the inner circle.

- **Sport-specific:** Use this variation in soccer sessions. Participants in the inner circle have soccer balls, which they hold in their hands and throw to the participants in the outer circle, who head the balls back. After heading, the participants in the outer circle move in a clockwise direction to the next cone to receive another ball to head back. On command the group can change the direction of the run to an anti-clockwise movement.

About the Author

Anthony Dowson received a post-graduate certificate of education and a master's degree in sport science from Loughborough University and teaches physical education at Whickham Sports College in Gateshead, England. Also the coauthor of *Fun and Games,* published in 2005, Dowson coached soccer for seven summers in the United States for Major League Soccer camps. He has earned numerous coaching awards for basketball, tennis, soccer, cricket, volleyball, badminton and rugby and has been a director of A Level PE at numerous institutions. He also owns SHAPE Performance, a business offering services and consultancy in sport, health and physical education. Dowson is a member of the Football Association (FA), the Association for Physical Education, and the British Association of Sport and Exercise Scientists. In his leisure time, he enjoys playing soccer (he has played semi-professionally since 1998), fitness training and playing other sports.

You'll find other outstanding physical education resources at
www.HumanKinetics.com

In the U.S. call 1.800.747.4457
Australia 08 8372 0999
Canada. 1.800.465.7301
Europe . . . . .+44 (0) 113 255 5665
New Zealand . . . 0064 9 448 1207

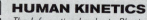